More Praise for *Designing the Smart Organization*

"A path-breaking work! Deiser creatively uses learning theory and practice to recast the practice of strategic management and demonstrates the concept through remarkable case studies from ten prominent companies."

> —Larry Greiner, coauthor, *Management Consulting Today and Tomorrow* and *Dynamic Strategy-Making*

"Deiser clearly, effectively and accurately points out how organizations must reframe how they design learning processes to thrive in today's rapidly changing world. A variety of interesting cases show how to do it."

> —Edward E. Lawler III, director,
> Center for Effective Organizations,
> USC Marshall School of Business, and coauthor,
> *Built to Change*

"A truly insightful book that I highly recommend for any corporate leader, senior executive, or consultant involved in strategy, organizational change, innovation, or HR who is looking to create organizations that last. Deiser makes us not only look at the practice of learning with new eyes, but he also tells a variety of concrete case stories from major global players that flesh out the concepts of this book with great clarity and relevance."

> —Daniel Dirks, executive vice president
> and global head of human resources, Allianz Group

"Deiser does an excellent job in making us think about learning in novel ways—as an enabler of organizational change, cultural unification, strategic renewal, or just plain survival. Everybody who wants to make a difference in business, government, or other organizational worlds should read this book."

> —Immanuel Hermreck,
> executive vice president human resources,
> Bertelsmann AG

We are pleased to offer a free downloadable Instructor's Manual for *Designing the Smart Organization*, including sample syllabi, chapter summaries, and additional case study materials, as well as chapter-by-chapter comprehension questions, in-class discussion questions, essay prompts, and PowerPoint slides.

To access the manual, please visit **www.wiley.com/college/deiser**

DESIGNING THE SMART ORGANIZATION

How Breakthrough Corporate Learning Initiatives Drive Strategic Change and Innovation

Roland Deiser

JOSSEY-BASS
A Wiley Imprint
www.josseybass.com

Copyright © 2009 by John Wiley & Sons, Inc. All rights reserved.

Published by Jossey-Bass
A Wiley Imprint
989 Market Street, San Francisco, CA 94103-1741—www.josseybass.com

Readers should be aware that Internet Web sites offered as citations and/or sources for further
information may have changed or disappeared between the time this was written and when it is read.

Jossey-Bass books and products are available through most bookstores. To contact Jossey-Bass directly
call our Customer Care Department within the U.S. at 800-956-7739, outside the U.S. at 317-572-3986,
or fax 317-572-4002.

Jossey-Bass also publishes its books in a variety of electronic formats. Some content that appears in
print may not be available in electronic books.

ISBN-13: 978-0-470-49067-9

Cataloging-in-Publication data on file with the Library of Congress.

Printed in the United States of America
FIRST EDITION
HB Printing   10 9 8 7 6 5 4 3 2 1

Contents

Figures and Exhibits

Figures (Part One)

Exhibits (Part Two)

For Kathrin, David, and Una

Introduction

It has become common sense that the competitive success, if not the mere survival, of most of today's organizations is in large part dependent on their ability to learn, to innovate, and to change on an ongoing, sometimes radical basis. Given this, one might think that the "learning imperative" would have already led to a steep rise in the importance and reputation of corporate learning and development activities as a key strategic organizational practice, on equal footing with finance or marketing and high on the agenda of the Chief Executive Officer (CEO).

However, in most companies the corporate learning agenda is still struggling to get an adequate voice in the boardroom. The practice of learning does not have a seat at the table when it comes to shaping the business. The Vice President of Learning and Development is usually part of a Human Resource (HR) function that itself suffers in most organizations from a lack of clout and perceived business relevance. The fact that some companies have introduced "Chief Learning Officers" (CLOs) or even corporate universities seems to suggest otherwise, but a little scratching on the surface reveals that, in many cases, it's just a new label for the old training department.

The primary reason for the ongoing marginalization of learning is that the debate about the value and contribution of learning is driven by a restrictive understanding of the practice, one that has its roots in a "school-based" approach to qualification and training. While traditional education and people development remain important, the true challenge large organizations face today is to create and manage enabling architectures that systematically build strategic and organizational capabilities—such as speed, responsiveness, responsibility, innovation, and creativity—into the company's DNA.

This leads us to a new and ambitious concept of corporate learning that has little to do with the traditional notion of training and education. As a transformational business practice, corporate learning has to leave the classroom and become a *business practice*, with the focus on initiatives that nurture, develop, and leverage a company's strategic competence.

To support this argument, we will look at the universe of learning with fresh lenses. We will show that it is not just a back-end qualification process; the very nature of learning is rather about innovation, change, and transformation. Learning is not just about the acquisition of cognitive and technical skills; it includes social, political, and ethical competences. It doesn't happen only in the classroom—classrooms are actually pretty dysfunctional learning contexts—it occurs everywhere because it is at the heart of our daily struggle to make sense of the world and succeed in complex contexts. And most important, learning is not restricted only to individuals; it is a fundamental process that drives the development of large-scale systems. Using learning to acquire personal skills and insights is great and important. But the learning challenge of the twenty-first century is much greater: How can entire corporations, industries, even societies learn to be more strategically competent systems, so that they will ultimately survive in balance within their relevant ecosystem?

Who This Book Is For

This is not a book just for experts on learning. It is for everyone who has a keen interest in how to shape larger systems in a way that they become flexible, agile, and innovative. As such, the book has relevance for anyone who works in organizations and is faced with the challenge to learn and change. The framework of the book makes it useful for experts and practitioners alike, as it connects conceptual thinking with concrete cases from leading global corporations.

Because the topic of strategic and transformational learning is growing in importance, the book will appeal to senior executives and managers who are involved in the domains of strategy, organization, change, innovation, HR, or general management, especially in large, complex organizations. The concepts and case studies in the book will likely inspire a broad scope of consultants, especially those whose practices focus on strategy, organization, leadership, change management, and innovation. Offering a new and unique contribution to strategic and transformational learning, the book provides a rich source of case study materials for academics, researchers, and students in the field of management science, sociology, and organizational science. It may be used as a textbook to discuss the cases, both in undergraduate and graduate business and organizational behavior courses. It should also be invaluable for those involved in offering executive education and other learning services.

How to Use This Book

The book has two parts that can be read independently. Part One is conceptual; in it I present the arguments for a new perspective on the identity of learning. Part Two contains ten case studies from global leaders that serve as benchmarks in creating organizational learning architectures for strategic innovation and transformational change.

The two parts of the book can each stand on their own, as can each case study in the second part. However, the chapters and case studies are linked to the degree that they reframe the meaning of learning, specifically learning in large-scale systems. When I reflected upon how to allocate space in this book to conceptual considerations and stories from practice, the cases were the clear winners, because conceptual thinking without the life-blood of practice remains stale and academic. The cases also help illustrate the argument from a variety of angles. However, practice without reflection remains just a story, and the conceptual frameworks presented in Part One help guide thinking. Therefore, the two parts belong together, and you are welcome to read them as best suits your needs.

Chapter One opens with a brief look at some major forces that drive a new "corporate learning imperative"—such as massive changes in the overall business context, the ascent of the knowledge-based economy and society, the changing basis of competitive advantage, the empowerment of the periphery, and the emerging globally networked co-creation clusters that require a different approach to strategy and leadership.

Chapter Two responds to this learning imperative by exploring the universe of learning from the perspective of creating an effective business practice. Looking at the phenomenon of learning though three different lenses, we can recognize the current restrictions and the significant future potential of the practice. First, by analyzing very briefly the nature of learning processes, we see that learning cannot be sufficiently explained through the mechanistic model of unilateral knowledge transfer between teacher and student. Learning is an interactive, highly contextual process that leads to new interpretations of the world and creates social fabric. This has significant implications for the design of learning architectures. We then turn to the various dimensions of learning. We investigate not only the cognitive aspect of learning, which is dominant in the educational system, but also the emotional, social, political, and ethical dimensions of the concept and make them practical for corporate use. Third, we look at the critical contributions of learning, extending its traditional focus on people excellence to a new focus on organizational and strategic excellence.

Chapter Three builds on these extensions of the conventional learning paradigm and introduces a hierarchical five-step model that integrates learning interventions with increasingly strategic business processes, extending the stakeholder universe of corporate learning to interorganizational networks. By doing so, we can witness the transformation of corporate learning from an educational to a strategic leadership practice. The chapter closes with concrete examples of advanced and unorthodox learning interventions that foster organizational and strategic excellence.

Reframing the identity of corporate learning is not without consequences for the players who serve the field. The conventional set of vendors—business schools, training firms, consultancies, coaches, software providers, and others—naturally reflect in their practices the current paradigm of learning. Chapter Four explores the strategic impact of a redefined learning practice on the various players and the required reconfiguration of the overall customer-vendor relationships.

Finally, in Chapter Five, we examine the interplay of the new learning paradigm with the strategy process in large organizations. Like today's practice of corporate learning, the practice of strategic management must also rethink its traditional planning paradigm, which has become dysfunctional in face of discontinuous change. As a result, we unveil how the two practices converge—learning as a strategic process, and strategy as a learning process.

Part Two of the book presents a collection of case studies of transformational corporate learning adventures from large and complex organizations, most of them global leaders in their fields—organizations like Siemens, ABB, EADS (Airbus), Novartis, BASF, PricewaterhouseCoopers, the U.S. Army, and more. The cases are quite diverse in demonstrating how companies have addressed various challenges they face, but they have in common that they are all large-scale learning initiatives that required smart learning architectures to make the entire system learn. Each of the cases is unique, because each context is unique. But they are also generalizable to situations many companies face, because they all model universal principles about designing learning architectures that go beyond the traditional narrow thinking of what learning can accomplish.

The cases are told as "war stories" rather than polished "success stories" and provide rich material for analyzing the success factors and challenges related to large-scale learning projects. They are examples of ambitious corporate learning endeavors that inspire and challenge the way most of us think about the learning function. They can be food for discourse in the executive suite, and they are great teaching material in executive education programs and business education in general. Together with the chapters in the first part of this book, it is my hope that the case studies will contribute to transforming today's definition of corporate learning and elevate the practice into the arena in which it deserves to operate.

Why *Corporate* Learning?

We all pay lip service to the importance of the educational sector, and at least in the United States we know that our educational systems are in desperate need of repair and innovation. Other books on learning might address the current state of our schools and universities and how they treat learning. Instead, I focus here exclusively on corporate learning.

I do this because the rapidly changing context in which large organizations have to act today puts on them a tremendous learning pressure. Failure to learn is not an option; continuous innovation and reinvention have become imperative for survival. If individuals refuse to learn, they may become unemployable—that's bad enough. But if large corporations refuse to learn, they can do much unintended harm to themselves and their environment. For the sake of us all, who depend on a healthy economy and on organizations that shape this world responsibly, it is important to raise awareness about the learning imperative. Learning in the comprehensive sense in which I define it is not just a luxury on which we cut back in difficult times. Learning is the lifeblood of sustainable organizational effectiveness and innovation, and done well, it leads to responsible industry leadership.

Further, I believe that any conceptual innovation in learning that is strong enough to transform the practice will be driven by corporations, not by the incumbent players in the learning and education space. Unlike in the academic world, learning in corporations is highly contextual as it is designed for impact. It naturally addresses multiple dimensions and domains of learning. Companies are more likely to realize the limitations of the current paradigm of learning, and as ultimate customers of the education sector, they have the means to drive paradigmatic change.

Finally, corporations—especially large and global ones—are major political actors that create much of the context in which they and we live. As such, they carry a responsibility as global citizens and have ultimately to legitimate their actions. They can become responsible actors only if they gain a better understanding of who they are and how their actions affect the world, and vice versa. The process of continuously developing an understanding of this dynamic is nothing else than the essence of ongoing learning. Unorganized, this learning remains accidental, and organizations miss out on the rich opportunities that come with it. Organized in the form of smart corporate learning designs, this learning enables companies to lead industry transformation by creating a context that benefits the entire stakeholder universe and the larger political and ecological context we all depend on.

PART ONE

Conceptual Foundation

CHAPTER ONE

The Corporate Learning Imperative

We live in turbulent times that are scary and exciting at the same time. It seems that the complex global system of interdependencies we've created over the past hundred years or so is suddenly cracking at the seams, creating massive concussions that reverberate throughout the world and challenge the very basis of our political and economic foundations. The leapfrog developments in technology and communications infrastructure open up tremendous opportunities to reshape how we deal with the world, but they are also threatening and potentially destructive if we lag behind in our ability to deal with complexity, assess the systemic impact of our actions, and govern global phenomena. We have to learn as individuals, organizations, and political systems to understand the emerging opportunity spaces and capitalize on them in ways that will lead us to a new quality of a global society in ecological balance with the planet. If we fail to do this, the consequences may be dire.

Corporations—especially large corporations—play a major role in this picture. With their global reach and powerful governance structures, they contribute significantly to the context they—and we all—live in, so they bear an increasing responsibility to act as global citizens. However, they are themselves under pressure to master these turbulences in a way that lets them thrive—or at least survive. They are faced with the imperative to develop new capabilities to more effectively deal with disruptive environments—or even better, to shape them. As in an evolutionary model in which the fittest organisms survive, corporations need to make their ability to learn a core part of their organization's DNA, so that they can be naturally smart, responsive, flexible, and responsible. If they succeed in doing so, they can keep up with, if not outrun, those changes that might otherwise remove them from existence.

Five Forces That Drive the Need for Learning

The driving forces behind the corporate learning imperative are numerous, and they reinforce each other. Let us explore the five most important drivers that pressure organizations to learn more deeply and in a different way and that force all of us to fundamentally rethink our notion of learning. They are:

- Massive disruption of the business context
- The rise of the knowledge-based organization
- A competence-based view of strategy
- The growing importance of the periphery of organizations
- The transformation from self-contained hierarchical organizations to "flat" and globally networked co-creation clusters

Massive Disruption

We are in the midst of disruptive change. The complex brew of rapidly advancing technologies, globalization, ecological megachallenges, and most recently the global breakdown of the financial markets leaves virtually no industry untouched. Take, for example, the automotive industry, which is slowly but with certainty reaching the end of limitless growth and needs to introduce radically new technologies. Or look at the media industry, which is wrestling with digital copyright issues and the substitution of old media with Internet-based models of production, distribution, and consumption. The pharmaceutical industry is being revolutionized through bioengineering and genetic technology, and the energy business needs to transform itself toward clean technologies of generation and consumption. And there is banking, which will not be the same once the dust of the financial crisis of 2008–2009 has settled.

In contrast to incremental change, which we can follow and understand as it emerges from familiar patterns of industry behavior and context evolution, discontinuous change surprises us. It comes out of nowhere, radically reconfiguring and rewriting the rules of the game. Because discontinuous change is so unfamiliar, the new rules are not yet clear; established response patterns are inappropriate; and it is hard to react to it adequately. In the wake of disruptive change, companies that cling to old business models may get destroyed, those who reinvent themselves survive, and new ones that embrace and invent new paradigms create new industry spaces.

Disruptive change that reinvents industries may be scary, but it is part of the game. As the Austrian economist Josef Schumpeter pointed out in his seminal work more than sixty years ago, "creative destruction" is the innovative power behind long-term economic growth and development, and as such it is at the heart of capitalism.[1] The pace of industry change through radical innovation may have accelerated recently, but we have seen it before, for instance, with the explosion of groundbreaking inventions that happened within a few decades at the end of the nineteenth and the beginning of the twentieth century.

But disruptive change today is different, because it is striking at more fundamental levels. We are seeing massive changes in the overall social, political, and economic contexts, all at the same time, and on a global scale. The past quarter of a century has been a period of breathtaking turbulence and disruption. The 1980s decade of Ronald Reagan and Margaret Thatcher launched emphatic industry deregulation in the Anglo-American business universe, unleashing the power of the free market with all its benefits and ugly excesses. In 1989, we witnessed the fall of the Soviet Empire, ending a period of relative political stability and predictability and adding a further dynamic to the global economy.

In the mid-1990s, the Internet took off, transforming our global communication infrastructure, reframing business-to-consumer, business-to-business, and lately also peer-to-peer relationships while generating countless new business models in its wake. We saw the burst of the Internet bubble in 2000, which solidified the new medium, transforming the adolescent dot.com craze into a mainstream business reality with a radical impact on all aspects of our lives, comparable to the invention of printing or the discovery of electricity.

Just one year later, in September 2001, we witnessed the terrorist attacks on the Twin Towers in New York and on the Pentagon in Washington, D.C., which led to radical political changes in U.S. policy, resulting in two wars and rekindling religious fundamentalism as a global conflict conduit. The first decade of the millennium also saw the rapid rise of China and India as powerful players on the world stage, reshaping the global balance of trade, reconfiguring the production value chain of most corporations, and taking globalization to a new level.

And now, as we reach the end of the first decade of the new millennium, we witness a breakdown of the global financial infrastructure that is likely to end the period of ruthless Wall Street capitalism and reset not only the way we do business, but the way the global economy—and society—works. At the same time, we are finally starting to realize the seriousness of the ecological challenge that will transform in its own way the foundations of virtually all businesses and our way of life.

All this has happened at warp speed, more or less within one generation. Each and every one of these events has a tectonic quality about it; each hits against the others, and in their combined force, they put an almost inconceivable pressure on organizations to keep pace. The imperative to innovate and reinvent oneself in these changing contexts has become ubiquitous and permanent. The capability to learn is not just nice to have; it has become a key factor for survival—not only for people, but for organizations, industries, and our global society.

The Ascent of Knowledge-Based Organizations

But there is more: During the past twenty-five years, the foundations of Western economies have become more and more knowledge based. The value of products and services lies increasingly in their inherent intellectual capital, and knowledge workers are slowly becoming the majority of the workforce. The "rise of the creative class," as social economist Richard Florida puts it, is slowly changing the texture of Western societies.[2]

The ascent of knowledge as the strategic lever for value creation has huge consequences for the way organizations deal with this asset. The effective management of knowledge has become a key success factor for competitiveness. Companies need a clear understanding about what kind of knowledge is critical to the business model of the firm—both in terms of marketplace intelligence and internal competence—and they need appropriate policies and mechanisms to acquire, aggregate, and utilize this *relevant* knowledge.

This is not an easy task for organizations that have been designed to be efficient machines. While some knowledge can be treated like dead material and quickly processed according to an industrial paradigm, the bigger and more relevant parts of today's knowledge tend to be tacit and ambiguous. This type of knowledge rests in people and in practices and is closely linked with the context where it gets applied. It is harder to access and cannot be "managed" like a database of information. It needs to be absorbed and continuously reevaluated through discourse as it derives from multiple internal and external perspectives. It is of little use if it is not converted into shared meaning and sense-making organizational maps that then inform the organization's strategic response.

This leads to yet another knowledge management challenge: how to make strategically relevant information available to the right people in the right place at the right time. How do we involve stakeholders in a knowledge-generating and -disseminating process? And last, not least: How do organizations go about eliminating—or "unlearning"—obsolete or strategically irrelevant knowledge so they do not get overburdened with old and useless stuff?

We can see that knowledge management is much more than the IT-driven craze of the late 1990s that eventually gave the practice a mixed reputation. As John Seely Brown, the former director of Xerox's PARC and a passionate advocate for a new ecology of learning elegantly phrased it: information has a "social life,"[3] and if we do not recognize this fact, IT investments in learning and knowledge management fall short. Dealing with organizational knowledge in a way that makes "sense" is a comprehensive learning challenge. It requires a smart social architecture that connects the right people in settings that are conducive to sharing and collaboration, and a technical infrastructure that supports these efforts. Such an architecture may include knowledge-sharing policies, incentive systems, mechanisms to build trust, the encouragement of communities of practice, wikis, and the use of other social networking tools to connect the many internal and external resources that eventually constitute what is considered the real "knowledge."

Competence-Based Strategic Management

A third driving force that moves learning center stage in the corporation is the recognition that core competences constitute the foundation of a company's competitive advantage. The paradigm of resource-based strategy, which became popular at the beginning of the 1990s through the work of C. K. Prahalad and Gary Hamel, views the source of strategic advantage not so much as the result of a smart positioning in an existing industry space but in the distinct portfolio of the core competences of the firm.[4] Such competences can be brands, hard assets, distinctive processes, technological expertise, distinctive talent, distinctive access to capital markets, and more. They are hard to imitate and constitute the anchor of a company's identity. A significant part of these competences result from the company's "DNA," which often goes back to the founding business idea and is deeply embedded in the organization's historical practices. But there are also competences that may have been acquired over time, either through mergers and acquisitions, or through internal organizational learning and transformation processes.

The decisions about what competences constitute the core of an organization and how they should be orchestrated and developed lies at the heart of the firm's strategy and its learning challenge. Core competences constrain the room for strategic maneuvering as the success of new business opportunities depends to a large extent on how well they connect with the firm's competence portfolio. How companies perceive their core competences has also major influence on the partnership architecture of a firm. The definition of a company's competence portfolio determines what business activities need to remain within the boundaries (that is, within direct control) of the firm and which ones can be outsourced or delivered by partners in the value chain. The choice is always a strategic one, as it is based on assumptions about which activities can maximize value creation and can best leverage a company's position in the industry.

The importance of understanding, developing, and nurturing core competences creates a complex corporate learning imperative, beyond the domain of building skill sets. Aligning employee qualification with the strategic goals of the organization is an important element in managing the competence portfolio of an organization. But people-oriented "competence management" alone does not sufficiently address the larger learning challenge. Equally important is the smart design of structures and mechanisms that build and reinforce the core competence of the organization. Here, corporate learning must help create a strategic discourse about the industry dynamics, the company's capability base, and the business opportunity spaces that result from linking the two. This requires the design of dedicated spaces that foster learning about the company and about its environment, through smart and honest interaction with internal and external stakeholders. In other words, ensuring and leveraging a company's core competence requires learning activities that are closely connected to the strategy process, transcending the current role of the corporate learning practice.

The Growing Importance of the Periphery

The accelerating change in the corporate environment has a significant effect on the leadership capabilities required by an organization. Processes that require the formal involvement of several functions and multiple internal layers of control are not only slow and tedious, they create a culture of inertia and blind obedience to rules. While these processes may work in stable and predictable environments where rules don't change, they become dysfunctional in a fast-changing context that requires entrepreneurial spirit, flexibility, and real-time response. Large corporations that are hamstrung by lengthy internal processes and a culture of silos have a significant disadvantage compared to small and nimble competitors who don't have to make their way through a jungle of red tape. To remain competitive, large corporations have to let go of steep hierarchies and central control and instead empower the periphery of the organization. Decision power and operational leadership need to move to the external boundaries of the firm, places that are in direct touch with the real world.

Empowering the periphery is a massive learning challenge for large organizations. It requires a major reset of the cognitive maps of executives, managers, and employees alike. The top must learn to let go of operational control and become instead a body that provides identity and overall strategic guidance. The key role of senior leadership is to create the right organizational architecture that encourages entrepreneurship, strategic discourse, and cross-functional collaboration. Corporate learning can play a major role in reshaping the mindset from a command-and-control mentality to a primarily *enabling* role that creates an environment where the periphery can thrive.

Middle management that was accustomed to playing a role as transmission belt between the orders from the top and the execution at the bottom must become entrepreneurial. They need to learn to make their own decisions, challenge senior leadership with creative inputs they receive from the environment, collaborate across boundaries without previous approval, and lead in a spirit of responsible semi-autonomy.

Employees who have learned to accommodate themselves to a command-and-control culture that rewarded obedience and blind execution need to become decisive and take action when dealing with customer complaints, process flaws, or quality management.

And this is just the people part of the equation. Empowering the periphery also requires the design of enabling organizational mechanisms and policies that help create the desired leadership culture. It requires a learning architecture that facilitates the interplay of responsibilities along the vertical and horizontal lines of the organization and that helps capitalize on the learning opportunities that result from a larger and more consciously managed interface with the market.

The Emergence of Globally Networked Organizations

Smart companies have a deep understanding of how they can achieve optimal leverage by keeping value-generating activities for themselves while entering into partnerships and alliances for noncore activities. Focusing on the core and partnering for the noncore has organizational consequences that again put a learning pressure on companies—and this time a pretty complex one: Organizations need to learn to let go of operational control of non-strategic activities and learn to act successfully in networks.

Giving up control is a major challenge, one that has little to do with teaching knowledge or skills but with developing the social and political abilities to orchestrate a company's stakeholder universe. Many of the activities that were formerly performed within the boundaries of the firm are no longer controlled by only one player; they require now the collaboration of a complex network that often is dispersed all over the world and may include hundreds of players. In globally networked organizations, a firm's competitive advantage lies not so much in being the "best," but in its ability to co-create with others and to orchestrate this process of co-creation in the most efficient and effective way.

Performing within an interdependent network of equals requires different strategic and operational leadership skills than those used in a hierarchically controlled organization. The traditional leadership model of command and control works fine *within the boundary* of each organization of the network, but hierarchical power does not work *between* the members of a network that co-creates. The interplay between the players needs horizontal coordination and adjustment processes, and these follow the logic of leading without formal power.

In addition, a network is only sustainable if its members can create an overarching win-win architecture that provides enough value for each of them to stay committed to the network. With the exception of rare monopolistic relationships, the members of a co-creation network are typically involved in many different value-chain webs that may compete or collaborate or both. Leadership and influence in the network is not a function of formal authority, but a function of the ability to provide maximum value for the entire *community* of players. The most successful companies will be those that can position themselves best in the battle for premium customers, suppliers, and other network partners and that understand how to optimize processes and profitability *for the entire network* instead of only for themselves. While such an optimization process requires investments and commitments from all stakeholders, it also creates a sustainable network with a sense of joint ownership of the space and a high degree of mutual value-chain integration.

Given this trend, the corporate learning challenge of globally networked organizations involves nurturing the company's competence portfolio while at the same time helping to build a hard-to-beat collaborative network architecture. Developing the organizational capability to lead successfully as a *network player* is the basis for competing successfully in the new "flat world." The challenge is to create a learning process that emphasizes the development of the communicative and collaborative abilities of the organization in favor of the traditional unilateral treatment of external stakeholders.

This challenge extends the reach of the learning function beyond the boundaries of an organization. Any learning architecture that fosters interorganizational collaboration needs to include the stakeholders that are members of the collaborating network. Corporate learning must reach out to customers, suppliers, alliance partners, or regulators and design an enabling learning environment for the entire value web. Successful stakeholder orchestration, designed as an ecological space that helps a network improve its collaboration, is an invaluable capability that helps secure industry leadership.

The Learning Challenge

The five issues reviewed in this chapter force organizations and their leaders to fundamentally reframe their mindsets and rethink the way they operate today. They create a comprehensive learning imperative that demands much more than just the usual training and development efforts. The new learning questions are:

- How can we create organizational structures, systems, and cultures to cope with the new realities? How can we create robust designs for dealing with massive change?
- How can we exploit the potential of disruptive change as a learning opportunity?
- How can we excel in orchestrating the generation, distribution, and sharing of relevant knowledge across the internal and external boundaries of the organization?
- How can we improve our understanding of the core competences of the organization? How can we improve our understanding of industry dynamics and emerging opportunity spaces that allow us to leverage our competences? How can we enable an ongoing discourse about the resulting strategic rationale?
- How can we empower the periphery of the organization to improve our ability for real-time response? How can we design the outer membrane of the organization in a way that maximizes learning from and with our external stakeholders?
- How can we design learning spaces for the organization that help us to perform as leaders in a horizontally networked world? How can we help orchestrate the external stakeholders of our organization in a way that maximizes the value of the entire network?

These questions open up an exciting and novel universe for corporate learning. But capturing that universe comes with a significant challenge: how to transform the practice of corporate learning itself so that it can effectively respond to these learning imperatives.

The current identity of the corporate learning field is too narrow and restricted to take on this challenge. With its focus on HR processes and people qualification, corporate learning today provides an important contribution, but this role covers only a fraction of the full range of learning imperatives on the horizon. The forces we have discussed require responses that reach far beyond the domain of the traditional human capital practices—responses that address the way organizations operate and strategize, the way they do business. What is required are creative strategic learning interventions that not only shape the texture of their own corporation but have the potential to touch the external stakeholder universe as well.

The mission of a new and comprehensive corporate learning approach is to gently redesign the system—how it works internally and how it deals with its external environment. Its task is to help organizations and their people develop an understanding of their core competences, assist in creating the right networks, enable these networks to excel in co-creation, and find ways to best leverage the company's position within its stakeholder universe. Learning needs to create spaces of strategic discourse among stakeholders inside and outside the organization; it needs to "teach" horizontal leadership. It must encourage internal and external collaboration and then support that collaboration with intelligent, elegant organizational designs. In short, corporate learning has to become an *organizational architect* that helps anchor system capabilities in a way that makes corporations not only economically successful but also ethically responsible players in this globally interdependent economic, political, and ecological space.

Getting corporate learning to this point may sound ambitious if not impossible to achieve. However, when we take off the mental blinders that restrict us to a traditional notion of the learning domain and look more closely at the potential of a wider vision of learning, new paths open up that allow us to start reframing the identity of the practice and embark on a journey of strategic transformation of the corporate learning industry.

Notes

1. Schumpeter, Joseph A. *Capitalism, Socialism and Democracy.* New York: Harper, 1975. [Originally published 1942].
2. Florida, Richard. *The Rise of the Creative Class: And How It's Transforming Work, Leisure, Community and Everyday Life.* New York: Basic Books, 2003.
3. Brown, John Seely, and Duguid, P. *The Social Life of Information.* Cambridge, MA: Harvard Business Press, 2000.
4. Prahalad, C. K., and Hamel, Gary. "The Core Competence of the Corporation." *Harvard Business Review* (May/June 1990): 79–91.

CHAPTER TWO

Enlarging the Framework of Learning

Most of today's learning activities in large organizations happen in more or less sophisticated settings that focus on the qualification of the workforce and the development of leadership bench strength. These activities are driven by an honest commitment to learning that goes to great lengths to excel, but they are a poor response to the larger corporate learning imperative. They follow a narrow paradigm of learning, one that takes its identity from the institutional educational sector at large, with its focus on individual qualification. Consistent with this paradigm, learning is usually perceived as the domain of the HR function, tasked with employee skill development. Frequently acting remote from the business and struggling to get a voice in the boardroom, corporate learning is one of the weaker stakeholders in the power game of business functions. It comes as no surprise that when times get tough, learning is often the first to see its budget cut.

To master the learning challenges outlined in Chapter One, we need to look at the notion of corporate learning with new eyes and extend the current paradigm of the practice beyond its traditional boundaries. This chapter makes the effort to reframe our lenses to get a different, more comprehensive view of learning—both as a phenomenon and as an instrument to enhance capabilities. We will do this by looking at learning from three angles.

First, we examine the *nature of learning*. The common notion is that learning happens through the transfer of knowledge or information from experts and teachers to learners. This perspective does not do justice to the complexity nor to the important social implications of learning. It takes learning out of the individual and social context and treats the process as a mechanistic transaction.

A different, more appropriate approach is to conceive of learning as an interactive, highly contextual process. To help readers of this book understand the far-reaching implications of this view, we briefly review in the first section of this chapter some elements embedded in the nature of learning that make it a powerful transformational force.

Second, we explore the *dimensions of learning.* The current educational system in the Western world is almost obsessively focused on the intellectual, cognitive, and analytical competences. This obsession is closely linked with the dominant paradigm of scientific inquiry designed around the rational explication of the world and resulting in a mechanistic approach to dealing with it. While the emphasis on linear rationality has been the dominant way of Western thinking since René Descartes, we know that the cognitive domain is only one part of the equation—and not always the most important one.

The intellectual genius who blooms in secrecy has no impact on the world; he needs to act and get "in touch" with his environment. The expert who is not able to communicate her expertise to others in an inspiring way remains dry and boring. The smartest analysis of consulting firms remains moot if it is not put into practice in a complex web of corporate power dynamics. In other words, just being smart does not cut it; creating impact on our environment requires emotional, social, and political competences that enable us to make things happen in a context of competing interests.

Furthermore, acting blindly in our interest without a deep understanding of the interconnectedness of systems and the long-term consequences of actions stresses the balance of systems and is ultimately destructive. To assure our long-term survival, we need to put knowledge and what we can do with it into the context of moral responsibility and universal ethical standards. To get a better grasp of these multiple dimensions that learning has to address, we separate them analytically and look at each of them in more detail.

Third, we examine the three *domains* that corporate learning needs to address as a core practice for assuring an organization's ability to compete in complex and fast-changing environments: *people excellence, organizational excellence,* and *strategic excellence.* We all agree that there is no great organization without great people, but the best people cannot unfold their potential if they are hamstrung by poor organizational structures and cultures. People excellence and organizational excellence are two sides of one coin that need to be addressed together if they should come to life. But even great organizations with great people are doomed to failure if they rest on their laurels or rely on their previous successes. This is where strategic excellence comes into play—the ability to continually challenge the rules of the game, transcend existing business models, and orchestrate the organization's stakeholder network in

Figure 2.1. Expanding the Paradigm of Learning

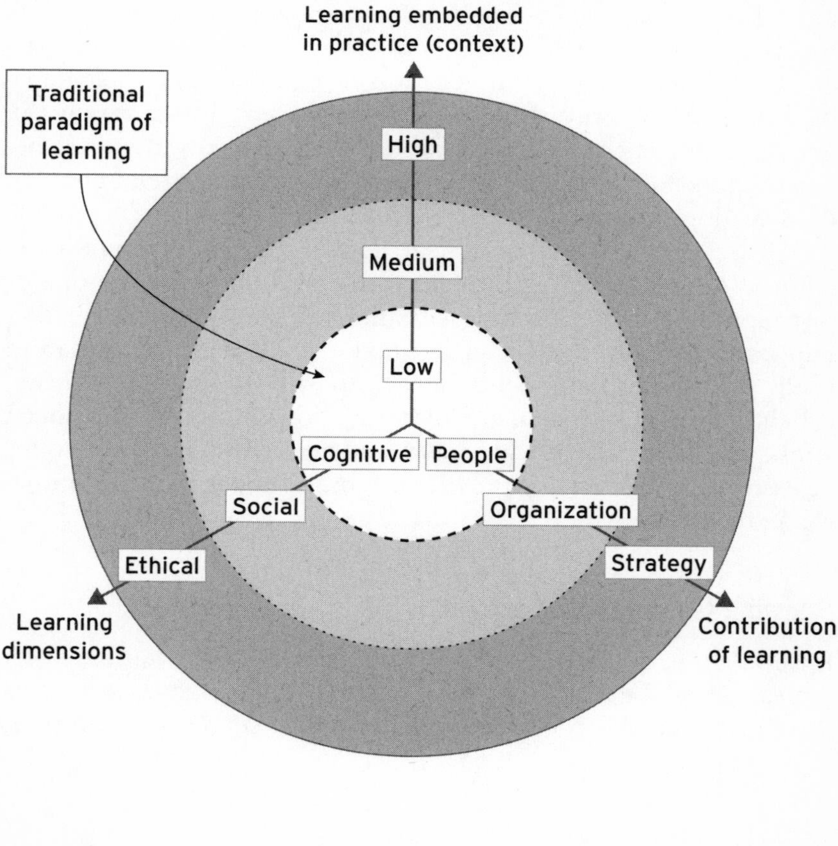

a way that leverages the firm's core competences. The third section of the chapter analyzes the three domains and shows the potential contributions that corporate learning architectures can provide to build and nurture all these abilities.

Examining learning from these three angles opens up a new universe for corporate learning and allows us to envision new development paths for its practice. Figure 2.1 illustrates the three directions learning can take.

The Nature of Learning

One of the most limiting constructs of learning starts with the assumption that information and knowledge are context independent and can be mechanistically transferred from the teacher into the student. We then measure the effectiveness of the transfer through tests and compare the student's knowledge before and after the learning intervention to assess if something has been learned. In this model, effective learning is defined by creating as little loss of information as possible. This mechanistic view perceives the student as a passive vessel into which the teacher funnels content. This model does not consider the specific context of the student, nor does it consider the context of the learning situation.

However, the nature of learning is that it is completely context dependent. Not only does the student bring his or her own context to the learning situation, the essence of learning happens through the social context of the learning situation itself. We cannot dig deep here into this fundamental issue, which is the subject of major discourse in philosophy and social sciences, but we will quickly cover some conceptual cornerstones of learning because they provide the basis for most of the frameworks that follow suit.

Learning Is Context Dependent

Except in very early childhood, learning never happens on a clean slate. Learning always happens in a context, no matter whether we read a book, listen to a speech, search the Internet, or discuss with friends or colleagues. Whatever the "true" reality may be, we always see the world through a cognitive and emotional filter that has been shaped by our previous experiences. We need these mental models and frameworks to make sense of the world. When we "learn," we connect new information with that which we already have and interpret this input on the background of our own history, which is our personal context. There is no objectivity in the world of human communication; whatever we learn, it is always biased and subjective, according to the specific context in which we think and live.

Relevant Learning Happens by Encountering Difference

Relevant learning happens through our daily encounter with the world, through our experiences and the interactions we have with people. As people always bring their personal histories and backgrounds to the table, each encounter is necessarily a meeting of different mindsets and different interpretations of the world. Encountering new and unfamiliar perspectives or situations shakes up the mental and emotional models that help us structure the meaning of the world. They are a threat to the old and familiar, and as such, they irritate us. However, such differences and irritations are the very source of learning. We learn where the familiar meets the unfamiliar, where different lenses to see the world collide, and we have to create a new and common meaning.

Differences of perspective are nothing that needs to be suppressed; on the contrary, if we would all know the same, think the same, feel the same, and had the same interests, no learning and no development would happen. However, we do have the tendency to negate differences or to "solve" them through unilateral power. While this may be necessary in order to act efficiently in our daily operations, it destroys the learning potential of irritation.

The art of designing great learning contexts is to optimize the degree of difference and irritation. If there is nothing new to experience, there is little to learn. But the same happens if there is too much difference—if you teach high school content to a first grader, even the smartest cannot learn. Creating "designed spaces of irritation" is at the heart of the learning practice, no matter whether the space is a classroom, an organization, or a business process.

Learning Creates Social Fabric

When people who have different perspectives meet, they both learn if they let their differences reframe their view of reality. But they learn not only as individuals; the process of negotiating different worldviews creates also a shared experience and constitutes a social relationship between the parties. In other words, meaningful learning creates a social fabric that connects the participants in a new way. Great learning designs recognize the power of this process and treat the creation of relationship networks that happen through integrating diverse perspectives as a goal that is often more important than the topical learning content.

Structuring the learning as mere knowledge transfer, in which the expert talks and the audience listens, wastes much of the rich potential of the interactive process. A restricted notion of learning that is based primarily on a one-way transfer of knowledge may have its role in a narrow realm of skill training and fact-based learning. But to fully exploit the nature of the learning process, the teacher-student relationship needs to morph into a discourse of equals who bring different perspectives to the table, with the expertise of the "student" being as serious a contribution to the learning process as the expertise of the "expert." To create real learning, a "teacher" needs to become rather a facilitator of a joint discovery of insights among various worlds of experience than a feeder of prefabricated knowledge pieces.

The Role of Boundaries to Demarcate Context

The diversity of perspectives does not always lead to learning and the development of productive social fabric—it may even lead to the opposite. We can see this on the individual level, when a person has a hard time letting go of prejudice or a certain mindset; it is even harder when we deal with larger-scale systems whose "frames of reference" are petrified in organizational structures and routines and in the way they do business. Systems have a natural tendency to close their boundaries to preserve their identity. They perceive "the others" as threat to their interests, and they naturally resist putting their established frames of reference to the test.

But boundaries between people, departments, or companies are the very space where learning happens; they are the place where difference is established. To experience the difference we have to cross or at least test these boundaries. This is a delicate act. Keeping boundaries closed like an oyster creates autistic silos. Abolishing them levels the difference and thus destroys the distinct identities of the players. Boundaries have to be semipermeable to allow for a productive interplay between the various sets of knowledge and mutual mental frameworks. Smart boundary design is one of the most delicate and most important tasks of a learning architecture.

This task becomes even more critical in light of the new dynamics that emerge in the move toward networked organizations and the resulting loss of direct control. Networks force companies to collaborate across boundaries as their formerly captive processes become part of a distributed co-creation process. Every company that has externalized elements of its chain that it previously "owned" knows how crucial it is to carefully design the new interface—the new boundary. Organizations that excel in creating smart architectures for the purpose of joint systems learning will become trusted leaders in their network and create an important strategic advantage.

The brief review of elements in the nature of learning demonstrates the importance of contextualizing learning interventions. In more layman terms: Learning is only effective if it happens embedded in practice. The traditional classroom setting is artificial and context poor; it leaves it to the student to contextualize learning "back home"—the familiar issue of learning transfer. Corporations are extremely context rich by their very nature, but we still conduct many corporate learning activities remote from their daily life. In the next pages we show that by conceiving learning as a core business practice, we are not only able to put learning into context, but we can also exploit the nature of learning for creating new and better organizational practices. Let us now turn to the various dimensions of learning.

The Dimensions of Learning

If you ask people on the street how they would define *learning*, most would say that it means acquiring knowledge about facts and technical skills in order to perform tasks. Digging a bit deeper, they might add that learning also has to do with the development of critical thinking. They will think about their school or university experiences, maybe about some corporate seminars, or about reading books. And this is it. They would not think about the learning that happens when children (or adults) play and discover the world through trial and error. They would not think about everyday learning experiences that make a person see the world differently, such as travel, encounters with fascinating people, or significant events in the life of a person. And they would most probably not think about the natural learning processes that happen in complex systems in communities, organizations, industries, or even societies. When organizations limit the definition of learning to this narrow and limited universe of what happens in traditional settings, they incur tremendous opportunity costs, as it obstructs their view of the potential of the concept. A narrow definition also allocates the practice of learning to the current institutional frameworks commonly thought to "own" the learning function—such as HR departments and business schools—but that are ill suited to address and orchestrate more complex learning challenges.

To overcome the blinders of the mainstream definition of learning, we need to take a closer look at various dimensions that come into play when we learn. These dimensions happen concurrently in every holistic learning process; I separate them here merely for analytical reasons.

Topical Learning

This dimension is closest to the traditional definition of learning, and it is also the easiest to deal with. Its objective is the acquisition of facts and knowledge about the world. Topical learning happens through listening to others who tell us what they know about the world, may it be through personal encounters, reading books, watching television, or searching the Internet. As such, this dimension lends itself best to the notion of learning as the transfer of knowledge. This type of learning requires minimal social interaction; much of it can happen though self-directed study. The didactical challenge lies primarily in structuring the knowledge in a way that it is easy to comprehend, and its success is measured by the learner's ability to reproduce facts, usually through tests and exams. It is the only dimension of learning that lends itself to objective assessments—people can either reproduce the knowledge or not. The ease and low cost of measurement is one of the reasons that have given this dimension a disproportionate importance among the dimensions in most learning institutions.

Analytical Learning

Acquiring knowledge about the world is important, but if we limit learning to this single dimension, we would be nothing more than a dumb database. To deal with knowledge in a meaningful way, we need to understand its context, assess its relevance, and interpret and analyze its deeper implications. To create new insights, we need to be able to take knowledge out of its familiar context, look at it from different angles, and establish creative connections with other contexts. While elements of this competence may be acquired through listening to various experts or reading about different perspectives on the same subject, it can unfold best in facilitated dialogue with teachers who understand the art of critical inquiry. Typical learning settings in the business world would be case studies in which the richness of participants' perspectives is used by a skilled facilitator to elicit various aspects of a case. However, analytical competence is hard to measure. Criteria are the depth of understanding and the breadth of perspectives on a subject, the ability to critically evaluate implicit assumptions and ideological biases in conformation, and so on.

The two dimensions of topical and analytical learning address the cognitive aspect of how to make sense of the world. The vast majority of formalized learning efforts are dedicated just to these two dimensions; topical and analytical learning represent the scientific-rationalistic paradigm that has dominated Western societies since the Enlightenment. They are important for the progress of science, and they provide a basis for dealing with the world in a rational way, based on knowing and assessing information. They are the undisputed domain of academic institutions. They play a key role in the development and nurturing of technical subject matter expertise, and they also have their place in executive education. However, restricting the notion of learning to its cognitive dimension separates it from the reality all learning is applied in: the social and political context.

Emotional Learning

This dimension of learning deals with the ability to gain a thorough understanding of oneself. Emotional learning has to do with personal growth. It includes insights into strengths and weaknesses, into the dynamics of one's personality, the ability to deal with one's emotions in a conscious and constructive way, and the capacity to reflect on the appropriateness of internalized standards. The overall objective of emotional learning is to develop integrity, authenticity, and a strong identity that is flexible and stable at the same time. This type of competence we acquire in a very different way. Insights about personal idiosyncrasies and the ability to handle them in a constructive way cannot be achieved through knowledge transfer and analytical sharpness. We achieve personal growth and a stable identity through meditation, through trusted friends who provide honest feedback, through personal coaches, or even psychotherapists. There is no objective method to measure the achievement of emotional learning; however, we can use subjective feedback and the assessment of our trusted social environment, because identity develops and constitutes itself only in interaction with others. This leads us to the next dimension of learning.

Social Learning

Social learning deals with the ability to interact successfully within one's immediate social context, in direct encounter with others. Successful interaction requires putting one's own assumptions and convictions into perspective by getting into the shoes of others and looking at the world through a variety of lenses. It also requires sensibility for social processes and the ability to act effectively within them, with an understanding how one's actions affect the dynamics of the network one is part of. This dimension of learning must happen, by definition, within a social context; its learning arena is the microcosm of relationships that we can directly influence. It does not follow the logic of knowledge transfer but the logic of interactive discourse. It deals not with the domain of rationality but with the domain of mutual influence. The dimensions of social and emotional learning are tightly connected; the stronger a person rests in his or her identity, the more flexibility he or she can afford in social situations. And social situations are the context in which identity is redefined on a continuous basis.

While the dimensions of emotional and social learning are underrepresented in the traditional world of "academic" learning, they find ample consideration in the corporate world of learning. It is widely recognized that leadership and collaboration require primarily emotional and social competences, and a plethora of specialized vendors offer coaching, personal and team development, experiential training, outdoor experiences that are supposed to get people in touch with their inner selves, and more. Other than academic institutions of learning, the field is practically unregulated and highly fragmented, not the least because of the difficulty of assessing qualification and results. This makes these dimensions no less important, however. Business schools, with their focus on the cognitive dimensions, play practically no role in this arena, although there is a growing awareness among executive education institutions that they miss out on an important market by not addressing the emotional and social universe of learning.

Political Learning

Social competence and emotional authenticity allow people to act successfully in the microcosm of immediate communication. However, this does not automatically mean that they are as effective in more complex environments, where relationships become indirect if not anonymous and require political savvy. Such environments require the ability to deal with people who are not just individuals, but who represent interests. Political learning gains in importance as the size and complexity of an organization grows. This dimension is rarely featured in the literature on learning; if at all, the term *political learning* is used in the context of civic education and political engagement—and it refers usually to topical and analytical learning about the traditional political domain.

For our purposes, we need a different, wider definition of politics, one that views the political sphere as everything that relates to power dynamics beyond the social microcosm of direct interaction. Under this perspective, the objective of political learning is to successfully act beyond one's immediate social context. It addresses the ability to understand and manage the interests of stakeholder groups and the power dynamics within and between these groups. Achieving political impact requires a deep understanding of complex stakeholder dynamics and the ability to influence these dynamics through direct and indirect interventions. As such, it requires analytical sharpness, emotional strength, and communicative competence—plus skills in the realms of power and diplomacy.

In contrast to the previously discussed dimensions, there are few if any intentionally designed spaces in which political learning takes place. The discipline of political science takes care of the cognitive-analytical aspects of this dimension, and there are college initiatives that engage students in community work, creating seeds for political engagement that may lead to political savvy and higher political participation. But there are few dedicated learning initiatives with the explicit objective of creating political competence in organizations. This is remarkable. After all, senior executives in large corporations spend a significant amount of their time navigating the slippery floor of organizational politics, and orchestrating stakeholder interests—a genuine political skill—is a key responsibility of every business leader.

Ethical Learning

The emotional, social, and political dimensions of learning enlarge the concept beyond the cognitive paradigm. However, excellence in all these dimensions does not necessarily lead to ethically responsible behavior. On the contrary, political competence comes often with ruthlessness, even corruption, undermining the productive interplay of the overall stakeholder universe.

The objective of ethical learning is to think and act according to universal ethical principles that take the larger societal and ecological context into account. It requires insights in the moral consequences of actions, not only for the immediately concerned stakeholders but for the larger universe we are all part of. The ethical dimension is of paramount importance for the long-term survival of systems, and it usually grows in importance with the power and influence of a stakeholder. It requires not only a deep understanding of the intended and unintended consequences of one's actions, but a moral consciousness that respects alien interests and takes them as seriously as one's own.

The ascent of corporate responsibility is a clear indication that the corporate world is beginning to understand its critical role in driving the development of this planet; globalization transcends national regulation and allows for a relatively easy movement of assets and resources across the globe. The global governance sophistication of Fortune 100 corporations exceeds the capabilities of most if not all national governments. With transnational power comes the responsibility of global citizenship.

But there is even a more mundane case to be made for corporate ethics: its increasing importance as an element of authentic branding. In times where products and even services become commodities, differentiation happens through trust and reputation—priceless assets if they can be achieved. To that extent, investments in ethical learning are not just charity but do provide tangible returns. As with political learning, there currently exist few if any designed learning spaces for developing ethical competence, neither for individuals nor for organizations. It is nevertheless a critical dimension for corporate learning.

Actional Learning

This last dimension may be the most important of them all. All of the competences mentioned remain moot if they are not enacted in the world. Real learning happens only when it becomes action, and it is through acting that we demonstrate learning. The actional dimension stretches across the six previous domains of learning. It addresses the ability to apply knowledge, draw practical consequences from analytical insights, execute intentions in a social environment, take risks, and implement ideas. This learning is the ability to apply all of the dimensions in the interest of having an intended impact on the world. It is closely related to entrepreneurship, to the ability to create a vision and realize it through a smart path of action.

Because actional learning is a kind of meta-dimension, we find it embedded in many learning settings as a more or less conscious element of the design. We find it in models of apprenticeship, which are particularly relevant in industries such as entertainment, specialized crafts, consulting, or natural science. We find it in executive programs that apply action learning elements to link learning with business issues; we find it in the training of technical skills. Although actional learning is pervasive, it deserves to be treated as a separate dimension because it does not always come naturally. In a way, it is the most relevant of all dimensions, because every learning happens through action, through experiencing the world. Designing experiences that allow inter*action* with the world is at the essence of the practice of corporate learning. Figure 2.2 summarizes the seven dimensions.

This brief exploration of the multiple dimensions of learning unfolds a universe that reaches beyond our intuitive connotation of learning. If we rank the dimensions by how strong they are anchored in educational institutions, we see a clear dominance of the cognitive domain, which is the dominant paradigm of the academic world. Less prominent, but still considered critical in the corporate world, are emotional, social, and actional competences, especially for managers and leaders whose performance depends on how well they master the social context. However, to satisfy these learning needs, corporations have to tap into a less regulated and highly fragmented vendor environment: the world of coaches, facilitators, and leadership

Figure 2.2. The Seven Dimensions of Learning

Topical Learning	Reproduce facts and knowledge about topics
Analytical Learning	Assess the context and meaning of knowledge; establish creative connections between different paradigms
Emotional Learning	Personal growth, self-management, authenticity, charisma, integrated personality
Social Learning	Role flexibility, self-distance, ability to effectively act within the immediate social microsystem
Political Learning	Ability to maneuver effectively within the dynamics of large systems; manage power beyond the immediate social context
Ethical Learning	Internalization of universalistic ethical principles, ability to think and act socially and ecologically responsible (global citizenship)
Actional Learning	Ability to act, take risks, implement ideas, apply all of the above for effective action

learning firms. Meanwhile, the political and ethical dimensions are entirely orphaned in the current notion of learning, without institutional home and with little awareness about their importance for strategic excellence.

The Three Domains of Corporate Learning

Let us now change the lens and see what learning can contribute to the most fundamental needs of organizations: people excellence, organizational excellence, and strategic excellence. All three domains are equally important, and smart corporate learning architectures can play a unique and central role in each of them. However, to capture this role, learning must step beyond its current key function as a provider of qualification services and begin to act at the core of the business process.

People Excellence

Creating people excellence is the undisputed domain of corporate learning. Learning has to ensure that the qualifications, skills, and competences of a company's workforce stay continuously aligned with the strategic requirements of the firm. This is a Herculean task on its own; accelerating technological change shortens the shelf-life of knowledge, and industry discontinuities force companies to continuously develop and change their business models. Also, strategic decisions may lead to a reconfiguration of the desired capability portfolio, requiring the development of new skills and new competences. This puts a significant pressure on organizations to stay cutting edge with its workforce's level of qualification. The pressure is exacerbated through the increasing importance of knowledge and expertise as sources of competitive advantage. Equally challenging is the creation of a great and sustaining leadership pipeline; it requires tools to recruit and retain the best leadership talent and support its development so new leaders can excel in meeting the complex challenge of managing in a globally networked, fast-changing world.

The tools to create people excellence through learning reach from traditional skill training to top business school programs, from carefully designed action-learning programs to coaching and outdoor team development exercises, or communities of practice. They feature advanced e-learning tools, sometimes even videogames and virtual platforms such as Second Life. The creativity and quality of didactical designs in the corporate settings are usually much higher than in the external educational system because of a higher pressure to create results. Corporate learning excels in the domain of people excellence.

Organizational Excellence

Creating people excellence is a key domain of learning; however, it does not address the learning and development needs of the organization. You may develop the best and brightest people, but they won't perform well if they are hamstrung by organizational inertia, multilayered hierarchies, cumbersome decision processes, or a culture of mistrust and intrigue. Corporate learning remains toothless if it does not get a say in the overall design of the organization.

Redesigning structures, mechanisms, incentive systems, and policies are among the most powerful tools of learning interventions. They can't rank high enough on the agenda of the corporate learning function. Organizing an enterprise in ways that foster discourse, cross-boundary collaboration, entrepreneurial risk taking, diversity, innovation, and more can be a much more efficient and effective intervention than spending money on training, coaching, and executive education while leaving the context untouched. We know that learning processes are stimulated and driven by creating a difference or an irritation in a system, and interventions can be created to do just this. Creating an organizational initiative that stimulates the right learning is more art than science; as every context is unique, it also requires diagnostic skills, political sensitivity, and design creativity and sophistication, but the rewards are a quantum leap richer than those derived from smart but narrow learning designs that focus on people qualification only.

Furthermore, corporate learning must contribute to developing and nurturing the right organizational capability portfolio. Such capabilities include not only people skills but the more deeply embedded core competences that can make a difference in the marketplace, such as speed of processes, technological expertise, precision engineering, large-scale distribution skills, mass customization, open innovation, brand equity, or whatever constitutes the core of competitive advantage. The challenge is to create a learning architecture that enables through its smart design a high-performing organization that excels in decision making and execution, is agile, and has a capability for continuous innovation and change.

Finally, corporate learning can play a particularly important role in supporting the success of a merger. Mergers and acquisitions frequently fail to realize their full potential because post-merger integration activities lack sophistication and are not designed as strategic and organizational learning processes. Under a learning perspective, every merger or joint venture provides an Eldorado of opportunity to reframe mindsets and to loosen up petrified structures. No function is better suited to provide platforms for discourse on the strategic meaning and the organizational implications of a merger. No other function has the organizational learning design expertise that is required to harvest the diversity of perspectives and cultures that comes with mergers.

Strategic Excellence

The third and most complex domain of corporate learning is developing strategic excellence by supporting a company's efforts to achieve and sustain industry leadership. There are some basic principles that organizations need to follow if they strive for strategic excellence, and this is where a smart corporate learning architecture comes into play. For one, companies need strategic sensibility; they need to stay alert to the dynamics of their industry to remain competitive in the present, and they need to sense discontinuities in their environment that may trigger radical change. In addition, companies need strategic creativity to respond to the industry dynamics by creating new business models that shake up the current rules of the game. They need to be able to identify opportunity spaces that result from the discontinuities and exploit them for their strategic benefit.

Staying alert requires the development and nurturing of sense-making skills at the boundaries of the organization that are in touch with the real world, as well as creating institutionalized spaces of irritation that can regularly stir up the existing cognitive maps. Exploiting emerging opportunity spaces requires the ability to look at the world through continuously refreshed lenses that see beyond the mainstream industry paradigm. And it requires a culture of bold entrepreneurship that encourages experimentation and allows failure.

A smart corporate learning architecture can help set up such spaces of irritation and design "sensitive touchpoints" in the environment to enhance continuous learning. It can also play a role in pushing for policies that foster organizational boldness through the design of protected "entrepreneurial spaces" that seek business model innovation. Such strategic learning designs help to fight "disease of the leader"—the tendency of leading corporations to rest with arrogance and pride on their success and remain stuck in business models and organizational routines that sooner or later become obsolete.

Furthermore, industry leadership is closely connected with the ability to maximize the performance of the value chain and the company's entire external partner network. This requires an architecture that engages stakeholders in an ongoing conversation to optimize the overall network design. Just as creating organizational excellence is a question of designing structures, mechanisms, processes, and policies that make the company learn, creating network performance is similarly a question of smart transorganizational design. However, this design cannot be imposed. Orchestrating networks requires network management skills that follow a different logic than hierarchically powered leadership. A smart corporate learning architecture needs to provide common spaces that instigate cross-boundary dialogue and ultimately create enabling mechanisms that foster collaboration, trust, and openness—important conditions for high-performing networks.

It is easy to see that the three domains—people excellence, organizational excellence, and strategic excellence—are closely interrelated and feed on each other. (Figure 2.3 provides a summary of the three domains.) People excellence drives organizational excellence (and vice versa), and organizational excellence affords industry leadership. Investments in one domain are likely to boost the other domains as well, as long as their interdependencies are consciously managed. Unfortunately, in many companies the interaction of the domains creates a negative loop instead. Bad leadership and skills deficits result in a low-performing organization, and a dysfunctional organization

Figure 2.3. Domains for Corporate Learning

People Excellence	Organizational Excellence	Strategic Excellence
▸Employee skill base aligned with desired capability portfolio	▸Organizational design (structures, mechanisms, systems, policies)	▸Strategic creativity
▸Developing and nurturing the right knowledge base	▸Develop and nurture the right capability portfolio	▸Business mode innovation
▸Talent management	▸Product and process innovation	▸Alliances and partnership management
▸Leadership development	▸Post-merger management	▸Stakeholder engagement and orchestration
▸Strategic HR system	▸Excellence in execution	▸Management of industry paradigm life cycle – fight the "disease of the leader"

inhibits people excellence. Poorly designed organizations lose in the battle for industry leadership, and a weak strategic position eventually leads to low performance.

It is the mission of a great corporate learning architecture to provide the overall framework for a concerted development of excellence in the domains of people, organization, and strategy. Establishing and managing such a framework is a conceptually challenging and politically delicate task; done well, it moves corporate learning center stage as a business practice that is key for the long-term survival of the firm.

CHAPTER THREE

The Integration of Learning with Business Processes

In Chapter Two we expanded our understanding of learning by discussing its context dependency, its multiple dimensions, and its potential contributions beyond the domain of people excellence. If we accept these premises, we need next ask how organizations can benefit from this expanded view of learning by integrating it into the heart of their business processes.

The common approach to learning positions the function in the HR department and tasks it for the most part with training and developing people. As such, learning activities happen on the margin of core organizational processes, and it requires a major effort to link them with the business. It is no coincidence that questions about proving the value of learning and aligning it with business requirements rank at the top of every CLO's agenda.

These questions become irrelevant when we transcend the current notion of learning and design everyday business activities as conscious learning processes. In other words, we create learning designs not just to shape the mindset and skills of employees and executives; we also design the structures, policies, and processes of the organization in a way that creates ongoing learning experiences that result in a smarter, more effective, and more ethical enterprise. This includes optimizing the interplay of the company's external partner network by reaching beyond the boundaries of the firm and designing a transorganizational learning platform for the relevant stakeholder universe.

However, expanding the learning notion from a people-centered HR function to a strategy-centered comprehensive enterprise function requires different capabilities, and it challenges the way learning is organized in most companies today.

Levels of Learning

To this end, this chapter introduces a five-level model of learning interventions, with each level requiring a more complex learning architecture. The five levels illustrate how learning can extend across the three domains of people, organization, and strategy by connecting to increasingly complex contexts, from qualifying individuals in a traditional educational setting to interventions that enable organizational change and eventually drive the business and the entire value chain of the corporation. As the levels progress, learning becomes more and more relevant as a core business function. Here's a review of each level.

Level 1: Standardized Learning

Standardized learning is the most traditional form of learning, the one we all know from our schools, universities, and corporate training events. It takes place in carefully structured didactical settings, usually with standardized professional teaching material that is scalable across a variety of markets. Standardized learning is entirely focused on qualification, and it addresses exclusively individuals, regardless of their affiliations. Assistance for transferring the acquired knowledge into specific actions that benefit the company or the business is usually not provided for and is viewed as the responsibility of the company and the participant.

Standardized learning makes sense if the topics are general, universally valid, and independent of any specific context. Examples are foreign language training, basic computer skills, writing training, or generic sales training. Some high-level education, such as the teaching of general management skills and specialized technical or functional expertise, also falls into this category.

Since the content is standardized, it makes no difference whether the programs are conducted within the company or offered externally, as an open enrollment program. Cost, quality of the content, and effective didactics are key factors in the selection of vendors. This form of learning is still the dominant business model for the executive education offerings of business schools—a segment that has become a significant revenue generator for many universities. It fits perfectly with the business model universities apply in their undergraduate and master's programs: lectures and seminars from expert professors who teach their carefully designed courses to exchangeable audiences. The market is very large, attractive, and very competitive, with universities, training firms, e-learning providers, and many more players competing for billions of purchasing dollars. Due to its context independence, this level of learning is an ideal candidate for outsourcing.

Level 2: Customized Learning

Customized programs attempt to connect the learning content to the specific context of the corporation. To achieve this, program designs are typically developed in collaboration with internal learning experts. Customization can vary in degree. At a low level, the framework of a standardized program is kept the same, but it is conducted with a group of participants who come from the same corporation, which allows the instructor to address specific issues of the company in the discussions and case studies. At a higher level of customization, the program providers hold interviews with executives, study the context of the corporation, and then devise a design in close collaboration with an internal team of learning experts. Customization here may also include the careful selection of the participant group to foster team building or cross-functional collaboration.

Customized programs attempt to consider the context of the participants and make it easier to transfer the lessons learned directly to the work situation. They are usually focused on qualification and individual learning, but they are a first step toward connecting with the context of the organization by using specific business challenges of the company as a learning conduit. As the participants of customized in-house programs come from one corporation, they allow a more open discourse about strategically sensitive issues. The programs can build a culture of trust that often survives beyond the event and becomes the basis for informal cross-functional and cross-business relationship networks that cut through otherwise tedious organizational structures and processes. "Alumni" from customized in-house programs often prove valuable. They can act as important liaisons for the learning function by providing input to improve the program and acting as ambassadors for certain topics. They may also form a network to continue to work on a certain agenda and connect their learning experience with organizational development and change initiatives they are involved in.

Business schools play a major role in providing customized programs. Prominent schools such as Harvard Business School, London Business School, or INSEAD make about 40 percent of their executive education revenues through in-house programs. However, many programs that business schools label as "customized" are often just a variation of their standardized offerings, as their business model allows for only a relatively low degree of customization. A higher degree of customization requires a thorough preparation for the idiosyncratic context of the company, and possibly follow-up activities in the company. It requires a sophisticated, highly flexible interface to manage challenging customer demands, and the dedication of a significant amount of time to activities beyond the traditional classroom involvement. And it requires professors who can not only teach but also work with experienced executives in an engaging and challenging way on their specific issues they face "at home." The few professors who have these capabilities have little incentive to put in this extra work if they do not get an individual consulting contract, but this is usually not in the interest of the business school. It comes therefore as little surprise that business schools are meeting increasing competition from specialized corporate learning vendors who focus their business models entirely on customization.

These first two levels are the undisputed domain of today's corporate learning function. They deal with qualifying individuals and teams so that they can perform better in corporate contexts. To that extent, they represent learning that contributes to people excellence. However, starting with Level 3, we transcend this common connotation of learning and enter a fundamentally different universe—the domain of large-scale systems intervention.

The focus of interventions shifts from connecting individual learning experiences with the organizational context (Level 2), to making the context itself learn.

Level 3: Learning as Driver of Organizational Change

At Level 3, learning drives the implementation of organizational change projects by designing and orchestrating a supporting corporate learning architecture. This requires more than just qualification efforts through training programs, although such efforts can continue to play an important role in a Level 3 learning initiative.

The task of the learning expert at this level is not so much the didactic preparation and delivery of content, but the development of tools, interventions, and policies that support and sustain the intended organizational change. In addition, change processes require a smart design of a process architecture that assures the right sequence of interventions and the overall consistency of the tool and policy kit. Every change architecture needs to consider internal stakeholder interests and actively involve them by assigning them roles and responsibilities and coaching them in the process. It typically includes workshops in which employees get together and work on topics related to the intended change—learning about themselves and their context while they work. It provides spaces for discourse such as town hall meetings, and it may include corporate communication campaigns, new policies, and more.

Level 3 learning is very different from the conventional classroom paradigm. It puts the learning space into the real life of the organization. It contextualizes learning by closely linking all learning activities with the immediate development need of the company. Through its emphasis on participation, change architectures have a major impact on the stakeholders of the learning process. Moving beyond mere qualification issues, Level 3 learning becomes an *organizational* challenge that requires the active involvement of line management and of corporate functions beyond HR.

However, as learning moves beyond the realm of individual qualification, it also moves beyond the established players of the learning industry. The integration of learning with organizational issues diminishes the role of business schools and training firms as "owners" of the corporate learning agenda. While they still play a role in delivering certain segments of the process, they become marginalized as their business model does not support the requirements of orchestrating complex change processes. As process design and facilitation become more prominent than content expertise, specialized change management consultancies, coaches, and trusted advisors enter the stage.

Level 4: Learning as Driver of Strategic Business Initiatives

At Level 4, the learning architecture is designed not only to implement internal organizational change; it becomes a key enabler in driving the business and fostering the strategic development of the company. Everyday managerial activities become elements of the learning architecture. Learning initiatives become business initiatives, and doing business becomes a learning process. Such initiatives can relate to strategy development, the optimization of business processes, the exploration of new business ideas, or the entry into a new market. These would happen anyway, with or without learning architecture, but managing them as a learning project makes the experience of operating in complex environments a hot spot for insights that can improve performance and trigger innovation. In other words, Level 4 learning increases the agility of an organization and fosters its strategic and operational excellence.

Action learning projects that use real business challenges as vehicles for learning are a good example of learning at this level. However, action learning frequently creates special project assignments on top of the regular business responsibilities of the participants. Business projects become a didactic tool for individual learning; the project results are nice to have but are not the purpose of the exercise. Real Level 4 learning turns this logic upside down by putting business challenges first and using learning principles to optimize the process of dealing with them.

Integrating learning with business issues requires an even stronger role of line management in the design and orchestration of the learning organization. Implementing internal change is still close to the HR function, which often includes a responsibility for organizational development; it deals primarily with the "soft" aspects of changing mindsets and creating employee engagement. Creating and nurturing Level 4 learning architectures, however, requires business acumen and positions the practice right in the core of the enterprise.

Level 5: Learning as Engine for Industry Transformation

Even if an organization excels in its organizational processes and business initiatives, its strategic success is ultimately dependent on the capabilities of its strategic partners. A chain is only as strong as its weakest link. Poorly organized and unsophisticated customers, suppliers, or alliance partners can create high transaction costs and diminish the performance of the overall network. Level 5 corporate learning deals exactly with this issue: how to develop the capabilities and optimize the performance not only of one's own corporation but of the entire network. To be able to play that role, the learning architecture needs to reach beyond the boundaries of the corporation and include external stakeholders that are relevant for the strategic success of the firm.

The challenge at Level 5 is primarily a political one: how to engage network partners to join and support a common learning architecture, and how to determine the common learning agenda. This requires a different form of leadership. Colliding perspectives and interests within a corporation can ultimately be solved through a top-level executive decision. But not so in a horizontal network of peers who have different roles but each needs to represent their own self-centered interests. How do you take the lead in designing a learning space that includes outside constituencies that cannot be controlled by the company's own hierarchical chain of command?

The answer is that Level 5 learning interventions are designed to genuinely support the learning processes of all participating players in a meaningful way. Level 5 can function only within the framework of a win-win architecture. This means that all involved parties need to have some insight into the rationale behind this model for learning. Great examples are learning projects that optimize collaboration across the value chain, for instance in the context of open innovation architectures, or platforms with outsourcing partners to improve the mutual interface management. Other examples are industry consortia that address standardization issues, or public-private partnerships to improve the infrastructure of the social and economic system.

Figure 3.1 summarizes the five levels and illustrates their increasing link to strategy and business processes. Note that the

Figure 3.1. Five Levels of Learning Linking with Business Processes

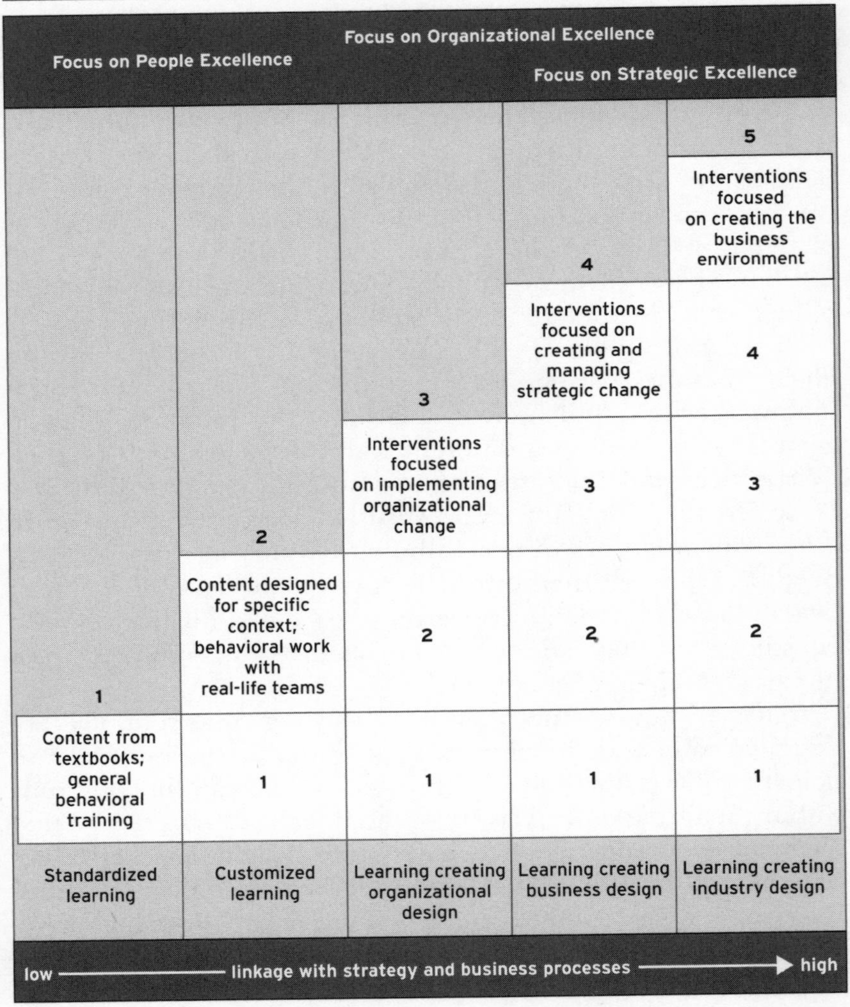

Focus on People Excellence		Focus on Organizational Excellence	Focus on Strategic Excellence	
				5 — Interventions focused on creating the business environment
			4 — Interventions focused on creating and managing strategic change	4
		3 — Interventions focused on implementing organizational change	3	3
	2 — Content designed for specific context; behavioral work with real-life teams	2	2	2
1 — Content from textbooks; general behavioral training	1	1	1	1
Standardized learning	Customized learning	Learning creating organizational design	Learning creating business design	Learning creating industry design

low ——————— linkage with strategy and business processes ————→ high levels are not mutually exclusive; in fact, they build upon each other and every new level has to contain elements of the previous level. The first two levels are limited to a traditional understanding of learning based on developing skills in individuals and enhancing productivity in existing teams; the higher levels facilitate the development of organizational capabilities and the creation of strategic competence.

The choice of the level has significant organizational implications. If companies limit their approach to learning to Levels 1 and 2, the responsibility for learning remains in its traditional space—in a training department that is usually a part of the HR function. After all, these levels of learning target the qualifications of people, not the capabilities of the organization. Ambitious CLOs who understand the importance of contextualization may continuously reach out to the business trying to maximize the relevance and impact of its learning activities, but by design they will always struggle with connecting to the "real world" of the business, and they will always have to justify their contribution to the bottom line.

The picture changes significantly the moment we move to Level 3 and beyond. While the first two levels require the design of an educational program that addresses the development of people, levels 3 and 4 require the design of processes and policies that address the development of the organization. They are learning interventions that aim for a conscious, didactically reflected change in the structure of actual business activities. While many companies have internal change projects and strategic business initiatives among their core activities to shape their daily life, they are rarely seen as learning processes because they lack a didactically smart design that leverages each process as a learning experience for the company.

Structuring business activities as learning processes cannot be delegated to the HR function alone; HR is usually not very well prepared for this task as their entire capabilities are focused on the domain of people issues. Levels 3 and 4 learning are *organizational* challenges that require the collaboration of a larger universe of relevant stakeholders within the company. They are impossible without cross-functional collaboration and the intense involvement of top and middle management—constituencies who usually have little or no functional involvement with learning issues. Advancing the learning agenda to these levels means deliberately transcending the organizational boundaries that tend to relegate the learning function to the ivory tower of a specialized department, where it struggles to be practical. They require reframing the notion of "learning" as not only the domain of learning professionals and HR departments but as a leadership practice that concerns the entire organization.

Level 5 then moves the domain of learning beyond the corporation and addresses the capabilities of the enlarged value chain the company is just part of. Today's smart companies may design their business as a continuous learning process, but their direct power to design processes usually ends at their external boundaries. In contrast, making customers, suppliers, or even competitors part of the learning architecture requires restructuring external nonhierarchical relationships and arranging the collaboration of stakeholders across the value chain.

Figure 3.2. The Impact of Learning Architectures on the Business System

Stage	Reference System	Key Players Within Learning Architecture	Impact on Business System	Perception of "Learning"
1 + 2	Human resource function	Learning and development department	Low	Functional responsibility
Internal Organizational Barriers				
3 + 4	Enterprise	All relevant stakeholders of the organization	Medium	Organizational challenge
External Organizational Barriers				
5	Enlarged value chain	Customers Suppliers Alliances Competitors Regulators	High	Strategic challenge

Figure 3.2 illustrates the implications of the various levels of learning interventions and the increasing strategic relevance of learning as it moves from lower to higher levels of complexity. It makes it very clear that learning needs to reinvent its identity to affect the business system.

Examples of Advanced Learning Interventions

To be able to play competently across the three domains—people, organization, and strategy—corporate learning needs a comprehensive portfolio of tools and approaches that can be diverse but have one thing in common: They are professionally designed to stimulate and enhance a learning process.

Figure 3.3 presents examples of interventions that cut across the three domains. These examples are by no means comprehensive; rather, they illustrate the potential diversity of a corporate learning portfolio. Methods that focus on individual competences, such as case studies, lectures, and leadership coaching, are familiar instruments from the toolkit of a traditional learning and people development function. Once we enter the space of building organizational and strategic competences, the interventions get closer to everyday business processes. What makes them

Figure 3.3. Some Tools and Interventions of a Comprehensive Learning Architecture

Individual Competence Focus		Organizational Competence Focus		Strategic Competence Focus	
Cognitive/ skill based	Emotional/ social	Internally oriented	Externally oriented	Value chain oriented	Innovation oriented
Lectures	Personal Growth	Cultural Change Projects	Benchmarking and Industry Research	Customer Visit Programs	Popcorn Stands
Case Studies	360-degree Feedback	Communities of Practice	Learning Expeditions	Value Chain Optimization	Corporate Venturing
Skill Training Programs	Coaching and Mentoring	Six Sigma	Business Projects	Learning Consortia	Destroy Your "Own Business"

different from being just a business process is their design as learning opportunities that maximizes the extraction of learning value for the overall system and their integration into an overarching system of corporate learning and development.

Let us take a brief look at some of the more exotic learning interventions that address organizational and strategic competence.

Learning Expeditions

Learning expeditions are carefully planned visits of a group of senior executives from a variety of functions to explore a strategically relevant issue. Such an expedition may include meetings with customers, suppliers, and regulators; it may include in-depth discussions with thought leaders and industry experts, or the visit of a series of cutting-edge innovators in an emerging technology space. The design of the learning expedition must assure a maximum of exploitation from the encounters of the group, including extensive debriefing and a careful examination of what can be utilized for better mastering the strategic challenge that triggered the expedition. Well designed, such expeditions are a powerful tool to open eyes and stay alert to external developments.

Customer Visit Programs

Customer visit programs are designed to achieve a deep understanding of the internal value chain of the customer and the role a company's product or service plays in creating value. Such visits allow a company to see "through the eyes of the customer" and redesign their own processes so that they provide true customer value. The visits are conducted by a multifunctional team, which may include manufacturing, product development, and marketing. The sales function plays no role other than providing the customer entry to assure a true listening and learning attitude. The cross-functional composition of the visiting team alone is a source of learning. A significant number of visits leads to a valuable database of customer intelligence, and it reframes the mindset of the organization toward a customer-centric perspective. Overall, customer visits are an excellent example for designing a systematic learning experience at the boundary of the firm.

Value Chain Optimization

This intervention creates collaborative spaces for members of a value chain for the purpose of mutually optimizing their processes and clarifying tacit assumptions about what provides value in the relationship. Tacit assumptions about the expected level of service can be major sources of avoidable transaction costs; taking a joint look at the cross-organizational process allows for a more efficient common process design than when individual players act on their own. In addition to the tangible cost savings, value-chain optimization exercises build trust and stronger relationships, and they help foster mutual understanding. But once again, their success depends on the smartness of the design built into the process in order to make this regular business activity become a source of sustainable organizational learning for the players.

Popcorn Stands

"Popcorn stands" are entrepreneurial assignments for leaders with high potential. They are noncore business activities of the corporation that have the potential to grow and become substantial, but there is no harm done if they fail (hence the name "popcorn stand"). They are not artificial exercises but operations that require real budgets and create real revenues. The executives get just-in-time support through a "board" that focuses not only on a traditional governance role but acts as a sounding and advisory board for the executive's learning process. Well designed, popcorn stands are a great way to foster entrepreneurial learning for the executives involved; well managed, they can also evolve into significant business opportunities for the corporation, in which case they can be folded into the business portfolio of the firm. If a company deploys a significant number of popcorn stands, it creates a contagious entrepreneurial culture.

Corporate Venturing

Corporate venturing is a focused strategic learning opportunity for organizations that own a venture capital (VC) unit. The process of scouting deals, assessing the strategic viability of business ideas, performing due diligence, and connecting selected deals to the portfolio of the firm is in itself each time a learning process. But there is much more: in most cases, startups and emerging companies are in need of professional management talent. Appointing young and promising leaders from the corporation as the CEO, CFO, or business development executives is an ideal way to expose them to an entrepreneurial environment and, at the same time, professionalize the startup. The young companies being funded also bring a fresh and unencumbered culture to large corporations, but it can only be harvested as an inspiring difference through a smart corporate learning design.

Finally, given that startups are usually funded by several VC units, corporate venturing is a great opportunity to build a network with other investors. Corporate co-investors are typically members of the same industry space that allows Level 5 learning; financial co-investors provide a different perspective on industry dynamics because they typically invest in a more diverse portfolio, which allows corporations to expand their horizons in terms of marketplace intelligence (Level 4).

"Destroy Your Own Business"

Learning initiatives that are designed to destroy one's own business are one of the boldest and most powerful tools for strategic learning and innovation. The idea behind this intervention is to anticipate disruptive business ideas by assigning the best team from the corporation to develop one. Although this may sound like a game, it is not. This tool puts a "heavy team" of bright and powerful executives outside their daily operations and asks them to try their best to come up with business ideas that undermine the core business of the firm. If they are successful, the idea is owned by the company, and the transition can be dealt with in a smooth process of "managed disruption." If they fail, the project puts the company nevertheless through a stress test that can ultimately strengthen its strategic capabilities. Again, the success of this depends much on the smart design of the intervention to maximize the learning inherent in this activity.

Although the examples discussed are generic, they illustrate a notion of corporate learning that reaches far beyond people qualification and the HR function. The case studies in Part Two of the book contain vivid examples of some of these as well as other advanced and innovative learning interventions.

Transforming the Corporate Learning Paradigm

Changing our lenses on the notion of learning does not come easily. If we prompt somebody with the word *learning*, we elicit powerful and often emotionally charged associations of childhood and adolescence experiences in the formal educational institutions. No matter how great those experiences might have been, they anchored in our minds and hearts an image of

Figure 3.4. Transforming the Corporate Learning Paradigm

Restricted Paradigm		Comprehensive Paradigm
Learning as people development	▶	Learning as strategic and organizational process
Focus primarily on cognitive competencies	▶	Includes social, political, and ethical competencies
Happens primarily in hierarchical expert-student relationship	▶	Happens primarily in horizontal peer-to-peer relationship
Transfers existing knowledge, trains desired behavior	▶	Puts existing perspectives and behavior into question
Focus on qualification for future application → requires learning transfer	▶	Focus on ongoing innovation, change and transformation → transfer is not an issue
Happens remote from practice	▶	Is embedded in practice
Learning is educational practice	▶	Learning is leadership practice

learning that is based on the cognitive domain and is related to individual qualification processes in a hierarchical teacher-student relationship.

We have used a number of conceptual angles to explore the various dimensions of learning and to expand the paradigm toward a practice that is deeply embedded in the context of people, organizations, and their environment. These angles help us to see corporate learning as a strategic and organizational process that shapes the texture of a company and the way it deals with its environment. Conceiving learning in this novel way transforms it from an educational to a leadership practice (Figure 3.4).

Transforming the paradigm of learning is a strategic task similar to the transformation of an industry. It requires the development of new business models and new products and services. It requires new capabilities, and it will shake up the established stakeholders who constitute the current state of the practice. It will enhance the role of some players and diminish others, both inside and outside organizations. It also calls for new players who are able to connect the dots and elevate the practice to a new level. But above all, it will create a radically new value proposition that addresses the heart of today's corporate and societal challenges.

CHAPTER FOUR

Implications for the Corporate Learning Industry

The shift of the learning paradigm requires a fundamental rethinking of the value chain of learning, the institutional framework in which learning happens today. Institutional frameworks are always a function of a dominant business model of an industry—in this case, the corporate learning industry. Reframing the business model shakes up the roles and the relationship network of the existing players. It will enlarge or diminish the role of existing players, and it may require new players with new competences. It will strengthen or weaken existing relationships, and it may require the development of new ones. At any rate, redefining the paradigm of corporate learning sends the practice on a journey of transformation that will eventually reshape the rules of the game of learning.

Internal Reconfiguration

We discussed in Chapter Three that extending the notion of learning from people development to a core business function has a significant impact on the role configuration of internal stakeholders. The current monopoly of HR with its inherent limitations has to give way to an orchestrating learning function that actively includes multiple stakeholders across the organization. This requires a new type of CLO with the credibility and seniority to design business processes as learning domains—a true C-level responsibility. Today, most CLOs are responsible for assuring the right skills and competences of the workforce. Their primary tools are well-designed "programs" in sophisticated didactical settings, mostly using a mix of classroom, e-learning, and project work. These learning interventions are their legitimate and undisputed domain—but they struggle with an image of being remote from the "real world," and they have to make continuous efforts to get attention for the learning agenda and to connect their activity with the business needs and the strategic thrust of the firm.

However, this focus on HR-driven programs overlooks the infinite number of *unstructured* learning situations and opportunities that exist throughout the organization and its extended value chain that are currently not regarded and defined as learning and therefore remain untouched. We know that learning happens somehow, but we don't know what type of learning happens and how its results are utilized to improve performance, effectiveness, or innovation. In contrast, higher-level learning interventions identify the places of "natural learning" that yield the highest "return on learning opportunity," both in terms of strategic relevance and leverage potential—and then design them accordingly. Learning requires irritation, so the major task is to design the right irritations, not only by providing intellectual/conceptual/cognitive discourse platforms but by systematically exploiting the encounters that happen in the life of companies, across internal boundaries, and with customers, suppliers, competitors, and other relevant stakeholders inside and outside the organization.

To illustrate this shift of perspective, let us take another look at the connection between the domain of learning and everyday business processes. "Business-driven learning" is a popular phrase that means that the needs of the business should guide the content and the design of learning. To align learning processes with a company's strategy and its relevant business issues, learning programs are developed according to business imperatives, through interviewing executives, considering the strategic plans, and seeking approval from the key constituencies. The result is usually a highly customized program design (see Figure 4.1) that represents Level 2 in the five-stage model we discussed in Chapter Three.

Figure 4.1. Business Needs Determine Learning Content

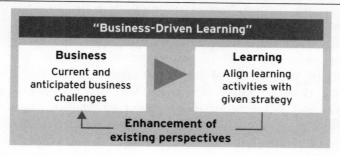

Figure 4.2. Learning Experiences Inform Business Activities

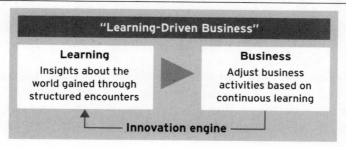

But we can also conceive the act of doing business itself as a continuous learning process. In a radical sense, we can turn the current mental model upside down and say that "learning drives business." This means that new insights about the world— technological innovation, competitive dynamics, emerging customer needs, and more—have an impact on the business model and on the way a corporation organizes to compete (Figure 4.2). The learning challenge is to design our business encounters with the world in a way that they maximize insights, and then design processes that turn the insights into strategically reflected organizational activity.

It is easy to see that companies that *consciously* drive their business through learning will gain a sustainable competitive advantage, as they develop much better antennae for weak environmental signals and they learn to think and act strategically faster than their competition.

Establishing an effective link between learning and business process requires more than that the learning function simply "listens" to current business needs. Many CLOs try to gain acceptance for their function by aligning their activities as closely as possible with the strategic direction they receive. Corporate learning support is critical for executing strategy, but limiting the role of learning to a mere alignment function reinforces current mindsets and practices. It is as important that an organization develops the skill to "listen to its own learning," a major perceptional change that eventually creates an engine for continuous innovation and change. It requires that the stakeholders at the core of the business process become key players in creating *learning-driven business architectures*.

External Partners for the Universe of Corporate Learning

As we said, reframing our understanding of learning has massive implications for the internal organization of the practice. Equally significant is the impact on the universe of service providers who currently constitute the relevant stakeholders of the corporate learning space.

It is a colorful universe, which includes major players such as Ivy League business schools that provide top-notch executive education, big training firms, global software corporations that provide e-learning solutions, media companies, conference organizers, and major international consulting firms. It also includes hundreds of thousands of coaches, trainers, motivational speakers, change facilitators, and more. As a rapidly growing multibillion-dollar industry, the space is obviously attractive, with low entry barriers and little regulation.

The current paradigm of learning is also reflected in the business focus and the related core competences of the vendor universe. Most service providers gather in the narrow space of cognitive and skill-oriented individual qualification. This territory is the domain of business schools with their standardized and customized programs for executive education, of training providers large and small, and of the entire e-learning industry. It is a crowded space, but understandably so—after all, it is the space where most of the corporate learning budget is spent today.

If we extend our notion of learning toward the emotional and social dimension of individual and small team learning, the field gets much thinner. Learning that targets personal growth and social competences does not lend itself to scale; it requires intimate settings that allow working on self-perception and relationships. The key players in this domain are personal coaches and specialized training firms. Because this space is less scalable and less profitable, it is extremely fragmented, with vast variation in quality and professional skills.

If we extend our dimensions further, to the domain of political and ethical learning, the space becomes pretty empty. Some coaching for very senior executives may include the careful analysis of power dynamics to prepare for executive decisions, but there are no significant players who would focus their services on making people politically savvy. Even less is offered in the dimension of ethical learning. While compliance training may at first sight address ethics, the subject is largely taught as a topic and thus belongs into the cognitive category, like languages, information technology skills, finance, or project management.

If we look at more complex learning architectures that address not only the individual but also the organizational domain, we quickly leave the traditional arena of corporate learning. The learning function may get consulted in "soft" organizational change projects, as such projects have often a cultural change component and include elements of retraining and new skill development. However, change initiatives are usually structured in form of a dedicated project organization, with line managers leading the effort. The choice of external partners depends on the type of change project: large-scale reengineering projects that address the structures and systems of the organization are the domain of large consulting firms, while cultural change efforts are typically supported by highly skilled process advisors or organizational development (OD) consultancies who are experts in designing effective process architectures. While change projects are always major learning projects for an organization, they may not be designed as such, and the choice of the consultant is usually not the decision of the corporate learning function.

Finally, corporate learning has even less say when it comes to project initiatives that are designed to restructure or develop the overall business portfolio of the firm. These decisions are made by senior business executives who hire general management and strategy consulting firms to support them in their efforts. Most of these consulting projects remain analytical and conceptual; they produce smart reports that often collect dust on executives' shelves. Implementing strategic change requires reframing the mindsets of key stakeholders, aligning their perspectives, and mitigating conflicting interests. This is not the forte of consultancies that have their core competence in a highly analytical approach to strategy and organization.

The matrix in Figure 4.3 provides a heuristic summary of the learning universe and the positions of the most important

Figure 4.3. Key External Service Providers in the Extended Learning Universe

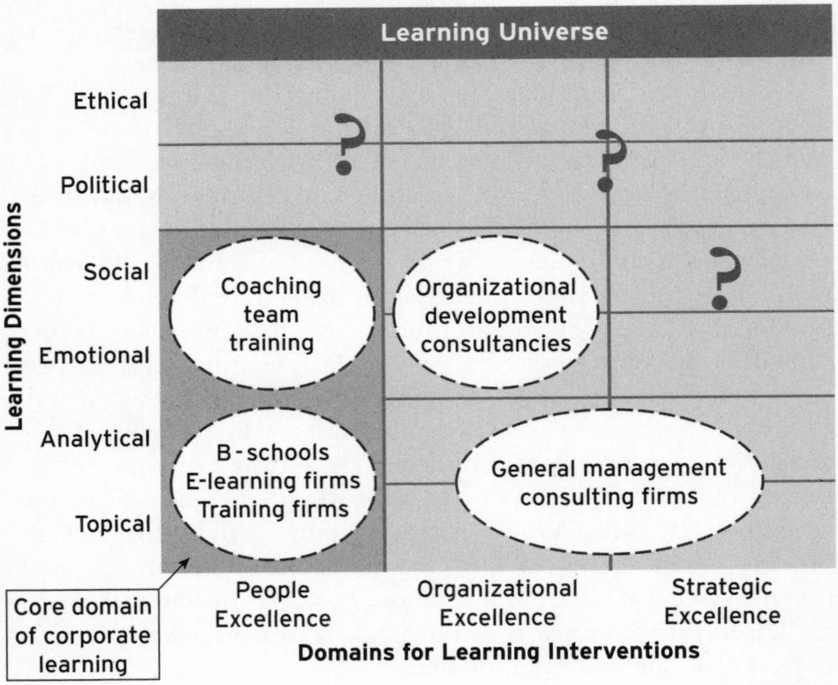

external service providers according to their areas of core competence.

Two issues immediately stand out. First, there is an ample white space that is currently not covered by any of the major vendors, yet it is the space that is probably most important for corporations in the twenty-first century: entrepreneurial innovation and the dimensions of political and ethical learning. While these are complex challenges, it is important to find ways to address them. Reframing the learning paradigm as we do in this book is a first step; it defines for the first time a comprehensive learning universe and we hope it will instigate a conceptual and practical discourse on how to get a better hold of this arena.

Second, we see relatively clearly defined segments that are the "home turf" of the various players. Business schools are great for cognitive learning on the individual level. "Hard fact" consulting firms are the vendor of choice for reorganization and business issues. OD consultancies know how to address the "soft" side of organizational change, and coaches help executives to reflect and develop their personalities. This separation is a reflection of the current state of the corporate learning industry, which does not reach much beyond the individual domain. It leaves many of the learning opportunities on the table: business schools stop short of real impact on organizations, training firms reduce learning to qualification, coaches have little effect on large-scale process design, and consulting firms don't understand the learning implications of their practice. OD consultants may be closest to understanding what it takes to build a learning architecture, but they often lack the business acumen required to be taken seriously by business leaders.

Nevertheless, each of the players in the current corporate learning industry provides valuable contributions. Combined, these contributions create a patchwork of competences that could drive a comprehensive learning agenda. Let us have a brief look at the strengths and weaknesses of some of the more important external stakeholders.

Business Schools

Business schools tend to think that they own the executive learning space, and they do to a certain degree in the minds of many traditional learning executives. After all, they are supposed to be the temples of management science, and they are widely recognized as the home of the traditional paradigm of management learning. Sending executives to major schools with global brand recognition—or having these schools create a customized program—is always a safe bet for internal learning executives, and it is often the first step to get senior leaders to "learn." The real strength of business schools is that they are institutions dedicated to the advancement of knowledge in the field of management and that their faculty is paid to think about fundamental issues that remain elusive for executives with busy schedules. Great schools such as Harvard, IMD, INSEAD, or Stanford come with great learning facilities designed for an optimal classroom experience. Executives can dive for a week or two into an intellectual environment of reflection and debate, and they may come back inspired and energized to change things.

But business schools come with significant weaknesses—weaknesses that are likely to diminish their role as vendors of choice in the future. For one, management science itself is in the midst of an identity crisis, with prominent scholars criticizing the dominance of finance and quantitative research as not appropriate for the challenges companies face in the twentieth century. In their quest for recognition as a "scientific" discipline, business schools reward research excellence, not teaching excellence, and the few stars who combine intellectual brilliance with the skill of inspiring dialogue are often celebrities and in high demand. The academic culture is remote from the life of daily business challenges, and while it may be nice to reflect, it is hard to transfer these reflections to practice. In addition, most professors have a culture of telling instead of listing; they tend to create reusable templates of PowerPoint slides and canned speeches that they can recycle at a variety of audiences. Customization in terms of real adaptation to client needs is not the forte of business schools; their whole business model forbids professors to enter into a deeper and time-consuming relationship with a company—an important condition for more complex learning interventions. Business schools and their faculty have a role in a corporate learning architecture—but given their structural limitations it may not be the most prominent one.

Training Firms

Training firms may not be as sophisticated as business schools, but they bring with them the advantage of making corporate learning their one and only core competence. Unlike business schools, their trainers are not "distracted" by research and teaching commitments in graduate education. They focus entirely on the design and the execution of highly scalable training interventions. The services of large firms typically include consistency that is supported by professional training manuals, which assure a certain level of quality. Training firms are better in customizing content to the needs of a client, because the development of educational solutions is in the DNA of their business model.

However, also training firms come with their weaknesses. Their focus is entirely on people qualification—necessary for every organization, but not addressing the needs of an enlarged paradigm of learning. Training firms often lack the business savvy of consulting firms and the conceptual depth of business schools. Their competence is usually limited to the customization of content design, not the customization of the design of a learning architecture. As such, they reinforce a restricted paradigm of learning. Their services are valuable, but again only for a narrow segment of the learning challenge.

Organizational Development and Change Consulting Firms

Consultants who specialize in organizational development bring to the table competences that extend the traditional learning universe toward organizational learning. Their core competence is in designing large-scale change and transformation processes in which relevant stakeholders of the firm are included. They are experts in connecting the people domain with the organizational domain. As such, they have the ability to go beyond the analytical and conceptual dimension of organizational change and address the complex internal relationship network of a corporation. They approach projects usually from a systems perspective, with an understanding of relationship networks, organizational dynamics, and the impact of change interventions on the overall context. They typically act more as coaches and facilitators than as experts and analysts, engaging executives and employees in the change effort. Their approach fosters dialogue and horizontal learning processes that help address conflicting interests and perspectives and can transform an organization's culture. Their capabilities make OD consultants important players in a comprehensive corporate learning paradigm.

However, with their focus on the "soft" side of organizational change and their emphasis on facilitation, OD consultants are usually not sparring partners for senior executives in the "hard" aspects of restructuring and business development. As experts in *organizational* development, their perspective is generally restricted to internal issues of the company. They bring limited business acumen to the table and therefore have no credibility in the strategic or entrepreneurial domain of learning. Most OD consultants are organizational psychologists and sociologists, not strategists or business modelers. As brokers between people and their organizational context, they are closer to the HR function than to the business. Still, with their holistic systems perspective, they can be valuable advisors for creating comprehensive learning architectures.

General Management Consulting Firms

General management consultancies bring strong analytical and diagnostic skills to the table, together with intimate industry knowledge. As such they are the preferred partners for senior executives on issues of corporate development. Working at the heart of business issues, they are not perceived as members of the corporate learning space. They share the view of business leaders and position learning as a tool to align people competences with the strategic and organizational requirements of the firm. Their projects are always learning projects, as they deal with increasing a company's understanding of industry dynamics, the optimization of business processes, the integration of an acquired firm, and so on—but they are not perceived and designed as such. Their role in a corporate learning architecture can be critical, but it needs to be developed and orchestrated.

But general management consulting firms also have their weaknesses when it comes to fostering a comprehensive corporate learning agenda. While they have credibility as trusted advisors to the business, their own business model makes it difficult to use this relationship for large-scale learning initiatives. Their strength is analytical expertise, not facilitation. Like the OD firms that have little expertise in the "hard" aspects of business, general management consultancies have deficiencies in dealing with the "soft" ones. Their economic model is based on having junior consultants do the work and partners manage the client relationship. They are interested in maximizing the deployment of their workforce, so they have little incentive to enhance internal capabilities that could make them obsolete or would cannibalize parts of their business. Young, bright MBA graduates may have great analytical skills, but they are not partners in facilitating politically sensitive change processes.

Coaches and Trusted Advisors

Finally, we need to consider a segment of players that is growing in size and importance in the field of executive development and learning: coaches and trusted advisors. Coaches help executives to reflect on their activities and assess their context in a very personal and intimate setting. As such, they can be major influencers of mindsets and perspectives, and they can foster the development of emotional intelligence. Trusted advisors who focus more on the business side of the equation act as sounding boards for strategic and organizational challenges, and they contribute to executive decision processes through their experience and their ability to listen and understand. They have the ear of major decision makers and so can provide a significant contribution at sensitive spots of a learning organization.

However, the coaching industry equally comes with its own set of issues. It is an unregulated industry with virtually no entry barrier. Any laid-off executive can become a coach or advisor, and there is no way to control quality other than by reputation. Great coaches are in high demand and therefore hard to get. Their work is not scalable and they have no backup who can substitute for them. Their domain is usually limited to the emotional and political learning of individual executives; they have no role in designing and facilitating larger-scale learning initiatives.

This brief journey through the strengths and weaknesses of some important stakeholders of the corporate learning industry shows clearly that no current player is able to cover the requirements of a more ambitious practice of learning. It is not good enough to buy programs from the shelves of business schools or hire a consulting firm to help. Designing and maintaining learning-driven business initiatives requires a collaborative effort not only within the corporation but also among the various service providers. Each provider brings an important piece of the puzzle to the table, but it is only one piece. Vendors tend naturally to pretend that they can provide the entire solution, and they view other service providers as competitors, even if they have complementing capabilities. Large-scale reengineering firms don't want to deal with coaches, business schools have a hard time connecting with OD consultants, and so on. To create a vendor universe that supports a new paradigm of learning, we need to instigate a collaborative mindset across the various segments and players of the chain, and we need a knowledgeable corporate hand to orchestrate that process.

The configuration of the vendor universe will remain as it is today as long as the practice of corporate learning and development is defined as it is today, and it will change only when demand patterns change. We can see tendencies of that change beginning, with "hard fact" consulting firms trying to gain "soft fact" competences, with business schools moving into providing consulting services, and so on. We also see the emergence of third-party integrators who understand the structural deficiencies of the corporate learning industry and try to aggregate vendors with diverse competences in an effort to provide comprehensive solutions, although they are still operating within the narrow definition of learning.

The space of corporate learning, like every other industry, is in transition. Redefining the learning paradigm will create disruption, exposing the industry's strengths and weaknesses and highlighting the contributions and limitations of each current player. It will create new players, and it will also affect the roles and responsibilities of the internal corporate functions. If we want to transform the practice of corporate learning by creating learning architectures that drive organizational and strategic excellence, we need to anchor learning as a core capability and a core process at the heart of the corporation. To do so, we need to equip the learning function with the necessary reputation and competences to orchestrate that complex web of internal and external stakeholders. As noted before, this is a C-level role that requires diplomatic skills, a deep understanding of business, strategy, organization, and a generic understanding how to design learning systems. It is a role that requires sensitivity for the sweet spots of corporate learning and design creativity to exploit their potential.

CHAPTER FIVE

The Convergence of Strategy and Corporate Learning

Chapters One through Four reframed the paradigm of learning to encompass a new, comprehensive business function: creating organizational designs that foster learning and development for individuals, the organization, and the industry, for the purpose of achieving sustainable competitive advantage. We saw that such a perspective moves learning beyond the boundaries of HR and makes the practice a key player in driving the development of the business and the firm. This change in paradigm affects the identity of other functions, above all the practice of strategic management, which today carries most of the responsibility for corporate development.

Chapter Five examines the interplay between the strategy process and the practice of an advanced paradigm of corporate learning. The analysis reveals a surprising commonality of challenges. As the practices converge, we can see the newly emerging role of learning in the various domains of the strategy process. This allows us to review some of our earlier considerations through a different lens.

The Convergence of Strategy and Learning

In the old paradigm, learning and strategy have a clear and simple distribution of roles that determines their relationship: The strategy function analyzes market forces and comes up with a strategic plan. The learning function helps implement the strategy by qualifying the workforce for the intended strategy and, in some instances, helping to create the required cultural change. Other than that, the two domains live separate lives—not only structurally, but also culturally, through their distinct languages, value systems, relationship networks, and so on.

However, this situation is changing. Since the early 1990s, a new view of strategy has been emerging in response to the evolving limitations of the traditional strategic planning practices. Long-range planning makes sense in relatively stable, predictable environments. It loses its value in fast-changing, discontinuous environments. The new approach defines strategic management not so much as optimizing a company's position within an existing industry space, but rather as mastering an ongoing creative process of capturing emerging opportunity spaces. This process is based not only on rational analysis but also on intuitive feelings for industry discontinuities and on the creativity, guts, and operational capability to capitalize on them. It is rooted in a changing understanding of existing and required organizational capabilities as well as in the recognition that organizations need to build and orchestrate a complex web of alliances, partnerships, and stakeholders that constitute the relevant ecospace of the firm.

Another factor is also new: strategic management is no longer an activity solely confined to top management. Strategy used to be something secret, known only to the selected few, a game of smoke and mirrors. While secrecy remains necessary to a certain extent, an increasingly bigger part of the strategy process is leaving the smoke-filled rooms. The reasons are obvious: responsiveness in fast-changing times requires flat hierarchies and empowerment of the organizational periphery. Also, companies can no longer afford long time lags between strategy formulation and execution. Both issues require an earlier and much broader involvement of employees in all elements of the process.

In addition, as we discussed in Chapter One, value creation today occurs increasingly through clusters of "value nets" or "creation nets," adding a complex web of important stakeholders to the game. These new realities are transforming strategic management into a comprehensive *organizational process* that unfolds in intense action-driven dialogues across internal and external boundaries. This process requires significant sophistication in organizational design and stakeholder orchestration. In short, strategic management is evolving from a structured step-by step planning routine into a fuzzy, complex, and ongoing learning and innovation process.

The evolving perspective of the strategy practice sounds familiar. It goes hand in glove with the changes we discussed in the corporate learning paradigm. As strategic management becomes at its core a learning process, corporate learning becomes the key enabler of the strategy process. Ironically, the limitations of the traditional strategic planning approach find their equivalent in the limitations of the scholarly approach to learning that we discussed in previous chapters. To create an agile, strategically competent organization, *both* practices need to change.

Sadly, for the vast majority of corporations, the convergence of the two domains has remained—if anything—a conceptual insight only. In most corporations we still find a lack of mutual understanding between the two worlds. Little thought is given to organizational designs that foster the creative interplay between the functions. Without such spaces of designed encounters, it is very hard to overcome the traditional perceptions and their inherent shortcomings. Reframing of identities does not happen easily. It requires dialogue, reasoning, and joint action. The following thoughts are a first step toward such a dialogue. To do so, let us first look at the generic elements of the strategy process.

The Strategy Process: A Permanent Threefold Challenge

Common language is always an issue, especially when discussing subjects as ambiguous and in flux as the fields of strategy and learning. A very simple framework may help to create a common language and better link the key elements of the strategy process with the domain of corporate learning. It can also serve as an inspiration for innovative learning interventions.

The complex process of strategic management can be broken down into a set of three distinctive subprocesses:

1. The *strategy generation/development process* includes all activities that help companies develop strategic alternatives based on a thorough understanding of opportunity spaces that

reveal themselves when matching industry dynamics with the company's strengths and weaknesses.

2. In the course of the *strategy formulation/decision process*, companies must make strategic choices that favor one alternative (or set of alternatives) over the other, leading to decisions on resource allocation and external relationship development.

3. The *strategy execution/implementation process* assures that these decisions get implemented—with all their consequences for the company's internal organization and external relationship networks.

The three elements are not distinctive phases that happen as a sequence of clearly separated steps (although the rational of the traditional planning paradigm may suggest that). In the real world of organizations, the generation of strategic alternatives, strategic decision making, and the execution of these decisions are a circular, intertwined process that is only partly rational and controllable.

The good news is that the effective management of each element, along with a conscious and sensitive handling of the dynamics among the three, will create a positive loop of strategic and organizational learning. Managed well, this loop will lead to a quicker and more creative identification of opportunities, more courageous and bolder strategic choices, and greater efficiency and effectiveness in execution (see Figure 5.1).

Figure 5.1. The Dynamic of the Strategic Process

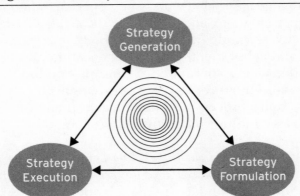

Dealing effectively with the three processes and their interplay is tricky, as each of the three elements has a distinctive logic, requiring its own leadership style, skill set, and attitude. A look at each of the three domains may help to better explore their characteristics, and consequently the role that corporate learning and development can play in bringing their inherent potential to life.

Strategy Generation

At its core, the process of generating strategy is about listening, asking, thinking, and inventing. It is an art (rather than a science) that unfolds by combining analytical skills, an intuitive understanding of interdependencies, lateral thinking, and creativity.

To generate a viable strategy, an organization needs to develop a thorough understanding of the context in which it is currently acting, how this context may change—or even disrupt— and what the company can do to play a proactive role in shaping the context dynamics to its advantage. At the same time, companies need to know who they are and what they could become—in other words, they need to understand their strengths and weaknesses, their core competences, and their potential.

But analysis and understanding are not enough. As important is the *creative process* that results from combining insights about external context dynamics and internal capabilities. Done well, such a process can give birth to bold ideas and visions for the future. It can inspire strategic moves that have the potential to redefine the rules of the game and sustain industry leadership. However, as we know, this last part is especially hard to do.

One of the major pitfalls when companies are trying to generate breakthrough or truly innovative strategies is that they always see the world through their own specific lenses—lenses that they develop over time through their distinctive history of dealing with products, markets, and the competition. The "genetic code" of an organization that initially led to its existence and its market success is at the same time its biggest inhibitor for radical innovation, as it obstructs the view to a potentially different reality. If a historically successful business model, with its products, markets, technology, and established relationship patterns, as well with its values, rules, and assumptions gets challenged through a different paradigm that claims to be as valid, companies get very irritated. And they tend to react to irritation with cognitive dissonance, conflict, defensiveness, and denial. But it's exactly this *irritation* that sparks new ideas. As we have reviewed, it's the creative and curious encounters with "difference" that have the potential to revolutionize old business models or even reinvent an industry.

In other words, *the process of strategy generation is primarily about learning:* learning about what goes on in the outside world, learning about the current capabilities and the potential of the organization, learning about different perspectives. Moreover, it means learning about one's tacit assumptions and cognitive maps and overcoming the natural defense and denial mechanisms against the "new."

The role of the corporate learning and development function in this process is obvious: For one, there are the educational interventions that aim to familiarize executives with the toolkit of strategic management and foster analytical skills and strategic thinking. But even more important: corporate learning is positioned like no other function to deal with the challenge of reframing perspectives. How? Through creating *designed spaces of irritation* that force companies to systematically listen to weak signals, listen to uncomfortable truths about themselves, encourage themselves to ask unconventional and uncomfortable questions, challenge their familiar assumptions, and make them reassess and redraw their cognitive maps.

The good news is that there are plenty such spaces of irritation out there that wait to be tapped into: customers, emerging competitors, new ventures with innovative ideas, unrelated industries with very different practices, foreign cultures—and last but not least, the company's own employees who deal with the outside world. Today, most strategic discourse happens in the remote settings of corporate strategy departments and boardrooms; places that are usually not distinctive places of irritation. They often lack the encounter with the outside world. Great learning designs understand which spaces provide the most value in terms of digestible differences, and they can create the right "stretch of alienation" that encourages learning and overcomes defensive patterns.

We talked about such learning designs in Chapter Three. They can be customer visit programs conducted by multifunctional teams, learning expeditions, innovative ways to glean the innovation potential of corporate venturing, benchmarking outside the company's core practices, and so on. In a nutshell, these are all about designing encounters across boundaries of systems that are usually not talking to each other. Part Two contains some case studies that exemplify this.

Strategy Formulation

Unlike strategy generation, the process of *formulating* a breakthrough strategy is about making choices, about political power, boldness, guts—and the conflicts that result from these dynamics. The logic of this process is in stark contrast to the logic of understanding and inventing.

When speaking about deliberate strategic choices, it is important to keep in mind that the strategic direction of an organization is always a combination of explicit executive intentions and the "blind" emergence of reality. It is impossible to control the entirety of organizational activities that contribute to the development of a corporation. Also, strategic choices are only partially rational (the great ones are often outright crazy at first sight). Information is always incomplete, things change the minute we learn about them, tacit assumptions and individual frames of reference put a bias on the understanding of "reality," and so on. So no matter how much care companies invest in the strategy generation process, there will be always an irrational, instinctive element to the decision.

The irrational element of strategic choices means nothing else than the validity of a choice can never be entirely backed up with facts and reliable predictions. The genius of a strategic move unfolds only in retrospect. This opens the door wide for political power games, as every choice can be challenged on the grounds that it is built on wrong assumptions or lacks rational justification.

What makes this process even more political is that each strategic choice comes with—sometimes pretty harsh—consequences for some of the stakeholders. Choices are about focusing on certain opportunities while dismissing or excluding others. Choices are about resource allocation, which means some stakeholders will gain, some will lose—at least from their own point of view. Strategic decision making is always about competing claims of potential futures, and these claims are driven by different assumptions and cognitive maps about reality as well as by vested interests of a sometimes complex group of stakeholders, who include both internal and external constituencies.

The role of the corporate learning function in this process is more delicate. The logic of the strategy generation process (understanding, asking, thinking, and so on) suggests many "natural" spaces for learning. The logic of the decision process (deciding, choosing, competing, and so on) is about politics and power, and the traditional paradigm of learning (teaching, knowledge transfer, and so on) seems to have not much to offer here. However, under the new and enlarged perspective of the practice, the contribution of the learning function can be significant.

On one hand, there are again traditional educational interventions that focus on building social and political skills so that executives can better understand and handle the multistakeholder power dynamics of strategy formulation. But the key contribution of learning in this arena is *designing and facilitating spaces for constructive discourse*. To tame the destructive potential of strategic decision making and to capitalize on the diversity of perspectives of the stakeholders, organizations need spaces in which the different cognitive maps of the key players can be made explicit, where silent assumptions become a voice, and where the inevitable conflict that results from different perceptions can be folded into a common frame of direction.

Such spaces are particularly important when companies strive for radical innovation and for breakthrough strategies. Becoming truly different—this is what breakthrough is about—means not only saying good-bye to trusted practices and routines; it also includes accepting a great amount of uncertainty. Uncertainty creates fear and is a fertile ground for fighting over assumptions, as nobody can predict the future outcome. Radical change is also much more likely to threaten vested interests, and that, too, incites fear.

To succeed as the designer of spaces and as a knowledgeable facilitator in such a high-charged environment, corporate learning must earn respect as a trusted advisor for the top strata of the corporation. This may be a long way to go for some cultures, where learning is perceived exclusively as training, but it can be done as some of the case studies in Part Two will show.

Strategy Execution

The process of strategy implementation likewise follows a very different and distinctive logic. Execution is about making sure that change happens. It is about knowing where to go and telling people to follow that path.

New strategic choices usually mean change: change of the power equation, change of relationship networks (internal and external), change of resource allocations, change of skill sets, and so on. At the same time, the organization must let go: let go of old practices, old skill sets, old relationship networks, old resources, and so on. Strategic change means learning *and* unlearning at the same time, and usually the latter is harder to do. People and systems don't like to let go of familiar stuff, especially if things work fine, provide power and influence, and can get done with existing skills.

This element of the strategy process is perhaps the domain closest to the traditional learning function. When learning executives talk about their link with strategy, they are usually referring to their role in the implementation process. The potential contributions here are manifold. For one, there are again traditional educational interventions, such as leadership programs, executive coaching, and so on, to improve the capability of senior executives in leading change. Second, strategic change is usually linked to a shift in the required capability portfolio of the firm. New skill sets need to be rolled out, and sometimes considerable parts of the workforce, and also customers and suppliers, have to be retrained. It is a classical role of the learning function to design and conduct large-scale retraining efforts.

In addition, the rationale of the strategic choice needs to be communicated throughout the organization and beyond. This is particularly important, because the new strategy will be successful only when it gets anchored in the minds and—first and foremost—in the hearts of employees. External constituencies also have to buy into the strategy. Customers, suppliers, and the peer companies in the distinctive "value net" of the organization are critical stakeholders of the implementation process. The learning function is ideally suited to create designs for town hall meetings that enhance strategic dialogue, to host a series of integrated, cascading workshops throughout the entire organization, and to integrate the discourse on the rationale of the strategic choice in all its educational offerings wherever there is a fit.

And there is more. What is usually overlooked in the course of strategy execution is the fact that the execution process itself is an indispensable source of learning. Execution is the litmus test of the viability of strategic choices. Strategies may fail because of weak execution, but they may also fail because they were the wrong strategic choices in the first place. The learning function can play an instrumental role in assessing the effectiveness of the strategy and making the process of execution a learning opportunity for the entire organization. It can do this by providing systems and mechanisms that allow harvesting the rich data of experiences with the new strategy, both within the own company and within the ecospace of the company's external "value net."

Finally, the learning function is ideally suited to assure that strategy execution is not purely a mechanistic top-down one-way street. Every strategic choice is based on assumptions—and bold, breakthrough strategies set out to conquer hitherto unknown territories. Enacting the strategy creates new realities, and these change the very context that had been the basis for generating the strategy in the first place. Monitoring and reassessing this context is an important part of strategy execution. It is a continuous strategic learning exercise linking the execution process directly back to the domain of strategy generation. Strategy execution may be about telling and making things happen, but it also requires listening and understanding. Does the strategy work? What is its impact on the organization and the company's ecospace? What can we learn about ourselves and the industry while implementing strategic change? The insights from the execution process not only generate new strategic alternatives, they may lead to new strategic choices—and smart learning architectures are needed to capture those.

Three Rationales, One Process

The three elements of the strategy process follow distinctive rationales that seem to a degree even incompatible. The ability to listen, inquire, and dream (Generation) is very different from the ability to decide (Formulation), and deciding is very different from the ability to implement (Execution). Each of the three domains requires different organizational enablers (see Figure 5.2).

But despite their different rationales, the three elements of strategic management and the potential role of learning within them nicely illustrates the interrelatedness of the processes. The challenge of a great organizational learning design is to create an architecture that effectively combines and balances the three elements of the strategy process. Too much focus on listening at the expense of decision making and execution is usually fatal. Stubborn execution without sensitive antennae for the effects of the strategy can lead to disaster.

Figure 5.2. Three Fundamentally Different Rationales Within the Strategy Process

	Generation	Formulation	Execution
Dominant Logic	Listen, understand, think beyond, dream	Choose, decide, be bold	Tell, know, lead change
Dialogue Culture	Investigating, understanding, creative exploration of ideas	Reasoning, arguing	Convincing, explaining
Role of Learning	Create spaces of designed irritation and strategic dialogue	Enable and facilitate spaces of constructive discourse	Create spaces for skill and mindset alignment; reflect on experience
Typical Interventions	Learning expeditions, customer visits, idea labs, think tanks	Top executive forums strategic retreats	Cascading workshops, town hall meetings, change projects
Conflicts	Ignorance towards the unknown / unfamiliar	Different assumptions, perceptions; power issues (horizontal)	Organizational inertia, power issues (vertical)

Once companies start to see the dynamic cycle of strategic management as an organizational learning process, and once they start to consciously and systematically exploit the learning opportunities inherent in each of the three domains, they can begin building sustainable strategic competence, a capability that is crucial in fast-changing times when it is not so important to make the *right* strategic choices but to develop the capability for continuous strategic innovation and change.

The good news is that the three domains feed on each other, so that learnings in one domain bleed through to the others. Building strategic competence follows the logic of a positive loop, but the hard thing is to get started. It takes tremendous energy for a jumbo jet to get rolling and finally get into the air. But with every mile the plane moves ahead, less effort is required, until the plane is on cruise control.

To achieve mastery in the strategy process, organizations simply have to nurture the learning imperatives that naturally unfold in the three domains: understanding the context, understanding one's own organization, asking uncomfortable questions, envisioning alternative worlds, learning to dream the impossible, overcoming the limitations of restricted cognitive maps, making these maps and their underlying tacit assumptions discussable, having the guts to move into unknown territory, and creating a sustaining culture of discourse on strategic issues throughout the organization and beyond.

Nurturing these learning imperatives comes not through preaching them in management seminars. It takes organizational structures, mechanisms, and policies that systematically link the strategy process with the respective learning issues. It requires the creative design of spaces that foster encounters across boundaries that can consciously lead to irritation, dialogue, and inquiry— and ultimately risk taking and entrepreneurship.

It is up to the chief architect of the corporation—the CEO—to insist on linking strategic management with a learning architecture. It is up to a new breed of CLOs to advise him as a subject matter expert on how to design such systems and fill them with life.

PART TWO

Case Studies

This part of the book contains ten case studies from major global organizations that cover a wide range of learning initiatives. The cases are diverse and shed light on corporate learning challenges from a variety of angles. They appear in no specific order.

The following brief abstracts provide an overview of the key issues and challenges of each case.

Case 1: Innovating Learning Through Design and Architecture (UniCredit)

UniCredit is the third-largest bank in Europe, with activities in more than twenty countries.

The company is the result of a breathtaking series of mergers and acquisitions, which made it grow from 16,000 to almost 180,000 employees in fewer than five years. Such growth brings major challenges in strategic and organizational alignment as well as in cultural and political integration. Case 1 tells the story of UniCredit's architecturally unique Torino Learning Center, an environment that has been created exclusively for the purpose of systematically enhancing transformational learning. A highly flexible and adaptive space in combination with cutting-edge multimedia technology encourages intensive peer-to-peer discourse, fostering the post-merger integration process. We describe in detail the features of this "enabling learning space" and how their design contributes to challenging mindsets, unfreezing perspectives, building relationships, and imagining new ideas.

Case 2: Top Executive Leadership Learning (Siemens)

Siemens is one of the world's leading engineering conglomerates, with about 460,000 employees in 192 countries.

In most large organizations, the members of the executive board and the CEOs of major market units rarely perceive a personal need for learning. Having reached the top of the organization, they are typically beyond internal talent management systems, and their role in traditional learning architectures—if any—is as mentors, project sponsors, and providers of strategic guidance for the learning agenda. Case 2 tells the story of how the strategic and organizational transformation of one of the world's largest corporations was designed as a carefully designed leadership learning process. The project significantly affected the mindsets and the collaboration culture of the top eighty-five executives of the firm and changed the culture of strategic and organizational dialogue. The initiative also created an invaluable network of committed senior leaders for the future agenda of corporate learning initiatives in Siemens worldwide.

Case 3: Phoenix from the Ashes: How a Corporate Learning Initiative Reinvented an Ailing Business (ABB)

ABB is one of the world's leading engineering companies.

Companies in serious financial trouble seldom if ever look to their learning and development group for answers. The usual thinking is that spending money on organizational learning and development would not contribute to rebuilding a sustainable business. Case 3 contradicts that view. It tells the classical tale of a business unit that was close to extinction. Facing massive layoffs and near-bankruptcy scenarios, employees and executives teamed up in a learning process that led to a reinvention of the business model. Today this unit is one of the most profitable and fastest-growing businesses of the ABB group. The case makes a convincing argument for utilizing a comprehensive learning design to guide cultural transformation that realigns strategy and organization alike. It also provides interesting insights into the political and strategic dynamics of a complex change process.

Case 4: Healing Post-Merger Chasms: Creating Corporate Values from the Bottom Up (EnBW)

EnBW is a utility company operating in Germany, Central Europe, and Eastern Europe.

Managing integration and cultural unity are key challenges when dealing with mergers, acquisitions, takeovers, or fundamental changes in leadership or strategic direction. Many organizations end up doing little or nothing to redefine their vision or establish new corporate values to motivate and guide employees. Case 4 presents the story of EnBW, a German utility company with 21,000 employees and more than six million customers, which after its formation following a merger experienced years of cultural disunity. The solution came when the company's corporate academy spearheaded a far-reaching initiative to redefine the company's values using a bottom-up campaign that invited nearly 1,000 employees to participate in choosing new values. The case demonstrates well how change is instigated not so much through "rolling out" messages in traditional settings, but by designing a comprehensive *organizational* process that introduces dialogue and reflection into the fabric of the entire company. The EnBW experience is also a great example for a post-merger integration project without labeling it as such.

Case 5: Designing Customer Centricity for Multiple Market Segments: The *perspectives* Project (BASF)

BASF is the world's largest chemical company.

Corporate learning has long been involved in educating staff, especially marketing and sales, on the elements of customer service. However, these programs seldom raise the fundamental question on how a company structures its business processes to drive them from the outside in. Case 5 tells the story of *perspectives*, a strategic initiative that fundamentally challenges the role configuration between supplier and customer, reaching deep into all functional elements of the organization. At first glance, BASF's *perspectives* project may seem like just another effort to improve customer relationships, but as the case unfolds, we unveil the architecture of a deeper transformational learning initiative that truly reinvents formerly unquestioned routines and opens up new and exciting opportunity spaces for the company and its customers alike. The case is a great example of a corporate learning initiative that has had a major impact on value chain dynamics.

Case 6: Transforming the U.S. Army Through an Informal Leadership Learning Network (U.S. Army)

Many organizations have launched communities of practice with the hope of fostering knowledge sharing, connectivity, and the exchange of best practices among employees, but few have had an impact on their organizations as much as Case 6 demonstrates. It takes place in the U.S. Army, normally a bastion of hierarchical command and control, and focuses on a grassroots effort initiated by a small team of Army commanders to create an informal network to share ideas and learn from each other to improve their leadership capabilities. The case relates how and why the commanders launched the network, how they designed its architecture to invite participation and sharing, and the steps they took to build a user base, gain acceptance, and grow the community into what has become a highly respected forum for knowledge and training that is today fully endorsed and operated by the Army. The case also offers some interesting perceptions into the type of organizational environment that may ultimately be necessary to develop a successful informal, self-organized, horizontal network.

Case 7: The Executive Hero's Journey: Going Places Where Corporate Learning Never Went Before (PricewaterhouseCoopers)

PricewaterhouseCoopers (PwC) is one of the world's largest professional services firms.

Case 7 tells the story of Ulysses, a project launched in 2001 in which small cross-cultural teams of senior PwC partners take a four-month leave of absence to go on a challenging field assignment in a developing country. Their challenge is to make a sustainable positive impact on a complex economic and social issue. Together with nongovernmental organizations (NGOs), community-based organizations, and intergovernmental agencies that have agreed to work with PwC, the executives must take on a specific project in a local community that is struggling with the effects of poverty, conflict, and environmental degradation. Ulysses effectively sends PwC executives on a hero's journey in which they must meet severe challenges. The experience addresses numerous strategic issues of the firm, such as personal growth for its key talent, corporate responsibility, cross-cultural collaboration, the development of networking and relationship competence, political competence in terms of multistakeholder orchestration, and the creation of a sustainable corporate brand that is differentiated by the quality of relationships with clients, colleagues, and the broader community.

Case 8: Managing the Strategic Asset of Cutting-Edge Technological Expertise (EADS)

EADS is the maker of Airbus and is the second-largest aerospace company in the world.

Because of the level of high technology required in all its products and services (airplanes, rockets, satellites, jet fighters, missiles, drones, and so on), research and engineering capabilities at EADS are key differentiators in their market. Managing the expertise of 1,000 researchers and more than 40,000 engineers is of major importance for this organization. Case 8 sheds light on how EADS approaches this tall challenge though an integrated effort that combines learning interventions, talent management tools, and organizational systems and processes. To assure retention, the initiative created a separate career ladder for experts that is parallel to management, with its own set of rewards and benefits tailored to this group. EADS also put in place several programs to encourage communication, networking, innovation, and knowledge sharing among the experts and the rest of the company. The case is a great example of strategic competence management in the high-technology space.

Case 9: Leadership Learning as Competitive Strategy in the Chinese Market (Novartis)

Novartis is one of the world's leading pharmaceutical companies.

Global corporations tend to standardize their learning and development programs everywhere they operate. They base this on the belief that it is necessary to foster large-scale uniformity of values and cultural unity. However, a more networked approach to globalization requires flexible cultural adaptation that allows for difference while strengthening an international perspective. Novartis recognized that it had to use a different strategy in its operations in China, where talent shortages, high turnover rates, and a non-Western cultural mindset presented the company with significant challenges in attracting, developing, and retaining managers. Case 9 tells the story of how the company established a dedicated China Learning Center and partnered with Beijing University to adapt its leadership development programs for the Chinese context. The payoff has been a tremendous increase in retention and a growing globalization of Novartis's Chinese executive leadership.

Case 10: *First Choice:* The World's Largest Customer-Focus Initiative (Deutsche Post DHL)

Deutsche Post DHL is the world's largest logistics company, with 550,000 employees in more than 200 countries and territories, which makes it one of the largest employers in the world.

Case 10 presents the story of *First Choice,* a learning initiative of unprecedented scale that combines customer focus with employee engagement. The case spells out how Deutsche Post constructed a global learning initiative that systematically helps every business unit identify inefficient processes and, using Six Sigma, fix them. Meanwhile, elements of the initiative are designed to help the company's more than 50,000 managers conduct workshops with their employees to precisely define customer service in words and deeds. The case offers a lesson in how to design architectures for very large scale change management, what anchors are required, what didactical tools are vital for success, and how to measure results. It's a lesson about the power of process and simplicity when it comes to dealing with scale.

Exhibit P2.1. Case Study Overview

Company	Key Topic
UniCredit	Enabling Bricks and Mortar Architecture
Siemens	Linking Strategy with Top Leadership Development
ABB	Business Transformation and Reinvention
EnBW	Post-Merger Integration through Values Generation
BASF	Organizing for Customer Centricity
U.S. Army	Communities of Practices for Real-Time Learning
PricewaterhouseCoopers	Leadership Learning Creates Authentic Corporate Responsibility
EADS	Assuring Expertise as Core Competence
Novartis	Balancing Globalization and Localization
Deutsche Post DHL	Customer Focus, Employee Engagement, Process Excellence

Innovating Learning Through Design and Architecture

Unicredit

Meaningful learning that yields sustainable impact both on people and the organization requires sophisticated design efforts—a kind of "soft architecture" that creates an effective process of individual and organizational learning. Elements of such an architecture include the stakeholder composition of the participants; the choice and sequence of topics; the choice of media; the mix of expert-led information transfer, peer-to-peer exchange, and experiential activities; and more. Designing great learning interventions is an art that requires a deep understanding of the learning process, and learning professionals usually put much effort into it.

But the success of learning depends on more than just getting the soft components right. It also requires a "hard architecture" that enables and supports the intentions of the learning design—the structure of the space within which learning happens. The traditional classroom is designed for a certain type of teacher-student interaction, and it reinforces instruction-based learning. An open circle of chairs suggests a very different kind of learning, one that invites interactivity and dialogue. Although there is much awareness about the importance of the "hard" setting of a learning environment, we still find that most learning takes place in uninspiring conference rooms and classrooms, places where people are happy when it's over.

Not so at UniCredit, one of Europe's leading banks. The following case tells the story of the bank's "UniManagement Executive Learning Center," a unique architectural space that was created with one and only one thing in mind: making learning an experience people won't forget. A testimony to the Italian feel for design, the center's architecture inspires a passion for learning and discourse for people from the moment they walk in. No other corporate learning facility translates so emphatically the social and psychological requirements of collaborative learning into architectural design. It has significantly changed the way executives perceive learning. It has moved learning center stage.

UniCredit is the result of a series of major mergers and acquisitions that brought various corporate cultures and many nationalities under one corporate roof. In providing an environment that is conducive to challenging mindsets, unfreezing perspectives, and fostering dialogue, the center plays a key role as an integrating platform that forges a new and joint identity among the company's leaders.

———

Imagine a vast theater-in-the-round open space, nearly dark except for a few small spotlights that shine down on the crowd of 400 people. The group forms a huge doughnut-shaped circle around a speaker standing in the middle, holding a microphone. A light zeroes in on the speaker as he addresses the people, slowly rotating a full 360 degrees to ensure he has a chance to look everyone in the audience right in the eyes. Then, around the perimeter of the crowd on all sides, a half-dozen movie screens begin showing a film as music blasts from loudspeakers. It's a fast-paced multimedia show that bombards the audience with images and messages all around them.

This is not a rock concert, nor an IMAX show, nor an interactive drama staged at an alternative playhouse. It is the annual

UniManagement Center's Agora hosting a large group meeting

leadership meeting of the top 400 executives in the UniCredit Group, one of the leading banking institutions in Europe, with 177,000 employees and operations in twenty-two countries. The meeting is held in the company's UniManagement Center, in Torino, Italy, a facility expressly designed to support a modern, interactive, and participatory form of corporate learning.

Guided by the vision of UniCredit's Head of Corporate Learning, Anna Simioni, with the involvement of the American architectural firm MG Taylor, the UniManagement Center opened its doors in January 2007. From its flexible open space areas on the ground floor to its specially designed work and conference rooms upstairs, everything about this facility has been created with a radical dedication to foster interaction, communication exchange, collaboration, and learning among the bank's diverse leadership ranks to create a unified culture across the bank.

Small group interacts at workshop in the Agora

The Rise of UniCredit

Based in Milan, the UniCredit Group was created in 1998 from the combination of nine leading independent Italian banks into a single corporate entity. The mergers went smoothly, largely because CEO Alessandro Profumo had already earned an excellent reputation as head of Credito Italiano, one of the larger entities included in the deal. Since the initial mergers, UniCredit has expanded rapidly, thanks to a potent entrepreneurial vision, a pan-European drive, and considerable good timing.

Today's company is the result of a breathtaking series of additional mergers and acquisitions across Europe that happened between 1999 and 2007 as governments in Central Europe and Eastern Europe sold off banks in the trend toward privatization of previously nationalized companies. The thriving UniCredit Group made the most of these opportunities, buying leading banks in Poland, Bulgaria, Slovakia, the Czech Republic, and Turkey. The group's crowning coup was its 2005 merger with Germany's then-number two bank, HypoVereinsbank Group

(HVB), a deal that also added Austria's market leader Bank Austria, with its vast eastern European holdings, into the mix. This fully confirmed UniCredit's identity as a European player—not just a diversified Italian bank—and launched yet another wave of acquisitions that extended all the way to Kazakhstan.

Throughout these years of international growth, UniCredit created unity by applying a specialized business model every-where it expanded. Even if business activity in a new country was not significant enough to replicate the full scope of UniCredit's offerings, the company ensured that every bank's staff included retail, corporate, and private wealth management specialists. In contrast to a universal banking model, where any customer can be served by any bank employee, people who came to UniCredit would meet with the most *appropriate* advisor to their needs.

All told, the bank grew from 26,000 to more than 177,000 employees in less than seven years, provoking major challenges in strategic and organizational development as well as in integrat-ing the diversity of management cultures and eliminating age-old European prejudices. To meet the challenges, UniCredit went to considerable lengths to train local staff, investing heavily in commercial and professional instruction. They opened training departments in every newly acquired bank and created corporate leadership and executive development education programs to meet the needs of their leadership competence objectives. What was lacking, though, was a spark that could ignite the transforma-tive power of learning and create a new, exciting sense of shared identity for this international, multilingual banking giant.

The Creation of the UniManagement Center

Anna Simioni, a former management consultant, joined the HR division of Credito Italiano bank in 1997, shortly before the bank combined with other Italian banks to establish the UniCredit Group. In 2006, she was offered the opportunity to become the bank's Head of Corporate Learning, responsible for ensuring that company members acquire and strengthen the skills they need to operate in an ever-expanding arena. She accepted the appointment under one condition: She would be able to create a new learning center that could be designed to raise the experience of learning to hitherto unknown levels.

In a venerable nineteenth-century building in the business center of Torino, Anna collaborated with American architect Matt Taylor, a specialist in developing highly creative and innovative learning and work spaces, to completely redesign the interior of the building to implement her philosophy of corporate learning. Together, they envisioned and constructed the Torino Learning Center ground floor as an environment built exclusively for the purpose of systematically creating intensive peer-to-peer discourse. A highly flexible and adaptive space in combination with cutting-edge multimedia technology provided the opportunity for breakthrough learning experiences that shake up traditional perspectives on executive collaboration. A tour of the 5,000 square meter (53,500 square feet) building and how its space serves the learning functions provides a sense of the value this environment offers UniCredit.

Ground Floor: Opening Up Space for Energized Minds

Located at the corner of two streets in central Torino, the UniManagement Center resides in an impressive gray granite structure whose rough-hewn stone gives no clue as to what lies inside. The entrance to the center is angled right on the edifice's corner, so that you enter the structure on the diagonal. As you take the first steps in, expecting perhaps some type of sterile corporate interior, you may find yourself shocked by the perspective of an enormous open space—the Agora—that makes you feel almost as if you had entered a kindergarten classroom welcoming people to come in and play. It's not that the UniCredit's Torino Learning Center is childish—far from it. But from the moment of your entrance, it's clear this space represents an environment full of innovation, creativity, energy, and playfulness.

Passing by the receptionist's area, which looks like a large amusement park ticket booth, your eyes are drawn to a gleaming polished wood floor set on the same diagonal as the entryway. Inlaid into the blond-colored wood are "energy vectors"—lines of dark wood that pull the eye across the enormous open room—perhaps 200 feet or 75 meters in diameter—off into the opposite corner. The darker inlaid wood creates a diagonal arrow that cuts through a huge dark inlaid circle in the middle of the ground floor space. The dark wood circle looks something like the compass design on a map, but is also slightly reminiscent of the famous Vitruvian image of a man by Leonardo daVinci. There's something Italian Renaissance and globally thoughtful about the circle in the floor that is symbolic, while at the same time it clearly defines a large circular meeting space.

Thin wooden beams reach from the floor up to a simple latticework ceiling. Like scaffolding that hangs over the center of the room, the lattice visually frames the meeting space below it. It is like a spider's web from which movable spotlights hang, directing their light onto the floor in a way that can clearly be moved around and adjusted as needed.

This central area of the ground floor is where large meetings are held, such as the one for the 400 executives mentioned previously. Anna and her staff also use it for the quarterly meeting of the Top 100 Executives at UniCredit, as well as numerous other events that bring in from 50 to 250 people. This open space is free flowing and flexible. Chairs can be set up around the circle or in rows facing a single direction in a more classical classroom

Mingling in the Agora

arrangement, all eyes facing front. Or there can be no chairs, making the room like a large loft space in which people can mingle, converse, and network.

Around the central meeting space, the rest of the ground floor extends out. Like a circle inside a square, the ground floor space includes corners and additional odd shapes partitioned off with movable walls and plants to isolate them from the central area. These outlying spaces are used for small group work that accompanies the plenary meetings of events held at the center. Following a talk, for example, people can break out and go off to a corner space where they can work on their assignments as a team. One part of the ground floor also has a balcony above it where groups can congregate.

Building a space that inspires and facilitates creativity, innovation, and teamwork was one of Simioni's primary goals. "Our concept here is that you create effective teams only when you have people working in a collaborative way on a very important and real issue that keeps them awake at night," says Anna.

A group meets in the garden team room (exterior)

A group meets in the garden team room (interior)

"Bringing executives to a fancy resort might make for a nice climate, but too often the work is not related to the job. It's easy for the people to collaborate but in the end, they don't care as much. It's easy for them to be nice to each other. What we do here is exactly the opposite. We pick the most burning issue for the team and ask them to work on it. The only way you can build teams is when you have an important issue, because that's when you get real energy that creates true team building."

The ground floor space facilitates a perfect match of form and function. With such vast open areas available, the ground area along with the balcony above it can easily accommodate ten to fifteen small groups, each working simultaneously in its own space. "This is an effective design for several reasons," Anna says. "The space facilitates their work in order that they can experience how nice it is to work together on a real matter, and it makes people come alive, elevating the energy and momentum which everyone can feel." Anna contrasts the design of the UniManagement Center with the usual type of meeting space: "When you have executive meetings in places like hotels and people scatter off into ten different rooms behind closed doors to do their teamwork, you end up with a facilitator bouncing from room to room to make sure people are working hard and are not confused or distracted. This is not effective. Here I can see nearly every group, and I can tell if there is a problem. I just have to look at a group to tell if they are getting work done, or if they are stuck or if people are getting up to get coffee. This space changes the nature and effectiveness of the collaborations. Here, you can manage the process of learning completely differently."

Group work in the Agora

The Art of Learning

Simioni's learning philosophy has been crucial to every aspect of the center's design, and central in her vision is the distinction between "learning" and "training," which she compares to the difference between art and science. *Training* is akin to science, because it focuses on facts and implies that somebody (the trainer) possesses information that he or she can transmit to trainees. A person who lacks certain knowledge or skills may need training, which is a finite experience, a building block. But while training may teach you a fact or how to do something, it does not change your behavior.

On the other hand, *learning* stems from people's personal experiences and emerges when they get involved in a dynamic of exchange. This why the center's activities focus extensively on using facilitators who challenge participants to enter into dialogue rather than having "trainers" or professors sharing the "pearls of their knowledge" with everyone by reading to a plenum. The facilitators and the open space are designed to make people interact, and consequently they start to think and work in different ways. By communicating and collaborating freely, people learn from each other, generating ideas and changing their mindsets in the process.

As in art, learning requires seeing things differently and understanding that which lies below the surface. Learning must go deeper than mastering facts; it requires active, deliberate participation and interaction. It needs to alter one's perceptions and sometimes one's deep convictions. Experienced, high-level professionals must have a chance to develop a new understanding of whatever issue is at hand and consciously choose to change their behavior. Simioni offers an example of managerial delegation. In order to handle delegation more effectively, a manager must first come to understand why he or she currently may not delegate. The process of exploring and thinking about the issue thoroughly and of tracking down the elusive personal answer produces an impact on your own behavior so that you can recognize when it is time to delegate.

Another element of UniCredit's learning philosophy is the value of fostering bonds. In a large or networked organization, human fabric or emotional bonding can't be created without direct contact. People need to establish an *emotional* connection to learn from each other, before virtual gadgets can work as multipliers and as reinforcement. If there is no emotional connection in the first place, there is no way to create shared learnings, even via the Web. That is particularly important for UniCredit because it doesn't have a history, and the most urgent issue is to create

Team creates a hands-on project

a shared identity among its diverse workforce and leadership scattered around twenty-two countries. Emotional connections are crucial for all companies in order to retain talent, which is a major issue that every industry faces increasingly today.

One of the other important factors in designing the center was the role that it needed to play in fostering ways to integrate the many banks from different countries that formed UniCredit. For an international company, all the processes and control systems in the world are no substitute for people sharing certain basic beliefs—without those, there will always be problems of compliance or integrity. The center is a huge equalizer, because everybody starts at the same point, even the people from the "old" UniCredit. When management teams from two or three different merged banks meet there for a few days, they have a chance to establish a different way of working together, leaving behind the oftentimes fierce competition or stereotyped prejudices they might have had for each other. They adopt a UniCredit identity.

Design Details That Create Energy, Dialogue, and Interactivity

The UniManagement Center is full of design details that reinforce Simioni's philosophy. Many elements have been included to provide a holistic experience that takes into account the many ways people learn, including the emotional component of learning, not just the cognitive. There is also a strong respect for the value of documenting the experiences so people can recall and relive them.

For example, one element is the abundant availability of large whiteboards that can be rolled about the room as needed. "We tend to make all our participants write a lot," says Anna. "In workshops where they appoint someone to take notes, the words belong to the note taker, not to the individual. Here, we have everyone get up and write on the boards. This activity changes the way people discuss and learn." Team members are able to print out what was written on the whiteboards, thus providing a record of the dialogues and brainstorms.

Teams meet to write up ideas

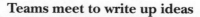

Artwork from teams

Scattered throughout the open space and hanging on the walls of the ground floor are many paintings and other types of art; professional artists are hired to come to the events specifically to create a work that captures the emotions, ideas, and reflections of what transpires in a session. The impetus for this is not only that it inspires people's creativity, but it enriches the entire experience of the participants and often synthesizes the essence of an issue much better than a written documentation. Simioni and her staff also ask participants to create their own art, and some of the better pieces from prior sessions hang permanently on the walls. In this case, doing art serves as a binding force that unites the teams and acts as a historical testimony of the successes they've achieved at the center.

Another holistic-learning design element is shelves throughout the facility filled with books of all sizes and shapes in many languages. The books include classic and recent business and management books, and also inspiring art books and interesting contributions from disciplines like biology or philosophy. Participants at workshops are welcome to make use of these as they desire—and they do. Anna notes that people often grab a book and flip through it when they go off into their small groups or even when they just take a break. The books act as inspiration and reminders of the vast repertoire of human knowledge.

Overall, much of the structural design, layout, and furnishings of the ground floor are intended to build discourse and create the energy of the meetings. The rationale for this again goes back to Anna's view that dialogue and debate contribute to real learning. "It's easy for people to disconnect when you're in a group of fifteen, as you can say, 'Well, there are fourteen others so I don't need to say anything.'" At the UniManagement Center, this is nearly impossible.

The Upper Floor: Rooms for Every Learning Style

A staircase and elevator take participants up to a second floor area that has also been designed to encourage and support active learning. This floor houses several rooms created to appeal to different types of learning styles for both group interaction and individual work. As Simioni puts it, "We try to leverage on the fact that each person has a gift for learning in different ways."

Thus, there are rooms designated for talking and conversation, for doing, and for reading and reflecting.

Conversation Rooms

The design of the conversation room has been inspired by the idea that people traditionally love to have conversations around a kitchen table. There's a kitchen island with a stove, microwave, sink, and dishwasher, for participants to brew up coffee, make food, or microwave popcorn. Beyond the island is a large open room with a table, but it's not the average corporate conference table. Designed by Anna, the large table is doughnut shaped with a hole in the middle. It provides space for about fifteen participants. The chairs are barstools that make it nearly impossible for anyone to avoid conversation. They are specially designed with seats tilted forward on a down angle, so as to force people to lean into the table, toward the other participants. The height of the chairs is such that people remain on eye-level even if they get up to walk around during a heated debate. Everything in this design makes it impossible to not be engaged. The room is ideal for all learning settings that require intense discourse.

Sitting around the table in the conversation room

Doing Rooms

The "doing" room is equally unique. Called the "energy room," the entire room is covered in a writeable white surface, from floor to ceiling, including the furniture. Participants can sit at the tables and write with markers right on the surfaces, but they can also write on the walls or they can lie on the floor and write on it. The design conveys the message to forget about all existing mindsets and prejudices and start thinking from a "tabula rasa"—a complete white space. It also conveys that no idea shall remain uncaptured; just begin writing and see where your brainstorms go. When the meeting is done, cleanup is easy too; soap and water clear all the surfaces.

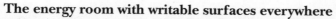

The energy room with writable surfaces everywhere

Quiet Rooms

The third type of room is the quiet room; it is available for reflection, meditation, and reading. People can go into this room to sit calmly, think about their work, or read a book. The rooms are furnished with comfortable, large, dark leather wing chairs, the walls are covered with jute fabric, creating a feeling of coziness and relaxation.

Team reflects and talks in a quiet room

Other Rooms

Additional rooms on the upper floor are available for other group activities. One of these rooms contains large square-shaped cardboard boxes that resemble children's stackable cardboard bricks in a kindergarten, but big. Some boxes are brightly colored with different hues on all sides, while other boxes display a statement on them in large, bold white type:

- Describe the biggest boundaries that you have crossed in your professional career so far.
- Describe your biggest travel adventure.
- Describe your biggest travel disaster and how you survived.
- Describe your dream destination. What, when, where, why, how long, and with whom?
- Describe the biggest insight about yourself that you've learned through travel.

Team uses cubes to create objectives and goals

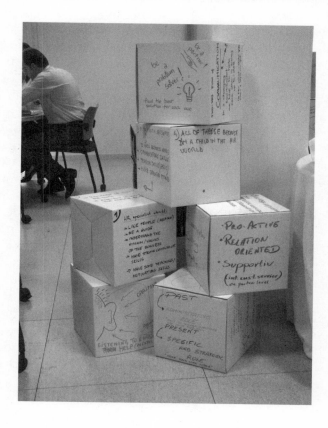

The boxes are like toys to inspire conversation and open up dialogue and sharing between people during group activities associated with the learning events.

While the ground floor space is used for the plenary sessions and team problem-solving work, the upstairs rooms are used for other types of development work that goes on at the UniManagement Center. They are frequently used by people who participate in UniCredit's Executive Development Plan (EDP). EDP is a dedicated learning initiative in which the company's top people (all executives and group talents) are invited to come to the UniManagement Center two or three times per year to work on a specific management issue, such as managing complexity and ambiguity, understanding the context and defining future scenarios, or giving and receiving feedback. The UniCredit Leadership Curriculum contains fifteen such workshops, intended to prepare the rising talents in the company for eventual leadership spots. These "learning labs" make heavy use of the three different upstairs rooms, as participants are invited to go into the room that reflects their preferred style of learning for at least two hours every day during the sessions. The learning labs use different rooms according to the phase of work the participants are in.

As on the ground floor, the upper floor has several unique design features to support learning. The most fascinating of these is a video camera setup created for the UniManagement Center in which several video cameras hanging in an isolated area of the upper hallway display on two screens images of whoever is standing there. One image shows the person from the front, the other from the back. The two images are, however, not shown in real time but with a slight delay from when the videotaping occurred. The pause allows you to step out of yourself for a brief instant to watch how you behaved a few seconds ago, so you can assess your actions and gestures and alter them if needed.

Explains Anna, "We usually see ourselves in a mirror, which is an instantaneous image, so you can't really judge yourself. Or you might see yourself in a video, but here again, the problem is, you can't change your behavior because the video has already been shot. With this setup, you see yourself in a way you have never done before. This arrangement lets you really see how it feels when you do something or act a certain way with other people." The center uses this to help managers get a better understanding of how they interact with others by letting them study their own body language and practice new behaviors.

The UniManagement Team and the Events

Simioni not only led the design of the UniManagement Center but also hired the learning team that conducts and facilitates the events. The team is composed of 90 percent UniCredit people, chosen from many of the company's locations—Poland, Germany, Bosnia, Austria, as well as Italy. Some of the learning team members had formerly been in the HR department, but most came from the business side, such as corporate planning or organization. They were selected because they had held senior positions in their prior jobs and know the field of banking. "Understanding the business is crucial," she remarks. "When you do something on consumer financing, for example, you have to understand the logic of it. You don't have to be an expert, but you need to understand the nuts and bolts of consumer financing."

Simioni uses her team to best leverage their personal backgrounds and work experiences. She notes that in the first months of the center it was not easy, because some members of the staff were afraid to play their new roles as learning facilitators. Having come from the banking side, they didn't know how to reframe their identity from subject matter experts to enablers who help others do the learning themselves.

Today, Simioni has confidence in her team, noting that they share the same passion she has for collaborative learning and for providing transformative experiences. She praises the aim of her crew to be a "step beyond" and to be the first example of the new transversal "UniCredit working style"—flexible, collaborative, cross-cultural, cross-divisional, and innovative. The staff is highly interchangeable, with many being able to take part in any event or workshop conducted at the center. What counts for Simioni is that the staff never hesitates to do whatever it takes to make events succeed. "We do whatever we need to, including taking the dishes out if needed. Our purpose is to make the participants focus on the work. This is about facilitating *their* learning and *their* collaboration."

The team is kept consistently busy, either planning a new event or running one of the workshops or meetings that take place on a regular schedule at the UniManagement Center. The largest of these is the previously mentioned Leadership Meeting, a two-day strategy session held every January for the top 400 executives in UniCredit. Each year's meeting digs deeply into a strategic issue that Simioni helps identify and then plans activities and speakers around. The 2009 theme was "Banking Reloaded: Understanding, Adapting, Leading," which investigated the root causes of the financial crisis from multiple angles and discussed strategic responses to the tectonic changes the financial industry is facing at this time.

Simioni begins planning for the Leadership Meeting in July when she makes the rounds of top executives to sound them out on what issues the bank needs to work on for the coming year. In these meetings, she updates them on the results of the work from the prior Leadership Meeting, so they can assess how effective it was and what ideas it might inspire for the upcoming year. The executives help her decide whether to have customers or experts at the meeting. She then creates a "draft outline" of the event and selects which experts to invite. Finally, she creates a short document for the top leaders to review and approve. Once the theme is selected, Simioni and her team have a few months to plan the agenda, create the activities for the plenary sessions and breakout groups, and prepare any multimedia needed to support the events.

With its large audience, the Leadership Meeting tests the UniManagement Center and the learning team to the max in terms of both the use of the space and the content of the event. Despite the large number of attendants, there is still a heavy emphasis on individual participation and the use of breakout teams to work on solving the challenges related to the theme or purpose of the event. Even with 400 people, group discussions and team problem-solving activities dominate the two days, proving Simioni's commitment to active learning and the goal of producing real results that affect the company.

In addition to the Leadership Meeting, the conference for the Top 100 Executives mentioned previously, and the fifteen EDP programs (which bring in more than 3,000 people each year), the UniManagement Center is in continuous use for other learning events. Says Simioni, "We host a mixture of global corporate events and specific individual and localized projects. For example, UniCredit acquired three banks in Bulgaria, and we managed several events at the center intended to facilitate their integration process. In another instance, one of the company's banks in Hungary sought to use the center to do team building with his management team, and the results were a great success."

In yet another learning workshop, the HR director of the UniCredit Consumer Financing Division worked with Simioni to devise a two-day workshop to introduce seventy of the division's executive management to each other and to have them jointly build a new strategy for their product lines.

For all these workshops, Simioni and her team continually monitor the sessions to ensure progress and results are being achieved. They make extensive use of the multimedia capability built into the center, with its networked connectivity and video capture capabilities. Events are often videotaped and edited the same day so a film can be shown to the participants at the close as a reminder of what was accomplished. If an event is more than one day long, Simioni and her team meet in the evening with the sponsors to discuss the results and make adjustments if needed in the following day's activities. For example, they may change the agenda and ask the group to rethink a strategy session or to return to their teams to do more brainstorming.

The UniQuest Program

One other program hosted at the UniManagement Center deserves special note. Called the UniQuest Program, it is an intensive six-month "learning journey" to develop the cream of UniCredit's talent. Anyone with three to six years working experience (of which at least one year is with the company) and the recommendation of their supervisor can apply to the program, but admission is highly selective. Each year, the company receives hundreds of applications from employees in its banks and offices across Europe. Following an intensive three-phase selection process, including an English proficiency test, analysis of a business case, and an assessment profile, only 100 people are chosen for the program.

The "UniQuesters" come to the UniManagement Center, where they are asked to work on projects of key importance for the company's business divisions (commercial banking, private banking, and retail banking), product factories, and competence lines. Identifying the projects is as much part of the process as is the selection of the UniQuesters. Each year, Simioni puts out a call to the senior executives in the company inviting them to submit ideas for projects they would be willing to sponsor. She typically receives about two dozen suggestions, out of which thirteen are chosen for the UniQuesters.

The program begins with a three-day kickoff meeting at the UniManagement Center in October, where the UniQuesters listen to the company CEO and speeches from each of the chosen project sponsors, who make a "sales pitch" trying to persuade the participants to work on their projects. This role reversal and power shift is instrumental in breeding a climate of mutual need and respect. "Top management" becomes a group of real people who need the UniQuesters, while the young managers have a fresh approach that is a valuable strength and a source of innovation for the sponsors.

The UniQuesters must then divide themselves into teams of eight, individually selecting the projects they want to work on while simultaneously arriving at a productive mix of people and skills on each team. Putting the teams together is like a chess game; the only rule is the teams cannot work on a project from their own division. With 100 people in the program, the process yields twelve to thirteen projects.

The teams then go back to their regular jobs, but can devote 25 percent of their time to their projects during the next three months. They have an assigned tutor and a development advisor from within the company to whom they can turn for advice. Then they return to the UniManagement Center in January for a status update, followed by three more months back home to finalize their solutions, which are presented in April. Given that the projects are real UniCredit challenges, the sponsors expect finished output.

According to Simioni, the program has generated excellent projects, with equally exceptional solutions generated by the UniQuester teams, many of which the company has implemented in its banks and financial services divisions. For example, one project team leveraged best practices from throughout the group to reduce retail delinquency, generating EU70 million in savings on recurrent costs. Another project resulted in the development of a new UniCredit financial product.

When the program is over, the UniQuesters return to their jobs, and while nothing is guaranteed, their experience conceivably helps them advance their future with UniCredit. As Simioni states, "The participants get to better understand our company, share our values, and learn something they would never had a chance to do in their own divisions. They also get very high exposure to top management and they build an incredible network of contacts in the company." Many UniQuesters become part of the talent pipeline, with possible advancement into the top 400 of the company.

Conclusion: The Strategic Value of Learning at UniCredit

No one at UniCredit doubts the Torino learning center has made a difference in the quality of corporate learning. By virtue of its extensive usage, hosting more than 13,000 days of learning time among 6,000 participants per year and growing quickly, it has clearly become a focal point for transformation, integration, and innovation.

More critical to this case, though, is the fact that the character of this facility has transformed UniCredit by creating a deep respect and appreciation for the value that learning can contribute to the company and its people. As Simioni states, "The more we are perceived as a tool for innovation and collaboration, the more we have a chance to make a difference in the company. And given that the banking business is changing dramatically in today's world, we can add value to the transformation instead of being the victim of cost cutting. The organizational support is there, because they've seen the results we can provide."

One of the most valuable lessons of this case is the power of the architecture that forces everyone who walks through the door of the UniManagement Center to engage and to collaborate. Much has been written about the benefits of participatory learning, interactive settings, action learning programs, and the importance of dialogue. Still, many current corporate learning events take place in spatial settings that have been built for the Cartesian paradigm of learning: an expert in the front, and listeners taking notes. Such settings require active efforts to overcome their inherent limitations; they work against a contemporary notion of learning.

We know that structure has an immense power as enabler of culture. Architecture can create boundaries or tear them down. The colors and the fabric of a room can energize or tire you. The design of rooms can encourage encounter or isolation, and so on. With its open spaces, "themed rooms," and countless other details, the UniManagement Executive Learning Center is an outstanding example of a company taking these insights seriously and applying them in support of a radical and emphatic commitment to creativity, collaboration, and discourse. These elements represent the essence of learning, Anna Simioni would say, not the transfer of content through the traditional teacher-student relationship, not endless slide shows with ten minutes of Q&A.

Learning is about thinking, being challenged, participating, and sharing ideas—and a physical space should not only allow but actively enable this. As Simioni frames it, "Putting adults in a classroom is not how we are built. Having a trainer teaching us how to behave will not make us change. There is no one who can make us learn by acting as a 'knowledge feeder.' You have to have a passion for learning and you learn by doing, by reflecting, and through discourse." The serious playfulness of the UniManagement Center enables exactly that.

About the Principal of This Case

Anna Simioni is Executive Vice President of the UniCredit Group and CEO of UniManagement, which provides leadership development and facilitates innovation and change throughout the group. She is also Head of Corporate Learning for UniCredit Group, which encompasses twenty-two countries and 177,000 employees. Before joining UniCredit, she worked eleven years in consulting in Italy, France, and the United States with Ambrosetti and the Forum Corporation. She is a graduate of Bocconi University and has attended the Advanced Human Resource Executive Program at the University of Michigan Business School.

Top Executive Leadership Learning

Siemens

In most large organizations, the members of the executive suite and the heads of the business units rarely perceive a personal need for ongoing learning. Having reached the top of the pyramid, they place themselves typically beyond the reach of internal talent and HRD systems, and their role in the corporate learning architecture—if it exists—is to act as mentors or project sponsors, or perhaps provide a pep talk in the learning agenda for lower echelons of managers.

Much of this situation is attributable to the fact that the world of learning is traditionally perceived as "preparation" for the real world. We learn to obtain job qualifications or to advance in our careers. Top executives have nothing further they can advance to—at least in terms of the traditional career path. They have already "arrived." They may pay lip service to the need for continuous education, and they may keep themselves abreast through reading and actively seeking opportunities to challenge their thinking, but they seldom participate as "learners" within the corporate learning system.

This is unfortunate, not only because top leaders are supposed to be role models. Their contribution to building high-performing and strategically agile corporations is key. They are the ones whose mindsets and behaviors determine much of a company's leadership culture, collaboration culture, performance, and strategic inventiveness. Common sense tells us that there are significant opportunity costs if top executives exclude themselves from consciously reflecting and developing their mindsets and behaviors within the strategic thrust and organizational context of their corporation. Still, apart from their roles as mentors or speakers, they remain the most elusive group of participants in corporate learning architectures.

The more impressive is the following case. It tells the story of how the eighty-five most senior executives of a 460,000-people company became part of a learning journey that significantly affected their mindsets and their collaboration culture, while addressing the most burning strategic and organizational challenges of the firm.

———

On a Sunday afternoon in October 2005, twelve of Siemens' most senior executives gathered together offsite, waiting for a workshop to begin. They had been handpicked to be the company's first leaders to attend the new Siemens Leadership Excellence (SLE) program, designed by Marion Horstmann and her small team of learning experts. The twelve participants were among the Siemens elite—division and business unit heads and directors of corporate departments, some of them responsible for billions of dollars of revenues, others with a global functional responsibility. At that time Siemens employed more than 460,000 people in 192 countries and territories worldwide, with revenues of more than EU100 billion, and some of these executives held positions with bottom-line responsibility equivalent to a Fortune 200 CEO.

Marion had personally selected these twelve to attend the first SLE program because they were known to be "maverick thinkers": demanding and critical leaders, people who would not hesitate to offer straightforward, no-holds-barred feedback while she "stress-tested" the pilot leadership program. She and her team had developed the program in roughly eight months, at the request of Siemens' new CEO, Klaus Kleinfeld, who had just taken over the helm of the company.

Horstmann was no stranger to the newly minted CEO. She had worked closely with him for many years as a senior partner with Siemens Management Consulting (SMC), a McKinsey-type internal consulting unit that aggregated many of the brightest minds of the corporation. Kleinfeld himself had founded SMC in 1996 with the mission to improve the profit margins and productivity of Siemens' multiple businesses through high-end management consulting services in the areas of strategy, organization, and operations.

The moment Kleinfeld became CEO, he asked Horstmann to take on the newly created position of head of SLE. The job title was no coincidence: Kleinfeld was very much aware of the importance of the company's leadership culture as enabler—or disabler—of strategic change, and he wanted nothing less than excellence in that field. He was keen to move beyond the rather rigid Germanic thinking, the silos, and the bureaucracy that characterized much of Siemens' culture at this time. Setting up SLE was a clear sign that the new CEO meant business and intended to make leadership a central issue of his tenure, and that he would stay closely involved in creating a different and new culture.

From the outset, Marion aimed high. She wanted more than a traditional leadership program designed and delivered by a business school or a specialized management learning firm. She wanted to engage and use the opportunity to transform the way Siemens worked. And she wanted to start at the very top of the corporation, where strategic leadership mattered most. In a nutshell, she wanted to bring the company's most senior executives to think more broadly, holistically, creatively—and to begin working more closely as a team of leaders on creating Siemens' future.

Never in the history of this company had such senior executives agreed to attend a leadership learning program—but she had managed to convince them to free their calendars and get them for an entire week around one table at an offsite location.

As the executives chatted and waited for the workshop to begin, Klaus Kleinfeld unexpectedly entered the room, appearing solemn and concerned. He handed each attendee the most recent issue of the notable and trusted business newspaper, the *Financial*

Times. Right there, above the fold on the front page, was an article announcing that Siemens was being looked at in an unfriendly take-over bid from a major hedge fund. He explained that the company was threatened with slow growth in its main markets, along with lag-ging profit margins and pressure from foreign competitors using lower-cost workers in China and India. Kleinfeld became gloomy and morose, and he told the executives that he needed their help to figure out what the company should do given the prospect of a takeover—accept the offer from the hedge fund, or fight and make efforts to avoid it through whatever new initiatives they could come up quickly to improve the company's sales and profits.

Everything about the moment, including Kleinfeld's sudden interruption, appeared real and believable—but it was fake, down to the famous pink paper on which the ersatz copies of the ven-erable *Financial Times* were printed, along with Kleinfeld nicely acting his part. The ruse was a planned maneuver to kick-start the workshop and shock the participants into deep reflection—and it was completely believable, because Siemens' share price was actually low enough that a takeover could easily happen if a suitor had been interested.

When the fraud was revealed to the executives, the CEO invited them to spend the next five days imagining what would happen to Siemens following such an unfriendly takeover. He asked them to work hard in this new leadership program to think about what actions they might take in their roles as top Siemens leaders to enhance the company's value to its shareholders and to reach the financial targets he was setting for the company. He instructed them to take a long-term perspective and to think not only about their own divisions or functions but about the com-pany as a whole. He asked them to reflect on a number of key questions affecting Siemens' future: How could Siemens maxi-mize its vast research and operational capabilities to speed its growth and revenues? What processes could they implement to ensure they did not miss out on new global markets? How could the company capitalize better on their reputation as leaders in information and communications, transportation, medical equip-ment, automation and control systems, and power and lighting—fields in which Siemens held a total of 120,000 patents, more than just about any other company in the world?

The Historical Context

For more than a century and half, Siemens had built a venerable history that put it among the giants of the world's engineering corporations. Founded in 1847 as one of the first companies specializing in electrical engineering, founder Werner von Siemens was the European equivalent of Thomas Edison, inventing breakthrough technologies for decades, including the telegraph, the electric dynamo, and the loudspeaker. For more than a century, the company had a record of many "firsts"—building the first European long-distance telegraph system in 1848, laying the first transatlantic cable between Ireland and the United States in 1874, completing the first long-distance European telephone cable in 1921, installing Germany's first traffic lights in 1924, and more.

The firm grew solidly from its start as the leading industrial innovator in Europe, creating electric railroad engines and streetcars, the first European subway system, the metal filament incandescent light bulb, data processing equipment, integrated circuits and semiconductors, the world's first pacemaker, the first GSM phone with color display, and more. Given this DNA, it comes as no surprise that a strong engineering mindset has dominated the culture of the company to the present day.

In deploying a global network for the telegraph, Siemens was already by the second half of the nineteenth century a very multinational company, with a presence in countries as far as China, Russia, India, Australia, and the United States—long before the term *globalization* was coined. But the growth toward a truly global conglomerate happened between 1980 and 2005. Numerous acquisitions, joint ventures, and partnerships—most notably the purchase of Nixdorf Computers in 1991 and the acquisition of Westinghouse Power in 1997—fueled Siemens' development into a company with hundreds of businesses in more than 190 countries, employing nearly half a million people around the globe.

In 2001, Siemens opted to be listed on the New York Stock Exchange, adopted U.S. accounting principles, and began publishing quarterly financial information and results on a per operating group basis. It made English its official corporate language and its office in Washington, D.C., became its chief lobbying representation.

In 2005, Heinrich von Pierer, who had been CEO since 1992, passed the baton to Klaus Kleinfeld. Coming from the helm of the company's U.S. operations, Kleinfeld had accomplished a great deal in the American market. Under his guidance in those years, Siemens U.S. had grown to 70,000 employees who brought in 25 percent of Siemens' total worldwide sales. Now, as new worldwide Siemens CEO, he sought to stretch the entire company toward new financial goals.

From his experience, Kleinfeld had developed a pronounced management style: direct, straight talking, hard working, and highly demanding of short-term results from expanded sales and better profit margins. As a twenty-year veteran of the company, he knew Siemens inside out and recognized that the company had the potential to exploit a rapidly expanding global marketplace. With its competence in power products and systems, transportation systems, medical and health care equipment, semiconductors and computer systems, electronic control devices, and industrial automation technologies, Siemens was ideally positioned to capitalize on population booms and urban growth in industrialized nations and, even more important, in the many emerging markets.

Becoming the global leader in enabling "megacities" as a comprehensive infrastructure provider was a compelling vision, combining corporate responsibility with growth opportunities, rooted in a solid base of core competences. However, Siemens would need a different kind of leadership culture: a culture of cross-divisional collaboration to realize synergies and create compelling solutions, a culture of operational excellence, and a culture of entrepreneurial hunger for growth and business excellence—all a stark contrast to the existing bureaucracy, silo mentality, and inward-oriented engineering mindset.

As former head of Siemens Management Consulting, former member of the Executive Board of the Medical Engineering Group, and then head of U.S. operations, Kleinfeld had ample experience and credibility in driving high performance and achieving business results. He believed firmly that "business excellence" could only be achieved through "people excellence"—a commitment to great leadership, outstanding management skills, and continuous people development. He had no doubt that the company needed both to strengthen the strategic skills of its top leaders, who ran the divisions, and put in place a rigorous program to develop the business acumen of its general and middle managers, who ran the business units and had to execute the strategy. And he knew that his former colleague Marion was the right person to lead this effort.

The Rationale for the Leadership Learning Initiative

Marion was keenly aware that she had to create a novel program that would challenge mindsets and attitudes and instigate boundary-spanning collaboration among Siemens' top executives in a way that had never happened before. In light of the existing culture, this was a Herculean task. For decades, the company's top leadership had come from its engineering ranks, and despite being one of the most global companies on this planet, it was filled almost entirely with German nationals, whose homogeneity of thinking yielded a conservative, slow-moving decision-making culture.

Division leaders and corporate department heads showed the tendency to work in isolation, one from another, focused on their own challenges. They managed their tasks with skill and diligence, but not all of them with regard for the corporate whole. They hardly cared to talk among themselves to establish corporatewide values or share leadership strategies or even to coordinate their thinking about how Siemens should allocate its resources and efforts to expand sales.

Above all, many of these leaders thought of themselves as being beyond "leadership learning," given their lofty and powerful positions in the company and their many years of experience as corporate executives. In fact, they had never previously been asked to take a leadership course before, because Siemens, like many diversified global companies at the time, did not have a formalized and integrated leadership development system, nor did it require its top executives to undergo any type of leadership training.

The History of Leadership Learning at Siemens

Actually, Siemens had a very short history in applying a systematic approach to leadership learning and development. Until the late 1990s, the corporate center had practically no role whatsoever

in executive development. Not unusual for a multibusiness conglomerate, all responsibility for learning and development was
located in the divisions, resulting in an uncoordinated patchwork of hundreds of programs. Recognizing the necessity to
create a more unified and cost-effective leadership learning system, Siemens created in 1995 a corporate department named
"Management Learning," with the mission to aggregate all leadership learning activities across the globe and across all divisions
into an integrated set of corporate programs.

The Management Learning Department chose to address
this challenge through creating a consistent architecture of
action learning programs, combining classroom-based learning modules with teamwork on real-life projects that would take
several months and that were designed to have measurable business impact. The programs for the upper management (level 2
and level 3) were conducted centrally in close collaboration
with Duke University and Babson College, whose faculty taught
the content modules and provided online support during the
project work. Programs for lower management (levels 4 and 5)
were delivered in the regions, with local providers, with a similar
design of combining content modules with project work.

Siemens' new management learning architecture quickly
became a benchmark for the action learning approach, but it
also soon revealed the limitations of this concept. After a few
years into the program, projects became less relevant, but they
still required significant time commitments from overworked
executives. It became harder to find senior project mentors—an
important element of action learning—and project results got
less and less attention as projects proliferated throughout the
corporation with no oversight or unified direction. Even if projects succeeded in yielding "business impact," they contributed
little to creating a unified leadership culture. And they did little
to help Siemens develop a talent pipeline—a major challenge in
a company of this size and diversity that needs the fuel of thousands of executives to run their businesses.

And there was one other important issue with Siemens
Management Learning. Although it conceptually intended to
include all executive levels in its architecture, the company's most
senior executives (level 1) remained elusive. They participated

as project sponsors for the level 2 programs, but they refused to become participants in a level 1 program in which they would learn as a group for themselves.

We mentioned earlier the very common resistance of this group to participate as "students" in corporate programs; in this case there was another, even stronger barrier: The top echelon of executives who headed Siemens' divisions and its critical corporate departments had not participated in the management learning program because then-CEO Heinrich von Pierer was not keen on getting this powerful group together.

Pierer had not always been so reluctant in this respect. Early in the launch of the action learning programs, he encouraged the Management Learning unit to design and conduct a program for the top tier, and they did. However, when the group met for the kick-off workshop in Feldafing, Siemens' Corporate Learning Center in the vicinity of Munich, the process soon got out of hand. In the course of discussing the current state of the corporation, its strengths and weaknesses, and viable perspectives for its future, the discussion focused more and more on the age-old conflict between headquarters and divisions, culminating in increasingly excited debates about spinoffs of business units, the radical reorganization of the corporate center, and the concrete hatching of plans for moving forward with these ideas. When Pierer learned about the turn events were taking at the workshop, he rushed out to Feldafing to calm heads, nix their plans, and hold the company together.

Since that event, the Siemens Management Learning department had never again attempted to include this group in a strategic learning exercise.

Designing Siemens Leadership Excellence: Concepts, Components, Connections

To task Marion Horstmann with reinventing leadership learning at Siemens seemed odd at first sight: she did not come from an HR background and had no expertise in learning and leadership development. Instead, she had been a partner in Siemens' Management Consultant Group; after that she had spearheaded one of the most visible companywide initiatives of the previous ten years: a program called Top+, which aggressively drove operational excellence by establishing clear goals, consequences, and metrics across all business units and regions, supporting them with a specific tool set that business units would be required to use, including benchmarking their processes and methodologies to grow their businesses. She had more than twenty years of experience at Siemens. More important, through her previous job, she knew and was known personally by virtually all of the company's senior leaders, which gave her great credibility to get things done.

Assessing the current state of affairs, with the action learning practice in decline, and the traumatic experience with the level 1 program attempt, her focus was clear: How could she rekindle the interest of the senior executives and create a program that would entice them back into learning? If the CEO wanted to move toward a higher ground of strategic and organizational leadership, the new culture had to start right at the top, with its top executives living the philosophy, walking the talk, and committing to their own high achievement. How could they be galvanized into thinking more strategically about change management and strategic innovation, improve their communication skills, and coordinate more tightly as a team of leaders? How could they enlarge their perspective to make decisions that benefitted the entire company, not just their own divisions or departments?

Marion and her team began sketching out a comprehensive and rigorous program that could challenge and inspire Siemens' top management. In designing what would be called the Corporate Management Course (CMC)—the highest level program in the Siemens Leadership Excellence architecture, which would be for level 1 executives only—she and her team were especially eager to ensure that the workshop would be immediately engaging and practical, with palpable results that created tangible impact.

One of the most crucial principles of the program was to create a kind of learning that combined the "hard" work on pressing strategic and organizational issues of the company with the "soft" work on the behavior and the personality of the participants. Instead of having business school professors teach content and discuss case studies, she trusted well-facilitated dialogue among experienced leaders to yield better results and to provide the equally important focus on personal growth and social competence. She trusted the power of executive coaches. In her view, Siemens had to commit to developing every one of its top leaders as an individual, and the surest, strongest way to accomplish this was to have experienced professional coaches working directly with them throughout the sessions. She wanted the executives to walk away from the experience with the sense that it was "about them" as much as it was about the company. They should feel observable personal growth, measurable in the way they would lead, communicate, and collaborate in the future.

The envisioned degree of personal coaching attention required an extensive use of outside resources. To guarantee each participant would have sufficient face time with an executive coach, each workshop was limited to twelve participants, with three executive coaches at their disposal. With this 4-to-1 ratio, there would be three groups of four participants working on burning issues of the corporation, sharing one coach per team who both facilitated teamwork and provided personal feedback on their leadership styles. This ratio represented a sizeable expense in hiring top-level coaches to attend every day of the six-day session, but Marion was certain the payoff would come in each participant's professional and personal growth.

In terms of what CMC would cover, Marion and her team designed an intensive retreat that addressed four topics she perceived as essential:

1. *Who are we?* One thread of the workshop was devoted to discussing Siemens' history and identity, competitive differentiation, and the cornerstones of its corporate strategy. A key goal in broaching this topic was to ensure that all executives shared the same *story* about the company. But another crucial objective was to motivate participants into delving deeply into discussions about Siemens' culture, the firm's commitment to high performance, and the possible strategies it might follow to improve sales and profit margins.

2. *How are we organized?* Another thread would review Siemens' structures and management processes, how its matrix worked, and the role that cross-business collaboration could play. The objective of this segment was to elicit a greater understanding

among participants about how Siemens could find new opportunities for its divisions and business units to coordinate and collaborate in ways that would maximize sales and profits.

3. *How do we work?* A third thread would tie into the company's Top+ program to ensure that the executives would master and utilize the business tools, such as strategy development, market and business analysis, target definition, business optimization and growth, process management, and controlling functions.

4. *How do we lead and communicate?* The fourth thread was designed to offer participants significant opportunities to work on their communication skills and leadership styles through both insightful group discussions and extensive individual work with their coaches. Time spent on this element of the program would help the executives strengthen their capabilities to motivate and guide others to set goals, get the results desired, and develop a clear understanding of conflict management. Since many executives at this level talk to the press and public, this segment would also help them become better communicators as spokespeople for Siemens.

By emphasizing all four threads, the program addresses leadership in a comprehensive way, including strategy, organization, business process management, and organizational culture, linked with overall personal growth (see Exhibit 2.1).

Exhibit 2.1. The Four Threads of Siemens Leadership Excellence

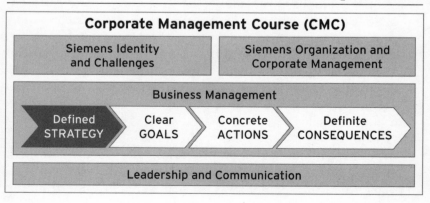

Another key element in the design was to invite the CEO and other members from the Corporate Executive Committee (CEC)—Siemens' Board of Management—to serve as session faculty at the workshop. Despite the high rank of the attendees—as division and corporate department heads—they nevertheless did not have regular contact with the CEC, and the program was a mutually beneficial opportunity to connect them. The board members would be able to talk about their experiences at Siemens, explain their thinking and decision-making processes, debate strategic options with the group, and learn about the perspectives of their best executives. In return, the participants would benefit through the opportunity to get to know some board members, enhancing trust and relationships, opening up new channels of communication, and sparking a renewed sense of commitment on both sides.

It took Spring and Summer of 2005 to finalize the agenda for the weeklong workshop and get the buy-in from various stakeholders. Exhibit 2.2 shows the text of a brochure that was created to describe the Corporate Management Course and its contents.

Exhibit 2.2. Brochure for the SLE Corporate Management Course

Dear Executive,

As a member of the Corporate Management at Siemens, your responsibility for Siemens as a whole requires a broad knowledge on developing pacesetting strategies, managing change, creating value, as well as communicating the "one Siemens" approach to our stakeholders. During the 6 days of the course you will be involved in challenging and highly interactive sessions. The content of the course focuses on:

- **The Future of Siemens: Portfolio and Performance, Operational Excellence, People Excellence, Corporate Responsibility**—What challenges will Siemens face in the future? What are the most pressing issues? You will obtain new perspectives on long-term strategy development by discussing upcoming changes in external business factors and global trends. The consequences of external changes for Siemens and for your own business are discussed. You will have the opportunity to discuss your views and examine the specific agenda and challenges of your own business area with senior Siemens management members.

- **Leadership Team**—Successful implementation of a strategy requires acting as a single leadership team. Therefore: a framework for effective "teams at the top" is introduced. Acting as a team, reviewing team performance, and improving team performance for the rest of the week will be a major task.
- **Corporate Management: Framing Your Role**—You will review the role of Corporate Management, analyze main stakeholders and discuss how to manage this relationship in an ever-changing complex business environment. Corporate managers also train their skills to effectively communicate to those key stakeholders.
- **Corporate Responsibility**—You will discuss the responsibility of corporate managers in shaping, maintaining and living the Siemens values.
- **Mastering Change**—Based on an actual Siemens case, you will, in a series of exercises and discussions, examine a change management process and learn how to apply best practices leading and managing change.
- **Leadership Style**—There will be many opportunities to take a closer look at personal leadership styles and enhance leadership skills in typical situations. Therefore you will learn about conflict management and practice how to motivate others to take action. To motivate people to action, you will practice skills for setting expectations, coaching and reviewing results.
- **Communication**—Having learned and practiced how to address different stakeholder groups, you will practice media communication—especially how to master difficult situations.

The detailed agenda for the week, which is depicted in Exhibit 2.3, shows the density of the program and the tight integration of the four threads. Change management issues figure prominently and cover strategy, organization, and personal behavior—not surprising in a situation where a new CEO wants to move the culture of his giant organization.

Exhibit 2.3. Agenda of the CMC Course

Sunday	Monday	Tuesday	Wednesday	Thursday	Friday
1–2 weeks prior: Individual coaching on 360° feedback	The future of Siemens: Challenges and opportunities Impact at the top: Creating a successful leadership team	Ambiguity and decision making: Using Siemens values as a guide External dynamics: Responding to the changing business environment	Stakeholder communication: Building deeper relationships	Stewards of change: Aligning people with the future Conflict management: Overcoming the barriers of change	Acting as voice of Siemens: Crafting media communications Leadership excellence: Creating a personal learning road map Wrap-up
lunch	lunch	lunch	lunch	lunch	lunch
Preparation and coaching Urgency for action: Creating immediate purpose Overview of the week: Corporate Management Course	Team learning: Observing your personal behavior Corporate management: Framing your role	Challenging the Siemens status quo: What does that mean for Siemens? Challenging the Siemens status quo: What does it mean for my business?	Mastering change: Case introduction and framework The beginning of change: Envisioning of the future The beginning of change: Formulating my strategy	Inspiration for the future: Motivating people to take action Coaching: Supporting the agents of change Mastering change: Putting it all together Learning from your team: Giving and receiving feedback	Optional: Personal coaching after lunch
evening	evening	evening	evening	evening	evening
Dinner/Get together	Shaping, maintaining and living the Siemens values	Leadership excellence: Integrating leadership into your everyday role	Fireside chat with a Siemens leader	Living team spirit (Team event with star chef)	

Launching the Program Amid Fear and Reluctance

Marion and her team slated the first program to take place in October 2005. Given the prior near-miss coup that had transpired years earlier in the famed workshop for level 1 executives, Marion was convinced that many board members of the company would be wary, if not completely distrustful, when they heard about the new Corporate Management Course. Some of the board members had been through a lot of change at Siemens, and they were especially suspicious of the course's intentions. There was widespread concern about the risks of having the company's highest-level executives once again gather at an event that could turn into a week of criticism, complaining, and finger-pointing, largely directed at them.

To counter these potential objections, Marion systematically approached each member of the Corporate Executive Council personally to explain what the program intended to achieve, particularly its learning value for the company's top executives. One by one, she discussed with board members how the new program was a meticulously planned, rigorous business exercise to strengthen senior leadership competences and help Siemens' top executives learn how to be more effective in strategic planning, change management, and teamwork. She reassured them that her learning team and the carefully selected executive coaches could handle the risk inherent in opening what might be the proverbial Pandora's Box of criticism, promising them that the results of the workshop would be positive and highly desirable.

In the end, she was able to obtain each board member's consent to move forward with the program. She attributes her ability to get past this hurdle to the fact that she knew most of the board members personally, and that her prior work at Siemens Management Consulting had earned her a great deal of credibility. Usually learning initiatives are launched by HR, and they are often met with suspicion, as executives believe that HR does not understand their businesses; in this case the board members knew Marion as the head of the totally business-oriented Top+ initiative, and they were familiar with her work ethic and the impressive results she had achieved. With each member's individual support, Marion was able to make a presentation about the new leadership program to the entire board and obtain a final approval.

Now green-lighted, Marion selected the twelve individuals she wanted to attend the first session. She decided to invite the "mavericks" of the top eighty-five executives—the ones she knew would be her toughest challengers. Should the program survive their criticism, the CMC would be offered to every new leader who was promoted into this level in the future.

Depending on the success of the CMC workshop, the SLE team would develop a Leadership Excellence architecture and adapt the CMC course design to the other four levels of Siemens management. It was clear that none of these lower-level management programs would fly unless the first CMC won the support of the topmost executives. Thus, the Corporate Management Course set the bar for a new type of learning discourse and reflection that the SLE programs could inspire for all of Siemens' management. As Marion put it, "For me, it was very clear. I had worked in a consulting environment for many years and I knew that the most important thing to drive strategy is to get the highest-level people behind it. You can't have the highest people not endorse a program."

In late summer of 2005, each of the twelve individuals received a personal invitation to attend the pilot session of SLE's Corporate Management Course. Many invitees responded with suspicion, unsure about the nature of the weeklong workshop and why they had been chosen. Some believed they were being singled out for "management reeducation" because their non-traditional leadership styles were well known to the board. News of their concerns made its way back to Kleinfeld, who began to wonder if Marion had made the right decision to pilot this first course using the company's top executives as the guinea pigs. He called two weeks before the course to ask her if she still believed it was the most prudent way to launch the program, suggesting instead that she consider using a group of middle managers. Marion persisted, and Kleinfeld trusted her enough to back off, agreeing to let her inaugurate the course as planned. Once again, her personal credibility played a key role in overcoming this last obstacle.

More than a Week of Inspiring Insights and Debate

The first session of the CMC went off as planned and intended. When Kleinfeld revealed the ruse about Siemens being considered in a merger to the attendees, they accepted the game as if it were real, suspending disbelief just as if the workshop were a theatrical drama in which they were asked to become the actors. Day by day, the executives attended the sessions, listening to the board members who openly shared their thinking, success stories, and concerns about the company's future. Participants discussed and debated Siemens' future prospects, the nature of the company culture, what changes and innovations they might be able to make quickly in their divisions and departments, and how their own creative leadership might contribute to improved results—all this while at the same time working with their coaches on their behavioral issues.

By the end of the week, the group had developed well-thought-out solutions to the simulated takeover challenge that Kleinfeld had given them. They presented a coherent, unified story, a specific plan, and clear recommendations they believed would persuade stakeholders that Siemens could meet its future better alone instead of being sold off. In short, they played the game all the way to the end.

Throughout the week, there had been no major personality conflicts and no destabilizing plans hatched to break up the company. In before-and-after group photos of all the participants, one can witness the transformation that occurred. In the pre-event photo, twelve men dressed in fully-buttoned dark suits and ties rigidly stand together, nearly identical in their emotionless blank faces. In the after-event photo, the members of the group sport open collars, no ties, and most of all, smiles and relaxed postures that reflect a week of comfortable togetherness and satisfying accomplishment.

The excitement of the learning experience sparked an energy that catapulted the impact of the learning initiative beyond anyone's expectations. Marion had bet high, and now it paid off that she had invited the most senior and critical leaders. They were so enthusiastic about the CMC program that they insisted to Kleinfeld that not only newly promoted level 1 executives, but also every single colleague at their level, should go through such a week so that they too could have the same learning experience. They committed to not revealing the *Financial Times* article ruse to any of their peers. And they wanted to see them go through the CMC as soon as possible in order to align the entire eighty-five top leaders to the same degree that they themselves had become aligned.

As this case study is being prepared, there is not one top executive at Siemens who has not participated in this initiative. All eighty-five top leaders of a 460,000 people company have engaged in a week of intense dialogue about the future of the corporation, and they simultaneously challenged their own behavioral patterns with their coaches.

And there were more pleasant repercussions. The executives left the program with a renewed commitment to Siemens. They were not simply pumped up by the workshop, as if it had been just a good motivational talk; they were moved into working harder and smarter for the sake of the entire corporation, taking on several actions to follow through on open issues the course had raised.

For example, in one of the workshops, the "Who are we?" conversation had unearthed the fact that Siemens did not have a robust up-to-date corporate "vision statement" that articulated the company's goals. Jazzed up at the conclusion of the program, they volunteered to work on developing one. Over the next few months, they corresponded among themselves and wrote a draft of a vision statement. The statement got board approval and has since been the vision statement for Siemens. It reads as follows:

> A world of proven talent, delivering breakthrough innovations, giving our customers a unique competitive edge, enabling societies to master their most vital challenges and creating sustainable value.

In addition, as more executives took the CMC course, the first group of twelve took it upon themselves to work with recent "alumni" to write up a new set of corporate values for the corporation. More than sixty Siemens leaders who had taken the CMC worked together over the course of 2006 and 2007 to propose ideas, debate choices, and settle upon three new core corporate values: responsibility, excellence, and innovation. These were accepted by the board and have guided Siemens ever since.

Perhaps the most palpable of all the repercussions from the CMC sessions conducted was a noticeably heightened sense of trust and teamwork among Siemens' top executive ranks. The trust could be seen in things as simple as the pact that the participants made to not reveal anything about the program to others, which was consistently upheld throughout the years, keeping the opening day a surprise for all future attendees. Even more important, the new culture of trust led to a new quality of strategic alignment, creating a more unified vision about Siemens and its outlook on the future. This alignment was so strong and unexpected that the Director of Communications of one of the Siemens businesses approached Marion one day after four division executives, all former course participants, gave an investor conference together. After listening to them talk, he facetiously remarked to Marion, "What have you done to these guys? I don't recognize them anymore. They all were telling the same story about Siemens when they talked on the call. How did that happen?"

The trust and alignment built up through the CMC workshops was seeping deep into the Siemens leadership culture. For most of the leaders who participated in the sessions, this was the first opportunity to work with their counterparts in a creative, open learning environment. They discovered that this type of learning allowed them to debate challenges they faced in their own divisions and develop shared understandings and ideas for improvement. The program's emphasis on long-term thinking and its holistic perspective transformed their vision of the company's future, while the executive coaching they received had a clear impact on their effectiveness as leaders and their ways of communication and cross-boundary collaboration.

Building Additional Levels of the Program

With the resounding success of the CMC program, the SLE team created a comprehensive learning architecture that included the entire chain of management. Between October 2005 and the fall of 2007, the team designed distinctive programs for four more leadership levels. To provide consistency in the courses and form them into an integrated, sequential ladder of leadership training, the team made two noteworthy decisions.

First, all courses would essentially cover the same four broad topics that the CMC course had covered: Who we are (strategic identity), how we are organized (structure and mechanisms), how we work (managerial processes), and how we communicate and lead (organizational culture and personal behavior)—though in varying degrees of complexity relative to the management level of the course. Focusing on the same four threads throughout all programs reinforces that participants at every level debate the same challenges and receive the same key learnings about Siemens, which ultimately contributes to a more unified leadership culture that shares the same values and delivers the same messages to stakeholders. In essence, the SLE architecture brands Siemens leadership in a way that no prior initiative had been able to accomplish.

Second, all courses rely on three key design principles that had taken shape when the original Corporate Management Course was designed. These principles are:

1. *Leaders develop leaders.* In the same way that board members got involved in the CMC as "faculty," the lower-level programs leverage the experience of Siemens' current leaders. Alumni from the CMC became faculty in the programs for level 2 and level 3, level 2 and 3 executives got involved as teachers in level 4 and 5 programs. Outside experts are brought in whenever an external perspective is useful, but by using Siemens' own internal wisdom, participants are not only able to experience firsthand the leadership persona and strategic thinking of the Siemens leaders they are working with; the resulting connections among the "teachers" and "students" also strengthen the ties among the company's leadership and align them on the topics they share in the courses—a principle that leads to a continuous reinforcement of the cultural change.

2. *See-Do-Teach.* All learning in the SLE programs has a tight connection to challenges participants face in their job today, eliminating the problem of transfer. Employing a principle they call

"See-Do-Teach," participants hear short plenary inputs that are followed by team challenges using real Siemens business situations. The approach assures that the program consistently reinforces meaningful learning that leaders can use in their jobs and model for their own reports.

3. *Challenge—Feedback—Support.* It is vital that all programs are designed to achieve visible professional and personal growth. They have to push participants' thinking about core Siemens issues by providing challenging topics for discussion and thought-provoking business exercises, while giving participants personalized feedback and support as they work on the problems. To achieve this, all courses provide extensive time for open-ended debate, discussions, peer-to-peer feedback—and, most important, private support time to work with the external executive coaches, who were used in the same 1 to 4 ratio in every course except at the lowest management level. To complement the coaching, each participant undergoes a 360-degree feedback review several weeks before the course to identify key issues of their leadership behavior. During the program, they work closely with their assigned executive coach to address these.

Exhibit 2.4. The Comprehensive Learning Architecture of Siemens Leadership Excellence

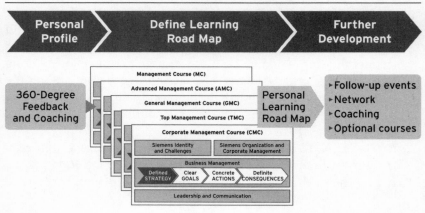

Exhibit 2.5. The Five Programs of the Siemens Leadership Excellence Architecture

Program	Key Learning Objectives	Target Audience	Duration
Corporate Management Course (CMC)	• Take responsibility for Siemens as a whole • Hold a long-term strategic perspective • Master change • Work as a team on the top	• Division executive management • Group executive management • Heads of large regional centers • Heads of corporate departments	one week
Top Management Course (TMC)	• Focus on the customer • Leverage your network • Deliver innovation and quality • Lead with edge	• Executive management in business units and regions • Division heads • Heads of regional centers • Other key corporate functions	one week
General Management Course (GMC)	• Internalize Siemens identity • Master complexity and ambiguity • Care for overall business success • Lead through people	• Experienced general managers • Subdivision heads • Heads of groups in regional centers • Comparable responsibilities	two weeks
Advanced Management Course (AMC)	• Think Siemens • Leverage my stakeholders • Translate my business strategy into action • Empower my management team	• Managers responsible for a function in a line of business • Managers with leadership responsibility to managers	nine months, including three months of distance learning, an onsite week, and six months of follow-up
Management Course (MC)	• Take a management perspective • Lead a team • Feel committed to Siemens	• Managers with leadership responsibility to individuals • Newly appointed top talents	three months, including distance learning, an onsite experience, and individual follow-up time

Given the regularity of topics covered and the three design principles, the SLE programs represent a consistent, integrated learning architecture that addresses strategy, organization, cultural change, and personal growth throughout the entire leadership population of Siemens, on a global scale, as illustrated in Exhibit 2.4.

Exhibit 2.5 provides an overview of the five programs that together constitute the Siemens Leadership Excellence architecture.

Ongoing SLE Value Crisis

In 2006, Kleinfeld updated his targets for the company in a program he called Fit_42010. It put a continuing emphasis on business excellence, people excellence, and added a new plank on ethics and corporate responsibility. At the time, Siemens was undergoing a crisis; compliance breaches had led to a number of resignations. To allow the corporation to start with a clean slate, Kleinfeld stepped down as well. On July 1, 2007, Peter Löscher, former President of Merck & Co.'s Global Human Health division, became the new CEO of Siemens.

Löscher opted to develop the existing strategy further to guide the company into the future. On the one hand, his vision sought to reorient Siemens into an integrated technology company having just three focal points: industry, energy, and health care. On the other, he aimed to turn Siemens from a rules-based to a values-based company. To drive the leadership needed for these endeavors, he fully endorsed the SLE program. An outsider and not involved in the origins of the program's philosophy or its content, Löscher could have asked for a new approach or at least for major changes in substance or format. On the contrary, he asked SLE to build on existing expertise to support the organizational changes through additional interventions and short-term programs for the highest leadership levels—with a special focus on collabora-tive leadership styles and strong customer orientation. His ongoing support for SLE was a clear indicator that the program could stand on its own as a powerful tool to foster strategic leadership and open up channels of innovation and teamwork.

In the years since, SLE has continued to play an integral role in developing Siemens' leadership to overcome the residue of the crisis and realign them to be forward thinking about the challenges ahead. By early 2009, more than 1,100 Siemens leaders have been involved in at least one level of the SLE program.

Conclusion: Leadership Learning as a Strategic Force

It is quite common that a leadership learning system systematically addresses the various levels of executives in a large organization. What makes this case remarkable is that the very senior executive group of one of the largest and most complex corporations of the world committed to a learning experience, and that they continue to carry the banner by volunteering cross-boundary work and by getting engaged in lower-level programs. It is the dream of countless CLOs and heads of Executive Development to get CEOs and top leaders involved in such a learning experience. But almost all of them fail in this effort, for reasons mentioned at the outset of this case study.

So why did Siemens' top leaders agree to put themselves on the spot? Why was Marion Horstmann successful in spite of the mixed reputation of the previous management learning programs?

Much of it has to do with the fact that the stars were aligned in an almost perfect constellation: a new CEO with the energy and vision to drive the company to new heights of performance and growth. A new and compelling strategic vision—enabling megacities—that required emphatic cross-boundary collaboration. And most important: the choice of Marion Horstmann to lead the effort. Only a person who enjoyed the unconditional trust of the CEO could risk a strategic learning exercise with top executives after the traumatic events of an earlier effort. Only someone with a proven track record as driver of the high-performance program Top+ could credibly insist on putting personal growth prominently into the learning agenda. Only a person with a companywide relationship network was able to convince this constituency to give it a try.

And then there is the holistic program design. Achieving sustainable impact in terms of alignment of strategy, organization, and leadership behavior requires more than a business school program or training in social competence. It is the unique integration of "hard" and "soft" that makes the difference: working on burning issues of strategy, organization, and operational efficiency in the setting of boundary-spanning collaboration while using this setting for reflecting on personal behavior with the help of top-level executive coaches. In addition, the involvement of board members as "faculty" creates a tightly woven texture of strategic, organizational, and cultural discourse that lives on in the firm's future "regular" business meetings.

The fact that each and every executive of the top eighty-five got involved sent a powerful signal to the organization, creating a buzz at all levels that Siemens is serious about leadership learning and development. It made it much easier to extend the program principles into an architecture that today comprises all management levels and creates a fertile ground for strategic change.

Ultimately, the SLE learning initiative has achieved a tremendous vertical and horizontal alignment across at the entire Siemens organization. It has become an indispensable brick for building a strategically creative and agile organization of the future.

About the Principal of This Case

Marion Horstmann is the CLO and Global Head of HR Strategy, Learning, and Leadership Development with Siemens. She received her degree in mathematics from the Technical University of Braunschweig, and attended INSEAD for her executive education in Strategic Management Tools & Systems.

Phoenix from the Ashes: How a Corporate Learning Initiative Reinvented an Ailing Business

ABB

One of the ironies of the practice of corporate learning is that it is usually one of the first victims of budget cuts when times are tough—but these are precisely the times when learning may be needed most. Companies that get into a downward spiral of stagnant growth and shrinking profits usually face a difficult general business environment, such as a recession, or the problems may indicate the demise of its business model. Both contexts represent major learning challenges for corporations, as they need to develop skills to better cope with adversity or reinvent the way they do business. But instead of responding to the learning imperative through dedicated strategic learning initiatives, corporate learning activities often get downsized and marginalized or at best kept at bay. The reason for this paradox lies in the common separation of learning from business issues, reinforced through the lack of business acumen that is pervasive in the world of HR and people development. As a consequence, learning is perceived as a luxury that we can afford in affluent times but dispensable when things get difficult.

The following case tells a story in which exactly the opposite happened: Faced with the dire options of either closing down or being sold, ABB Stotz-Kontakt—a business unit of the global engineering giant ABB—realized that their only sustainable way out of the negative spiral was a significant investment in a strategic and organizational learning initiative. They turned to ABB's internal Learning and Development unit, called *GoBeyond!*, for help in creating a radical cultural transformation process to realign strategy and organization and to rekindle a spirit of enthusiasm and entrepreneurial optimism among their disheartened employees.

And help they got. The learning journey led the business unit to new heights of success, both in terms of growth and profitability. Today, the previously ailing patient not only has a new lifeline but has become a benchmark in ABB for what is achievable through a smartly designed learning architecture that builds on the underutilized energy of people. Indeed, the ABB Stotz project is a paradigm for corporate learning that reaches far beyond the established notions of skill and competence development. Showcasing a learning architecture that combines the toughness of strategic turnaround management with emphatic employee engagement, the dramatic rescue of the ABB Stotz factory provides testimony to outstanding leadership and workforce commitment as well as to a highly effective approach to transformational learning.

———

ABB was established in 1988 when Sweden's century-old company Asea merged with Switzerland's similarly traditional Brown Boveri to form one of the world's largest electrical engineering corporations. Establishing headquarters in Zurich, Switzerland, the new company quickly became a global leader in power and automation technologies. Throughout the early 1990s, ABB developed a stellar reputation as a benchmark of a successful merger. Gradually expanding and decentralizing into more than 5,000 business units worldwide, its innovative business structure and management became a well-known story about successful post-merger management and globalization.

From 1999 to 2001, the firm was ranked number one for corporate sustainability in the Dow Jones electrical equipment index.

However, after a decade of being the darling of organization and globalization scholars, the downside of radical decentralization emerged. A lack of coordination among the group's relatively independent 5,000 business units soon generated enough chaos and in-house competition that the ambitious structure ultimately became self-destructive, and a life-threatening crisis hit the company in 2002. In response, the Board of Directors appointed Juergen Dormann as CEO and gave him the job of saving ABB.

Although Dormann eliminated thousands of jobs, he nonetheless managed to save the remaining 100,000 by selling off noncore businesses and resolving asbestos claims. He refocused ABB on its core businesses of power and automation technologies, and the company started to pursue business opportunities in Asia more aggressively. At the same time, Dormann redefined ABB's mission to stress environmental solutions as a key area of the company's products and services. The combined attention to efficient business processes, worldwide needs, and a stronger organizational culture put ABB back on track to success. In 2005, the ABB Group reported record profits and has done so consistently ever since.

Yet while the ABB Group as a whole was working its way toward a bright new future, one of its member companies in Germany was languishing in the past. In 2005, after more than a century of success, ABB Stotz-Kontakt had fallen to the point where it was threatened with closure.

The Turmoil at ABB Stotz-Kontakt

ABB Stotz-Kontakt GmbH is one of the principle players in the ABB automation products division. Headquartered in Heidelberg, Germany, the company develops and manufactures highly specialized low-voltage switches. The original company, established in 1891 in Mannheim, Germany, was named for its founder Hugo Stotz and was the first industrial company in its area of business. It became a part of Brown Boveri in 1928 and was integrated into the ABB Group in 1988 in the course of the merger. Many of its

2,000 employees had worked for the company for several generations. Allegiance to the local organization was strong, and its people had little sense of belonging to their globally prominent parent organization.

In 2000, ABB Stotz was a healthy company, with revenues of EU330 million, returning a solid double-digit profit. However, productivity and revenues had precipitously dropped in the following years, and there were considerable problems with innovation and quality. Rumors began circulating about closing down the factory in favor of an offshore production site. Closure would be an especially harsh blow to the local community.

Meanwhile, at the corporate level, the memory of the corporate ABB Group's brush with disaster three years prior was still fresh in everyone's mind. Corporate management believed that ABB Group could not afford to hold onto this unit unless it improved. It was decided that a final attempt to revive ABB Stotz would be made, and in June 2005, it was given two years to transform itself back into a premium member of the group.

Infusing New Leadership and a Restructuring

When Ferenc Remenyi joined the existing ABB Stotz management team as CFO at this time, he was fully aware of the gloomy situation, and he was determined to drive a full-fledged change and revitalization process. The choice of Remenyi was deliberate for many reasons. Not only had he spent his entire career in this industry, but more important, he had worked his way up the ranks. He had started in bookkeeping, progressing into sales and then management, where he continued to advance through hands-on experience. Though now their superior, he could truthfully tell Stotz employees that he had once been in their shoes and held their positions. In addition, Remenyi had experience—he had already succeeded in reviving a failing business. Still, in the case of ABB Stotz, Remenyi realized that the challenges were not a matter of figures. The firm's business potential was obvious; it was the company culture that was problematic.

One of Remenyi's first steps after he took office was to go and meet the people of ABB Stotz, because, "it's always about people." He even went to the factory at night to meet the people who worked the night shift. "These people hadn't set eyes on an executive in over a decade," he said, indicating his disapproval of the distance between employees and management that the regarded as a major impediment for a high-performance culture. Visiting the production facilities allowed Remenyi not only to assess the factory's situation with his own eyes; it also gave him the opportunity to engage into conversations with shop floor employees and directly launch his message of the change that he envisioned.

His style and his attitude in addressing issues were different from those of previous leaders and took the factory workers by surprise. When he saw that the factory facilities were messy and dirty, he refused to take this issue on as a management responsibility. Instead, he suggested the people clean it up. This may sound trivial, but it was symbolic and presented workers with a new perspective. If they wanted to build a more positive future, they could not rely on others to take care of business. They would have to take fate into their own hands; they would have to get involved and take on responsibility.

Naturally, Remenyi's first steps involved some judicious restructuring. From the start, it was clear that layoffs would be inevitable to reduce otherwise fatal business costs. A brief analysis revealed that to create a leaner structure in administration and production, approximately 15 percent of employees would need to be laid off. But instead of just moving ahead with firing people—and creating an even more gloomy spirit in the already disheartened workforce—Remenyi wanted to provide some visible symbols of hope for a better future. To make a point, he remodeled the run-down entrance to the ABB-Stotz grounds as well as the administrative offices, and he had all washroom facilities renovated to counterbalance the trauma of the layoff announcements and convey a sense of investment in a long-term future.

The layoffs were just the first step. Deeper changes were still needed. To get back on track, ABB Stotz had to improve its products by increasing innovation and process quality. Some activities such as packaging and logistics could be shared between various business units, creating cost synergies and higher efficiency. But the company also needed to modernize its production machinery. The question was, How would they get the funds to do that? One thing was sure: ABB corporate management would not agree to such investments until the company had demonstrated greater capabilities.

To express the seriousness of change needed, Remenyi, together with his codirector, the works council, and labor unions, unified their voices and explained the dilemma in clear terms to the workforce. They painted a frank and sober picture of the genuine risk of factory closure. Faced with the scenario of a total loss of the company but encouraged by the perspective of building a future together, the employees agreed to work overtime without any pay increase. The factory started to lower its costs, but more significant, this joint sacrifice began to spark a collaborative mindset for change throughout the entire firm.

Six months into the restructuring process, Remenyi recognized that the moment was right to raise additional momentum in the efforts to promote change. To move his transformational project on to the next level, he invited *GoBeyond!*, the internal learning and development unit of ABB Germany to come in and help. This action proved to be the decisive catalyst for multiplying energies for positive change.

The Origins of the *GoBeyond!* Team

Step back a few years. The radical and painful restructuring of the global ABB Group that had happened from 2001 to 2003 left deep cultural scars throughout the organization. Germany, which was one of the largest country organizations of the company, was no exception. One of the first victims of that era's cost cutting was ABB Germany's internal consulting unit. It had always had a good reputation as a center of expertise for topics like strategy, project management, and process optimization. But at that time, not being a core business of the corporation, it was declared a dispensable overhead.

By 2003, however, the dust had settled and ABB Germany seemed to get back on its feet. Looking at the cultural aftermath of the massive transformation toward an ultra-lean organization, German HR Director Heinz-Peter Paffenholz believed that it was time to begin addressing the trauma of the restructuring. The business atmosphere had stabilized, but a lingering sense of anxiety still pervaded within company walls; he felt it was now important to help employees rebuild their self-esteem, renew faith and pride in their firm, and build new strategic capabilities into the DNA of the organization.

Paffenholz decided that a new and innovative learning function was the best resource to pursue these goals. So he created a new unit called "Organizational and Human Resource Development," with the mission to help ABB's German business units counter the culture of wariness and caution inherited from the prior crisis. Michael Roehrig, an experienced organizational consultant, was brought in to lead the effort. The Executive Staff Manager of ABB Germany HR, Volker Stephan, had worked with Roehrig previously and was confident that his capabilities as an expert in leadership, organization, and cultural change would effectively serve their needs.

Roehrig's approach to driving organizational change had its theoretical foundation in systems theory. In stark contrast to a mechanistic, expert-oriented approach that trusts expertise and top-down power mechanisms to decide and implement desired change, the organic, resource-oriented systems paradigm stresses the importance of interaction between the various elements in the social network of the organization, and it trusts that people already possess the resources they need to solve their problems. The approach involves:

- Uncovering the sources of problems through dialogue and self-exploration rather than through external expert studies
- Encouraging reflection and ownership rather than selling ready-made solutions
- Promoting diversity and orchestrating differences rather than forcing standardization
- Adopting a holistic viewpoint rather than focusing on partial initiatives
- Increasing the ability to cope with complexity and ambiguity rather than ignoring complexity through promoting simplistic perspectives

As Roehrig explained, "The 'I know what's best for you' type of traditional instructor-led training is inappropriate for experienced, already knowledgeable managers. Instead, learning interventions can offer different perspectives, raise awareness, and help people develop new insights from exploring their issues. Looking behind symptoms, challenging mental models and engaging others are important elements to develop systems thinking." In his view, the true role of change-enabling learning professionals is to provide ways for business leaders to enhance their own abilities to *sense* situations and to *make sense* of situations. Conceptual frameworks and experiential learning activities are the supporting tools managers need in order to build their own capabilities in dealing with ambiguities and building shared leadership. With this philosophy in mind, the new learning unit summarized its mission as "to promote and facilitate change by fostering insightful, shared leadership."

Roehrig recruited two additional external consultants and three consultants from the former internal consulting unit to form his team. No trainers or subject matter experts were brought on staff, as it would be more cost effective to hire them only as needed, when specific expertise was required.

The team's business model was rigorous; it was conceived to operate as a cost-covering, customer-focused internal consulting business—nothing else would have been accepted in the tough business climate. Although under the generic umbrella of HR, it would be a rather independent unit, employing its own consultants and earning its way by charging ABB business units for its services. Roehrig would have to prove that his team was capable of competing with the best external consulting firms, because ABB businesses would in no way be obliged to use them.

To refine his unit's business model, Roehrig investigated similar practices used in other large corporations and benchmarked with renowned external consultancies. He knew he would not get preferred treatment from ABB, especially not in these difficult times; he needed to meet the highest competitive standards in the industry, or he would be soon out of business.

In its first six months (June to December 2004), the unit focused primarily on defining and establishing itself. "You mustn't rush through the early stages of a process," Roehrig underlines, explaining that a fundamental concept in change management is to take the time at the beginning to get things right; thorough exploration is crucial, and things will doubtlessly move faster later on. "Begin right and you are easy," was his motto.

The first challenge for the team was developing a brand of its own so that it could position itself as a center of competence for learning and change. Organizational and Human Resource Development was not a very attractive label that lent itself to creating a brand, so the team set out to define a more distinctive vision and identity that could be easily and convincingly communicated to customers. Eschewing hierarchy, all members of the team engaged in dialogue until they ultimately reached consensus on a new name: *GoBeyond!* The moniker translated the team's passionate belief that their work was about challenging mental models and organizational boundaries, but also about surpassing the limitations of traditional corporate learning approaches. In this spirit, they added a tag line with a message to potential customers: "Embrace change and win the future."

GoBeyond! adopted a strong customer focus. "Every contact with a customer is a moment of truth and should make a difference," says Roehrig. "People have to walk away from each and every of our learning interventions with the realization that they have gained new insights which will have a tangible impact on performance." *GoBeyond!* presented itself as a knowledgeable partner that would push its customers toward previously unexplored territory and accompany them on the journey. Moreover, above and beyond supporting a customer's actual change project, the team's activities would build organizational capabilities to safeguard the viability of the corporation by promoting a positive attitude about change that would be profound and long lasting.

Having found a suitable new name, the team embarked on a campaign to communicate its message of change, its offerings, and its approach. They created a series of high-quality brochures about *GoBeyond!*'s learning and consulting services; they illustrated them with specially conceived images of superimposed cutouts that appeared to escape "beyond" the frame of the picture. Photos and statements from Paffenholz and Stephan testified to top management's endorsement of the unit and its mission.

To find out where the learning unit could be most effective, Roehrig and Stephan visited ABB's twenty-five German worksites. Stephan's presence signaled corporate support for the learning unit's initiatives, providing prestige to an otherwise commendable but unglamorous fact-finding trip. The two met with ABB business leaders, investigated their business and change challenges, and presented *GoBeyond!*. They then went home, and the learning team used their input to design new leadership development programs and to revise their frameworks for organizational development and change.

By the end of 2004, six months after its inception, *GoBeyond!* launched three new management development programs: "Start Ahead" for new hires, "Step Ahead" for first-level leaders, and "Lead Ahead" for middle managers. The speed at which the learning unit was able to design and deliver these programs was directly related to its being composed of seasoned consultants. They knew how to zoom in and select the right method for a specific situation, and they could build on the stakeholder dialogue held with all business units, so actual program creation was a relatively short process.

The learning team's biggest challenge was to establish the *GoBeyond!* approach to change among ABB managers. This was not a program in which you could lean back and listen to a business school professor or play experiential games. Leading change in this approach required commitment and engagement. Participants had to be fully involved in what Roehrig refers to as a "co-creative learning journey." There were no checklists of "dos and don'ts," no shortcuts to success; *GoBeyond!* believed "learning by doing" was indispensable. Successful change requires a time investment for building shared meaning and should actively encourage resistance or different perspectives. In a nutshell, *GoBeyond!* told ABB leaders that if they sought change support, they had to be at least willing to change their own leadership culture!

GoBeyond!'s Intervention at ABB Stotz

In mid-2005, ABB Stotz was already actively involved in some major change efforts, but Remenyi was convinced that most of the company's managers had yet to be brought into the scheme. He formally hired *GoBeyond!* in October 2005 to work with his managers. The steps they took were as follows.

Step 1: Build a Foundation for Strategic Repositioning

After explorative meetings with Remenyi and his codirectors, which created a mutual understanding of the general project objectives and *GoBeyond!*'s methodology to address them, *GoBeyond!* went to work. Knowing about the importance of buy-in from ABB Stotz's most important internal stakeholders, Roehrig suggested kicking off the project with a high-level leadership workshop with the company's twenty most senior leaders attending. The support and involvement of the top twenty would be essential to drive and support the envisioned organizational change.

The session began with a brief exploration of people's perceptions about the company's status and future prospects. Once their opinions were on the table, the company's top team laid out their view and predictions. In addition, Heinz-Peter Paffenholz, who besides his HR director role was also the ABB Germany board member responsible for Stotz, voiced strong corporate support for change, conveying the group's care and concern for the company. Paffenholz had started his own career in ABB at Stotz many years before, which allowed him to be even more authentic and passionate about this.

In order to coinitiate the case for change, the group formed a shared understanding around questions like:

- What are reasons, triggers, and conditions for us to start a change initiative?
- What are we going for? What is our idea of a good future?
- How are we going to get there? How are we going to utilize the diversity of our people?
- What must we learn on the way?

Their discussion also served to review the restructuring efforts that had taken place during the previous six months and to highlight their connection to the strategic changes that were still to come to bring back stability and profitability. Targets were kept deliberately open and vague at this stage to leave room for innovation and concretion that was to emerge from the change process itself. The intention of this segment of the workshop was to set the right tone and to develop a shared understanding about what needed to happen.

Once the "case for change" was established as a shared perspective of reality, the management group started to identify the concrete challenges the company was facing. With the conceptual and methodological support of the *GoBeyond!* team, the group analyzed the strategic and organizational challenges from a variety of perspectives. Tapping into the diversity of their experience, they thoroughly discussed the key issues and challenges that they had to consider if they wanted to create a viable future for ABB Stotz. A dynamic model of the interplay between the organization and its environment served as the basis for a joint analysis of the trends and developments that people expected for the next three to five years. To encourage their passion for change, the group engaged in a visioning exercise and produced theatrical expressions of a good future for Stotz around questions such as:

- Looking back from the future, what groundbreaking changes have we achieved?
- What amazing inventions and innovations are now available to us?

The group also explored the enablers and barriers of their existing culture by reflecting how they currently dealt with power, ideas, decision making, differences, change, or accountability, and how they would have to change to be successful in the future.

This activity laid the cornerstones for building the strategic agenda of ABB Stotz for the next two years. It also generated a shared understanding of the specific challenges that needed to be tackled. Roehrig explained, "People usually know where changes need to be made, but they may need help to bring this awareness to the surface." He continued, saying that the role of the learning consultant is not to provide solutions but to enable their emergence by acting as facilitators and translators. The art of enabling learning interventions is creating the conditions for solutions to emerge out of the social system, based on the belief that the knowledge and wisdom to make the best choices is available within the system. Enabling people to generate ideas and solutions is also the most effective way for generating commitment, because people develop a stake in what they create.

By the end of the first day, the managers had identified the areas where ABB Stotz had problems and needed to change. They synthesized these issues into eighteen guiding questions, such as:

- What are our core competences and how do we develop them?
- How do we create value for the customer throughout our company?
- How can we as leaders create the conditions to make this strategic change real?

Working on these questions would be the basis for a process to actively explore the company's future rather than getting stuck in extensive analysis.

The discussions made it clear that the most important need for change was in the area of company culture. Employees had to stop focusing on an idealized past and redirect their sights toward responsibly and energetically creating a viable future. Remenyi had symbolically introduced the notion of personal responsibility when he had addressed the messiness of factory facilities as an issue to be solved by the employees. Now the managers could fully appreciate how personal responsibility was a nonnegotiable condition for change that had to be integrated into the company culture. Another cultural issue was the underlying gap between the company's local and global identities. It was time for the local organization to recognize the positive aspects of being part of a large corporation rather than wallow in negative feelings caused by threat of a corporate-level decision to close the site. The leadership team began to see implications of the needed cultural shift: that they as leaders would have to change themselves.

The second part of the top management workshop was held after six weeks of reality testing the strategic agenda. It was dedicated to explore the interconnectedness of the strategic challenges. Working on a specific challenge would affect the range of possible answers to the others, and a shared understanding of the overall system dynamics would assure a coherent impact of the various change projects. This strategic dialogue helped also identify the leverage forces in the strategic agenda and would later provide guidance for how to best organize project work.

Eventually, the group consolidated the strategic challenges into four clearly defined change work projects that needed to be completed. Project titles were created to address the heads, hearts, and hands of people, and for each project an initial mandate was created, addressing issues such as:

- What should be created, generated, or produced by this project (three to five guiding objectives)?
- Which three to five main topics or processes have to be designed or resolved?
- Who in the organization will be affected by this . . . and who should contribute?

For example, one of the projects was entitled "Stotz are We." It tackled the strategic challenges involved in creating a change-embracing culture in the organization, ensuring shared leadership and engaging all employees in the process. Remenyi himself took the lead for this project.

The learning team encouraged the managers to agree upon a transparent two-year project architecture for the change program. Roles and responsibilities were clarified, and the entire project was named "Fit for Future" or "3F." The team members committed to engage in the project work, and four of them chose to personally lead the four projects. They set up clear schedules for their work, with the four project teams regularly meeting on Monday, Tuesday, Wednesday, or Thursday, with the steering team meeting on Fridays, thus ensuring the alignment of the activities in all four projects.

A summary of the entire workshop design is shown in Exhibit 3.1.

Step 2: Kicking Off the Change Program

As one result of the workshop, the top twenty executives agreed that it was critical to broaden the base of involvement to multiply energies for the change initiative. They decided to invite eighty additional employees from the company to join their teams, from all levels of hierarchy and across all functions. At the time, ABB Stotz consisted of roughly two-thirds blue-collar workers and

Exhibit 3.1. Objectives and Outcome of First Management Workshop

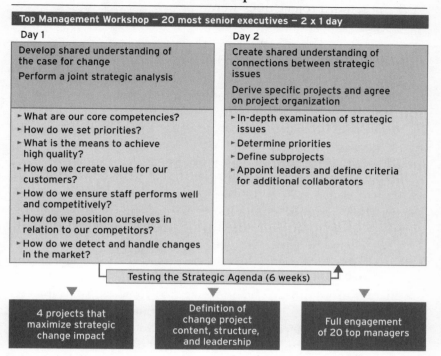

Top Management Workshop – 20 most senior executives – 2 x 1 day	
Day 1	**Day 2**
Develop shared understanding of the case for change Perform a joint strategic analysis	Create shared understanding of connections between strategic issues Derive specific projects and agree on project organization
► What are our core competencies? ► How do we set priorities? ► What is the means to achieve high quality? ► How do we create value for our customers? ► How do we ensure staff performs well and competitively? ► How do we position ourselves in relation to our competitors? ► How do we detect and handle changes in the market?	► In-depth examination of strategic issues ► Determine priorities ► Define subprojects ► Appoint leaders and define criteria for additional collaborators

Testing the Strategic Agenda (6 weeks)

4 projects that maximize strategic change impact	Definition of change project content, structure, and leadership	Full engagement of 20 top managers

one-third white-collar employees. Together with Remenyi, the *GoBeyond!* team set the criteria and decided on principles for a representative selection. Individuals could apply to join a project, or supervisors could make nominations.

On March 16, 2006, the twenty participants from the first management workshop and the newly invited eighty team members held a one-day Fit for Future (3F) kick-off event. The leadership team had met the day before to ensure their shared understanding and to prepare for their role as change enablers in the kick-off.

The day began with informal conversations around given questions that gave people an opportunity to connect and to approach the issue of upcoming change. In the next session, entitled "Marketplace for Change," the twenty managers explained the reasons for change and responded to questions and comments in a marketplace setting. Employees were encouraged to wander around and tune in to different leaders who each made their case for change. Employees reflected on these discussions with questions like:

- What did I understand from this session (content wise)?
- What does that trigger in me (my inner and outer reaction)?
- What does that tell me about my way of dealing with changes?

Additional working sessions during the day included the whole group drawing pictures of the change journey that lay ahead, envisioning the change process as an expedition, and identifying "equipment and supplies" one would need to pack or "stuff that needs to be left behind." The leadership team also shared their insights from the process of jointly analyzing the company's situation and identifying the strategic challenges. The project architecture was discussed, and the different roles and ways to contribute in the change journey were explored and offered as opportunities to co-create the future.

In the afternoon, a poll was taken to measure the effectiveness of the learning intervention, with enough time left to react to emerging questions or issues that people wanted to raise. An impressive 96 percent of participants agreed with the statement, "This change process is crucial for the future of Stotz," and 92 percent said, "I have gained a very good understanding of my role in this change process." Change was clearly on its way, this time not only ordered from the top, but supported by a little army of 100.

An outline of the day's activities is shown in Exhibit 3.2.

Step 3: Set Up "Pathfinders"

To further broaden engagement in the change initiative and obtain greater involvement, the learning experts next sought to enlist a group of about twenty "pathfinders." These were people with good communication skills from all areas of the corporation who were asked to act as communicators and change agents throughout the company.

In addition to the twenty top managers and the change project teams, they would be a third important group to drive the process. As relays between the change project teams and the line

Exhibit 3.2. Objectives and Outcome of Fit for Future Kick-off Workshop

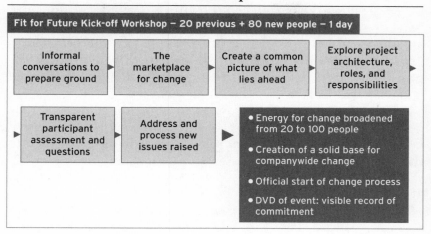

organization, they would provide their coworkers with information on the progress and serve as "sounding boards" to obtain feedback from their colleagues. Their rewards for participating were the opportunity to learn more about the initiatives and enjoy heightened visibility in the organization. Also, pathfinders would be given learning opportunities in communication, facilitation, and dealing with change. As a side effect, facilitation skills would be brought into all areas of the company.

However, some pathfinders found they were uncomfortable in their role, concerned they may be perceived as "spies" and lose social acceptance among their peers. To address this problem, Roehrig organized a special workshop for them. Consistent with the *GoBeyond!* approach, the pathfinders were first invited to voice their concerns. Once their worries were out in the open, the focus shifted to dealing with specific problems they perceived or encountered, identifying potential conflicts, and responding to individual learning needs. Remenyi joined the workshop to show top management support for the pathfinders and to show appreciation for their openness, and *GoBeyond!* consultants provided tailored learning interventions that focused on clarifying the pathfinder role and teaching special communication skills for the change process.

As follow-up, pathfinders attended monthly lunches with Remenyi in his role of being the leader of the "Stotz are We" project team, so that they could learn of new information first-hand. Such privileged advanced access to plans for the future was an additional reward for their involvement, and the pathfinders responded proudly. These monthly meetings were a safety feature in the project, since concerns or issues could be presented and dealt with before they gained momentum.

Through a cascaded discussion in all leadership teams, the approximately 120 managers of the company were engaged in dialogue sessions about their role and contribution as leaders in the change process. These discussions about linking leadership with project activities and the pathfinders' role were crucial for aligning all activities.

From this point on, the change program proceeded almost on cruise control. The team had sufficiently established the necessary conditions for all members of the company to become involved in the process. Everyone was part of either a leadership team, the project team, the pathfinder group, or a staff member invited by a project team to contribute experience and expertise. The corporate learning experts from *GoBeyond!* had fulfilled their mission as an enabler for transformational change. They pulled back and limited their role to offering facilitative support as needed and conducting review meetings with the managing directors, during which they assessed progress, reviewed new ideas, and made recommendations for next steps.

Exhibit 3.3 summarizes the contributions of the *GoBeyond!* team.

Exhibit 3.3 Seven Change Services Offered by *GoBeyond!*

1. Decision-making support
2. Design of overall project architecture
3. Workshop design and facilitation
4. Frameworks and tools for change project management
5. Training and coaching for people actively involved in the change project
6. Review of sessions and recommendations for route adjustments
7. Additional intermittent support

A Bright Outlook

It took eighteen months—not the expected two years—for ABB Stotz to produce the figures necessary to prove to ABB Group's management that retaining the business was a wise decision. The company had not raised its sales prices despite increased material costs, but it nonetheless had increased profitability through double-digit improvements in productivity. The secret behind this achievement was the radical cultural change: a newly energized and committed workforce had relentlessly worked on optimizing existing processes, reducing costs, and shortening delivery cycles. A new atmosphere of ownership, collaboration, and cooperation had created a spirit of optimism and pride that translated into positive action.

Now, when management discovered a problem, it was immediately communicated to all employees instead of being contained in the smoke-filled rooms of executive offices. In one case, two charged-up employees spent their weekend exploring a production problem and developed a solution by Monday morning. Their contribution was recognized in the new company monthly newsletter, *Hugo Extra*, along with a cash prize, which became the accepted prototype for this type of extra initiative in the company culture.

Further changes occurred gradually, step by step, as the project teams moved through the different stages of their work, coming up with strategic options, implementation plans, and monitoring measures for each of their challenges. External experts were utilized only where needed in a just-in-time and just-enough manner to keep the journey a shared responsibility of all Stotz associates.

The excitement of change got ample coverage in *Hugo Extra*, where employees could read straightforward and direct explanations of ABB Stotz and ABB Group strategies, along with clear information about the future of the company and the group. The newsletter was named after the notorious original founder of the company, Hugo Stotz, which reminded readers to celebrate the company's historical roots as a local family enterprise while now part of a global corporation. Articles highlighted onsite renovations, new products, quality improvements, and customer-focused initiatives, as outcomes of the 3F process. They were written in straightforward, accessible language. *Hugo Extra* has become a popular, friendly communication tool that has recorded company progress and made its achievements visible not only locally but also to the global ABB organization.

Finally, in July 2007, ABB Stotz held a party—a big party. The company was back on track and had proved its capabilities as a business. Revenues and profits were the highest in company history—and it had rebuilt its reputation both inside and outside the ABB Group. In return, ABB Group management announced it would make its largest investment in a production site ever at Stotz-Kontakt. New machinery would allow them to design and manufacture new products on the premises, laying the groundwork for further growth.

Conclusion: The Learning Team as a Strategic Force for Change

Among the thirty-nine projects that *GoBeyond!* designed and carried out in ABB Germany over a period of four years, the Fit for Future project conceived for ABB Stotz-Kontakt was one of its most remarkable achievements. Michael Roehrig, who has now moved on to the ABB Group level, where he supports the company's global activities in organizational development, attributes much of the project's success to the inspiring leadership of Remenyi, who not only allowed but encouraged the exemplary involvement of many Stotz employees in the process.

The project's results demonstrate convincingly the power of an approach that emphasizes finding and implementing solutions from within. While every project will be different, and context variables always require adaptations, a few simple principles have proven to be very effective elements of this type of organizational learning. They are:

1. *Get comprehensive stakeholder buy-in.* Change always has repercussions across a universe of stakeholders inside and outside the organization. Understanding the dynamics of this universe is critical, and engaging stakeholders in dialogue is an important precondition for sustaining change.

2. *Foster shared leadership.* A common understanding of the current reality and a shared vision of where the organization wants (or needs) to go are key ingredients for building creative tension and unleashing energy for change. The common intent, or purpose, of a core group provides the change process with leverage.

3. *Create a transparent process architecture.* Create a process that provides containers for joint exploration and co-creation. Phrase strategic challenges as open questions, inviting an exploration process. Organize change in stages rather than linear phases, and establish feedback loops. Allow opportunities and solutions to emerge on the way, and adapt the process as you go.

4. *Actively manage involvement.* Identify stakeholder groups affected in different ways, agree on appropriate involvement levels (decide, codecide, advise decision makers, contribute ideas and solutions, give feedback, be informed) and involvement purposes (quality and expertise, understanding and acceptance, competence building) and incorporate suitable involvement platforms into the process architecture.

5. *Make change practical and visible.* Integrate head, heart, and hand by having people take a stake in creating their future. Encourage practical applications, testing and prototyping new ideas as you go along and integrate learnings into your further proceeding. This includes emphatically communicating quick wins, no matter how small, to counterbalance the negative and symbolize investment in the future.

6. *Review how you are doing.* Provide for regular process reflection and actively invite feedback and experience sharing. Expect and encourage different views. Look behind symptoms and challenge mental models. Make learnings available.

Applying these principles, not only ABB Stotz but the entire ABB Group have benefited from the project's success. Case in point: in February 2008, ABB Stotz was asked to present its delivery improvement project to division managers worldwide, as a model for what others can accomplish. Here, as with any other benchmark, the key message of the ABB Stotz experience lies not so much in the impressive results and the new management processes. They are important, and without them there would be no story to tell. But the real significance of the ABB experience is that it provides a convincing example of the tight connection between human commitment and business needs—a valuable lesson to learn for all the business units across the global ABB Group. The story also shows how local tradition and global interests can complement rather than compete with each other.

About the Principals of This Case

Michael Roehrig is Group Vice President of Organizational Development of ABB Group, with a global responsibility of driving change through comprehensive learning architectures. Before moving to the firm's global headquarters, he was head of Learning and Development for ABB Germany and Central Europe. Before joining ABB in 2004, he was partner with Comteam AG, a leadership and change consultancy based near Munich. He holds a degree in business administration and strategic management from the Frankfurt School of Finance and Management.

Ferenc Remenyi is Senior Vice President and CFO of ABB Stotz-Kontakt. He has worked for ABB since 1977 and gained extensive experience in commercial project management. In particular, he has been involved in numerous large scale foreign projects (for example, finance director for a project in Saudi Arabia). Remenyi has held the position of CFO in a variety of ABB companies and has effectively managed several restructuring and change projects.

Healing Post-Merger Chasms: Creating Corporate Values from the Bottom Up

EnBW

Mergers can wreak havoc on a company's brand, vision, and values, whether the company is located in the United States, Europe, or elsewhere. While the strategic and financial gains in uniting two enterprises may improve their long-term competitiveness and profitability, the post-merger entity may not find integration an easy road. Chief among the challenges it must tackle immediately are how to unify and represent itself in the eyes of its customers and its employees. The first months and years of the new enterprise must be a time for unity, integration, and redefinition. Leadership must ask and answer critical questions, such as, What is the brand our two combined companies now represent? What vision of our business now drives us forward? and What values do we want our combined workforces to live by?

Such was the dilemma for the German energy company EnBW, which went through a series of mergers and acquisitions between 1997 and 2001. The rationale was to create a single strong company that could compete in a new European energy market in which none of the firms alone would have survived. The mergers eventually proved strategically sound. Today, a united

EnBW is Germany's third-largest energy enterprise, comprising sixteen energy-related businesses in electricity, gas, and renewable energy, employing more than 21,000 people and serving six million customers in Germany, Central Europe, and Eastern Europe. But the road to EnBW's current enviable position took many turns and caused the company to go through significant turmoil and structural changes before it found its equilibrium.

This case illustrates how EnBW's corporate learning academy created and led a crucial strategic effort to unify the company following the mergers, with a unique campaign that resulted in a redefinition of the company's values and the bringing together of multiple organizational cultures. The distinctive element in this case study is the bottom-up/top-down process that engendered the participation of more than 1,000 members of the company's workforce to help craft the values, disseminate them, and inspire buy-in from employees, management, and senior leadership. The concepts and methodologies described in this story are applicable to any organization seeking to reinvent or strengthen its values for the future.

———

When companies merge, it is reasonable to expect "some smoothing" will be needed to bring the respective corporate cultures into alignment. But when Badenwerk AG and Energie-Versorgung Schwaben AG combined their forces in 1997 to form a new company named EnBW, it was clear that "smoothing" would not be enough to bridge the deep cultural chasm between the management teams and workforces of the two organizations. The values each company had pre-merger survived in the minds and hearts of the employees much longer than expected, as the two energy firms attempted to join forces a second time to tackle the huge energy market opportunities that would become available when Germany deregulated its energy industry in 1998.

The seeds of EnBW's post-merger turmoil had been planted a half-century earlier. In 1952, the two German states of Baden and Württemberg were combined to form the country's third-largest state. Stuttgart, the former capital of Württemberg, was selected over Baden's Karlsruhe as the new state's capital. The political merger left a residue of rivalry that halted an attempted merger in 1994 and then clouded the atmosphere when the two firms finally merged in 1997.

Uniting the two firms brought apparent financial benefits, but the two company cultures were utterly incompatible. While employees from the Karlsruhe-based company displayed a progressive, market-oriented attitude well suited to facing the new challenges in the energy market, those from the Stuttgart-based firms tended to harbor predominantly conservative perspectives. In addition, the merged company had grown into a large, 13,000-person organization. Many EnBW workers resisted the changes; still attached to their original ways, each group worked in a sort of hidden culture, nostalgically yearning for "the good old days" when they knew what to believe in.

Between 1997 and 2000, EnBW barely limped forward. A further merger between EnBW and another German energy company, NWS, added even more operational and cultural disunity to the company; especially considering that NWS itself had been formed by a merger between two former independent utilities. In an attempt to finally gain stability, EnBW restructured its divisions into sixteen separate shareholder-driven business units. The change paid off for one business unit, Yello Strom, which profited from its independence to redefine itself as an innovator, using an upbeat, modern consumer-oriented marketing campaign. While consumers seldom view electricity as a product with character—it has no taste, texture, sound, or emotional association—Yello Strom brought it to life, promoting it as if it were tangy, smooth, musical, and cheerful. Their marketing revolution brought in more than 1.4 million new customers.

But EnBW's other business units did not rise to the challenge as quickly. They continued to adhere to a more conservative attitude, publicizing their attention to security rather than building a new consumer-oriented brand image. While their emphasis was justifiable—the businesses involve potentially dangerous power plants, gas networks, and waste treatment centers—they languished in the increasingly competitive German marketplace, stalling EnBW's profitability and growth.

Amid Tumult, Birth of the EnBW Academy

In 2000, EnBW's Board of Management (the German equivalent of the C-suite executives in U.S. companies) authorized the formation of a learning academy, the first corporate university in a German energy company. Having originated the idea for the academy and pushed for its creation, Dagmar Woyde-Köhler was appointed as its director. The academy was tasked principally with addressing the company's regular learning needs with training courses, seminars, and workshops for all employees.

But it was also assumed that the academy might design programs to foster the much-needed cultural integration over what had been essentially four different company cultures. Formerly the head of HR at EnBW, Dagmar was acutely aware of the need to harmonize the culture. Her philosophy—that "culture is the wellspring from which all other issues emerge"—convinced her that the learning unit had to reach beyond its traditional training boundaries. Her goal became growing the academy into a bona fide strategic actor to achieve cultural change within the corporation.

Dagmar's mission had to be put on hold for four more years. Between 2000 and 2004, the academy's role was limited largely to the usual task-oriented employee skill building and management development using a pool of trainers and coaches. During those years, the company's senior leadership and Dagmar kept taking the pulse of the company, but consistently agreed that EnBW was not ready for a major push to redevelop its culture in the midst of ongoing financial turmoil. Like many large companies of that era, EnBW had pursued diversification with a frenzy, acquiring numerous firms outside of its core businesses (including a shoe manufacturing company, a waste treatment business, and telecommunications agency), and it soon became painfully clear that diversification was the wrong strategy. Many German companies learned this same tough lesson, but unlike larger, wealthier organizations, EnBW did not have the means or financial leeway to successfully pursue such out-of-core diversification.

The Academy Tests the Waters

In 2003, the company brought in Utz Claassen, a new CEO who quickly made the tough decisions required to reverse the company's life-threatening situation. He sold off the superfluous businesses and refocused the firm on its core competences in energy.

To support the change efforts, the academy conducted its first baby steps to draw attention to cultural issues. In a program conducted in late 2004, it invited 450 people from the company's middle and top management to attend a workshop entitled "The Role of Management and Leadership in Change Processes." The program was designed to help leaders deal with the thorny issues of restructuring. Managers were taught how to maintain team cohesion despite the trying circumstances, including the divestitures and layoffs that had been determined to be necessary.

The program proved useful in promoting a degree of connectivity among attendees. Its success prompted the academy to host another event at the end of 2004 designed to further address cultural unity among the company's diverse group of professions. Labelled "EnBW Leadership Day," 650 managers listened as CEO Claassen and a fellow board member presented the annual corporate results, objectives, and strategies. Participants were then invited to share information about their respective business units and to discuss problems with their peers. Following this workshop, it became clear that people were finally opening up to recognizing the larger needs of the EnBW group of companies rather than just their own prior cultures.

Seizing the Moment

The restructuring decisions paid off, and by the end of 2004 the company had pulled itself out of the red. Now refocused on its core energy businesses and back on track financially, the time seemed right to bring the issue of company culture directly to the foreground. The two workshops had suggested that management was ready to tackle a more full-fledged cultural change campaign.

But what about the employees? Were they emotionally prepared to begin looking at the firm and themselves in new, more unified ways? One of Dagmar's early decisions about the design of the academy proved extremely valuable in answering that question. Unlike most other corporate universities in Germany, she had advocated from the outset that the constituencies of the academy include all EnBW workers, not just management and executives. This approach had put the academy in touch with employees at every level. The trainers, coaches, and consultants were continuously interacting with people in every business unit, and in their weekly staff meetings, Dagmar was able to acquire a thorough, comprehensive understanding of the company's cultural and political dynamics.

By the end of 2004, Dagmar assessed that the company was ready for a deep cultural transformation. In the intervening years, she had devised several ways to attack the cultural disunity. Her planning led her to believe that the most promising approach to strengthen the corporate culture was to redefine the company's values, an issue that had been largely neglected from Day One of the merger. Now, eight years later, EnBW still had no set of specific, meaningful values to guide employees. Without values to ground the cultural integration process, all further attempts to unify EnBW's people would be hollow and superficial.

Creating new values was particularly relevant for coordinating with the ten new corporate vision statements that Claassen had formulated when he became CEO. Published in December 2003, when the company was struggling with the divestitures, the statements redefined EnBW's purpose more concretely and prompted the company to craft a new corporatewide branding campaign in 2004. Coalescing around its core energy businesses in electricity, gas, hydroelectric, and other renewable sources of power (such as wind, geothermal, and biomass), EnBW presented a new face to the public as "The Power Pioneers."

Dagmar felt that new values would be a strategic corollary to enhance the rebranding efforts. "Our idea was that we needed to have a kind of mirroring going on *inside* the organization to ensure our people can deliver on our brand's promises. Effectively, the values are the bridge between our external promise and our internal behavior."

In addition, there was a very practical payoff in focusing on values: motivating employees to give their best for the success of the company. "There is frankly a real business case for having values. They reinforce the need to succeed. Even employees at the bottom line of the company understand there is a link between having a successful brand and keeping their jobs."

Choosing a Unique "Bottom-Up" Process

While the new corporate vision statements had been created in a top-down process, orchestrated by the CEO and the company's Board of Management, Dagmar firmly believed that creating and anchoring values had to be done from bottom up. In her view, new values could not simply be imposed on the people at EnBW. Given the multiple cultures from which they came, employees needed to have a hand in fashioning them. Getting people to accept any new values could happen only if they were engaged in their creation.

The academy devised a plan that would ultimately touch EnBW's entire workforce. She presented her bottom-up plan to both Claassen and the head of HR for their buy-in, and both approved it wholeheartedly. The three shared an exceptionally sound working relationship, with a great deal of trust and respect for the others' areas of expertise. Also, Claassen was familiar with the feedback received about the employees' emotional frame of mind, and he agreed that now was the time to launch the project.

The values campaign was designed to take place entirely under the auspices of the EnBW Academy rather than through the HR function or using an outside consulting firm. Process-wise, the academy would provide the leadership for the design of the various workshops, analysis sessions, and decision methods. The only limits on defining new values were that they had to fall in line with the vision statements and branding work. Otherwise, the territory was wide open for the employees to formulate values in whatever fashion they wanted.

One key element in the project's design was the ability to move quickly to build the values but allow the entire process enough time to become assimilated into the culture. In a company that by now had more than 20,000 employees, it would be foolish to rush forward by conducting a few forced meetings and then ram-rodding new values into existence. As a result, the campaign was conceived on a long-term schedule that would begin immediately and continue over roughly five years, from 2005 to 2010. To understand the architecture of the project, it is helpful to separate it into phases of activity, although they were not originally defined in this exact manner. For purposes of this case study, they are described as Phases 1 through 6.

Phase 1: Inviting EnBW Employees to Identify Potential Values

The first phase was designed to jump-start the process and give a large cross-section of the EnBW workforce the opportunity to take the first pass at creating new values for the company. It was named "Our Values Take Shape," and to launch it, the academy invited 800 EnBW employees (just over 6 percent of the company's workforce), to attend one of thirty-seven one-and-a-half day workshops hosted at various company locations throughout March 2005.

The initial group was comprised of 400 managers and 400 staff-level employees selected in proportionate numbers to EnBW's sixteen business units. Two-thirds of the nonmanagement group came from EnBW's technical and engineering professions— people who were not generally accustomed to the "soft task" of defining corporate values, but whose role the academy recognized as critical as managers. There were also representatives of the company's works councils (the German equivalent of labor unions).

Each of the thirty-seven workshops held approximately twenty-five people, with at least one member of each business unit represented. However, separate workshops were conducted for management and employees; despite growing optimism, the overall organizational climate was still full of years-old resentments. To kick off each workshop, participants were invited to talk openly and without guidance about the current state of EnBW's values. People immediately jumped at the opportunity to express their opinions toward the company, which often were critical. The process proved to be cathartic, as people released their old emotional baggage to make room for the real work of the workshops, usually without even realizing it. It also helped build trust among the participants.

Next, a senior representative of EnBW's marketing department addressed the group about the company's brand. Letting the participants know firsthand about how the new branding had been formulated and how it would drive the company's success proved extremely valuable. This session usually left people excited and enthusiastic as they began envisioning a vibrant "new" company as their future workplace.

The second part of the workshops began the serious work on proposing values. Participants split into teams of five people. Each team was instructed to draw a 2x2 matrix "value square," a tool designed to help them create discourse. In the first quadrant, the teams identify what they consider is a positive value for a company (for instance "cost awareness"). In the second quadrant, they write the opposite of that value (the negation of square 1, in this case maybe "lavishness"). The third quadrant contains a potentially negative element of the positive value in square 1 (usually an exaggeration of the value, such as "stinginess"). Finally, the fourth quadrant contains the positive aspect of the negative value from square 2 (usually a less radical version of the negative value, in this case, maybe "generosity").

This exercise accomplished several things: it opened everyone's eyes to the fact that positively connotated values always include a "darker" negative side and vice versa. This helped people begin to appreciate cultural differences—a key issue of the post-merger conflict. It also encouraged a discourse about the real content of each value, allowing people to dig deep into the semantics of the values they desired in the company. After each team had completed one or two value squares, they were asked to discuss two questions:

1. Where in the value square is EnBW as a company at the present time?
2. Where should EnBW strive to be in the future?

After the group work, everyone returned to a plenary session to share their chosen values. After discussion, the entire group reviewed the portfolio of values presented and selected those they believed were the most worthwhile for the company's future development. Any number of values could be selected as finalists for each workshop. In most cases, each workshop produced between five and ten values.

By the time all thirty-seven value workshops were over, a total of 260 value principles had been generated within a period of one month. Their effects resonated, as they were already sparking some dissolution of the residual resentments between the old cultures and nourishing thoughtful debates about the future. With their 800 participants, the workshops themselves resembled a microcosm of the very cultural unity that was sought. They laid the groundwork for the entire company to witness that the values campaign was a credible bottom-up process.

Phase 2: Letting the Values Naturally Disseminate

It was now important to allow sufficient time for the 800 workshop participants to return to their business units and share their experiences with their coworkers. To encourage "soft dissemination," the academy sent all workshop participants a copy of the value principles so they could see all 260 results, compare their own group's output with that of the other groups, and gain an appreciation for their contributions when the final values would eventually be chosen. At the same time, it was decided not to provide the entire workforce with a copy of the 260 values, so as to not diminish the specialness of the participants.

However, this "silent phase" began grounding the effort. Participants received no guidance on what to say or how to teach their peers about the values; they were simply naturally inspired to talk with their coworkers about "the value of having values." The uncontrolled "gossip about values" anchored the project culturally throughout the organization. People who were not directly involved in the workshops became more open to accepting whatever final values were to be decided, because they saw that the proposed values had been formulated by people like them.

In April 2005, the academy also gathered EnBW's senior executives and the Board of Management so they could familiarize themselves with the methods used in the Phase 1 workshops and review all 260 value principles.

Phase 3: Selecting the Final Values

The challenge now was to move the bottom-up process one step higher and begin selecting a final set of new values. The academy worked with the company's senior management to appoint a formal "Values Commission" whose task was to evaluate the 260 value principles and create a final set. The commission's members were carefully chosen to balance representatives from management ranks and the entire organization. It included eleven senior executives, one from each of the core companies, plus three employee representatives, a values program manager from the academy, a member of the EnBW marketing department, and Dagmar.

The commission conducted its first gathering in May 2005 and continued meeting for six consecutive weeks. An external consultant facilitated the meetings to guide the process and help the group assess, sort, and distill the 260 values. It was not predetermined how many value statements the commission would choose, nor the wording they would adopt, nor even how reliant on the prior 260 statements the members had to remain. However, the commission held the proposed statements in high regard, discussing each and every one as they walked around a conference room where all 260 had been printed in large type and hung on poster boards.

As a member of the Values Commission, Dagmar was able to see firsthand how her planning was paying off. She summarized the commission's meetings: "The task was not an easy one. Our objective wasn't to find the 10 best sentences out of the 260 statements that would become the EnBW principles. It was more to filter out of all the thoughts, suggestions, and propositions, a body of statements that could be representative *and trend setting* for EnBW. The basis for the decision-making process was never the personal preferences or interests of the Commission's members, but rather the interests of the entire corporation."

The commission ultimately condensed the 260 workshop statements down to a final set of ten, a coincidence to mirror the ten vision statements formulated in 2003. The commission took some literary license in crafting the final wording of the new value statements. They chose to begin every statement with "We" to reinforce that the entire company adopts the values. They also worded the final statements using parallelism in linguistic articulation rather than using an unplanned potpourri of recommendations. (See Exhibit 4.1.)

The final ten value statements echoed some of the values principles developed in the Phase 1 workshops, thus respecting the bottom-up process. The commission presented the final ten values in July 2005 to the company's Executive Board. In a noteworthy exhibit of trust, confidence, and recognition of the efforts put into creating them, the board members unanimously and immediately approved the final ten value statements.

Exhibit 4.1. EnBW's Ten Corporate Values

- We fulfill the expectations of our customers better than the competitors.
- We strive for outstanding performance through commitment and competence.
- We act consistently and reliably. Our word is our bond.
- We think beyond boundaries. We treat our partners with fairness, respect, and trust.
- We challenge and promote our employees. Management leads in a clear and straight way to success.
- We share our knowledge and see lifelong learning as the key to personal development.
- We always act business-minded and work to increase our company's value.
- We are pioneers paving the way for innovation within our business sector
- We see change as an opportunity and drive change processes decisively.
- We consciously act for the future, being aware of our particular responsibility for the environment and society.

Phase 4: Implementing the Values

The ten values now had to become embedded in the everyday lives of the workforce. For this purpose, the academy had to find a way to immediately engage all employees with extensive and intensive communications to encourage the positive changes that the company needed and desired.

Dagmar's plan of attack was to repeat the same bottom-up process she had tapped into before. The intervention of choice was a "Value Scouts" program developed in collaboration with a business consultant. For the program, the academy invited any company member, regardless of level or profession, to volunteer to become a value scout; the only requirement was that he or she demonstrate a sincere commitment to the new values. Asking for volunteers was key, because appointing people and forcing them to have enthusiasm for the new values would likely prove unsuccessful. Still, the academy asked managers to nominate people to become scouts, so that potentially good spokespeople would not be overlooked because of personal shyness. Nominees were approached and accepted only if they wholeheartedly volunteered.

Beginning in September 2005, about 120 value scouts attended two days of intensive training to prepare for their mission. During the remainder of the year, and through the early months of 2006, the scouts conducted a series of "value dialogues" with their coworkers and managers in their units. They spent at least one hour talking about each of the ten EnBW values with each group they saw. The scouts were in charge of moderating the discussions, keeping track of comments, and reporting back to the academy. Each value dialogue revolved around a "script" wherein scouts and their groups talked about how that value applied to and could improve EnBW's business. For each of the ten principles, scouts asked participants two questions:

1. How important is this principle for the success of our unit's daily business?
2. To what degree do we already practice it?

To make the answers visually powerful, participants were asked to place physical markers on a grid marked with a scale from 1 to 10. The visual representation of the many perceptions within in a group helped provoke heated debates as people sought to explain their positions or persuade others.

Ultimately, the value scouts conducted hundreds of dialogues. In all, between 2005 and 2006, each employee at EnBW participated in at least one hour of dialogue per value, thus ten hours per employee, which totalled 120,000 hours for the company's workforce of 21,000 employees. The program paid off in a big way. The dialogues themselves demonstrated the company's sincere commitment to a new openness and willingness to listen to its people. Just as the Phase 1 workshops allowed everyone to express their negative feelings, the value scouts encouraged participants to express their honest concerns about the company. Scouts reported that even people who were initially reluctant to speak got caught up in the dynamic. Some highly negative employees went into the obligatory meetings convinced they were wasting their time, given that the ten value principles had already been decided, but they came out amazed, making comments like, "This is the first time we've ever talked about these issues!" or "I didn't expect this to be so worthwhile!"

Scouts also reported the feedback they received in their value dialogue sessions. Rather than reporting to their unit's manager, they were told to bring their feedback to a "value coordinator" in their business unit, that is, a single person whose job was to collect the feedback. These coordinators then consolidated the feedback, ideas, and suggestions and reported them to their company head. The academy then held quarterly Q&A sessions where EnBW senior corporate management was brought into the loop.

By the end of this phase, more than 1,000 EnBW people at all levels had become involved in either the creation or dissemination of the values, while the remainder of the company had contact with the values through the dialogues. In essence, no stone had been left unturned to ensure that everyone at EnBW understood that the company believed in values.

The academy also conducted its first cultural survey. With the help of an external consultant, it sent a form to a 60 percent sample of the company's entire workforce. Most received and answered the questionnaire online, and those employees in the field who did not regularly use the Internet used paper questionnaires. The academy received a 60 percent response rate. Results were impressive, indicating an extremely high awareness of the ten values. However, what remained ambiguous was that employees were still confused about "how to live the values."

Phase 5: Living the Values

Incorporating the values into employees' daily lives was the next task. This effort had to be conducted in indirect ways because the academy recognized that the new values could not simply be drilled into people or directly enforced. Although the Board of Management echoed the values at every possible occasion, and the academy released various print documents and videos covering the values formulation process, the "value of the values" had to naturally seep into the corporate mindset and become a natural part of each worker's frame of reference.

One special emphasis at this time was encouraging the company's leaders to take a strong role in modeling the values. To assess how well EnBW's leadership was doing at this, all managers were instructed to record notes on all positive values-related changes they made themselves or observed in their business units. They were then asked to present their results at an annual management meeting in 2007. A few business units were able to present success stories. One manager spoke about using the values to guide effective quality management and CRM schemes, and another explained how his unit had improved several of their fundamental business processes.

However, most other business units had not done anything special about the value issues since the dialogue sessions. Reviewing the status of their efforts at this meeting was a strong reminder to refocus on the values. The meeting also acted to promote a healthy competition among business units and provided executives with a renewed opportunity to plan and commit to the coming year.

Phase 6: Individual Internalization of the Values

In 2008, a portfolio of smaller initiatives was aimed at moving the values deeper into EnBW's organization and reinforcing the cultural change process. The major thrust of these efforts was dedicated to shifting responsibility for the values to the personal level, reminding employees to adopt the values into their specific job. The academy interviewed numerous top managers, employee representatives, and the value coordinators to brainstorm how to best help employees keep the values alive. The general recommendation was to integrate values into normal business activities rather than addressing them as a separate issue. These are some of the ideas that were implemented:

- *Value cookies.* Participants of the academy's regular training courses were rewarded with a fortune cookie that contains not the usual Chinese proverb, but a value principle! In this way, values were brought to the surface in a lighthearted way, without any formal presentation or instruction.
- *Value checks.* Regional company managers dedicated parts of their regular group meetings to a "Value Check." To perform the check, people mark on a special visual matrix the spot where they think the company is in its journey to advance a specific value principle. This engendered group discussion and bolstered awareness.
- *Value exhibitions.* A consultant from the academy attended a regular business unit event where a small team of participants did fifteen-minute entertaining presentations on one of the value principles.
- *Value journey.* The "Value Journey" combined interbusiness unit learning and entertainment. All interested employees were invited to take to a quiz about corporate values. The top twenty "winners" spent two days visiting five EnBW locations and participated in a variety of activities. During the journey, no specific discussions about values took place, but values themes were continually recalled through soft communication and community-building events. For example, in a "value cooking" segment with a member from the Executive Board, a professional chef helped the group create a meal together, which metaphorically reinforced the idea that everyone nourishes teamwork. Participants were able to converse with managers and employees in the branches they visited and discover changes undertaken as a direct result of the value initiatives. The two-day journey was captured on film and distributed only to the "special" group of journey participants. Nevertheless,

the symbolic value of the journey spread to their coworkers throughout the company. The participants thus enlarged the network of EnBW value representatives and became additional ambassadors for the value process. Other Value Journeys are scheduled for future years.

The EnBW Values Campaign will not be completed until 2010. The academy has not fully planned further efforts in detail, as they believe it is wiser to react to developments as they come up from this point forward. Exhibit 4.2 provides a summary overview of the development and implementation process.

Exhibit 4.2. Values Development Timeline at EnBW

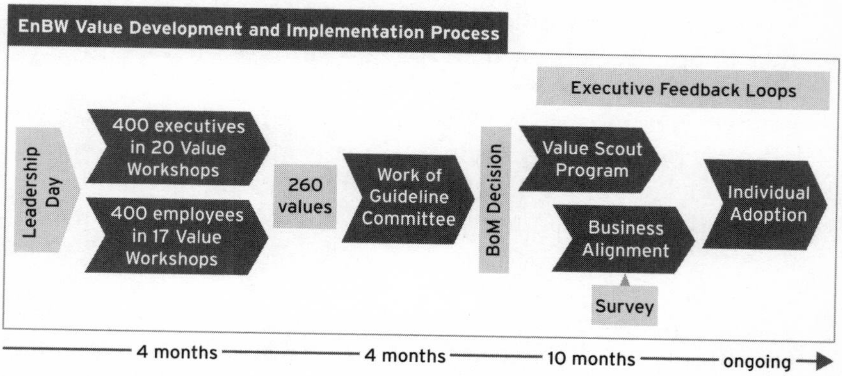

A Transformed Company

Although it is impossible to measure the specific impact of the value creation process on the company's financial results, the academy deserves credit for accomplishing a significant organizational transformation. In the program's second employee survey, taken in November 2008, employees rated the values as a highly relevant factor in their job satisfaction and feelings of commitment to the company.

Another indication of the program's success can be seen in the popularity of a DVD produced to document nearly every step of the initiative, including footage from some of the original values workshops, the values commission meetings, and some of the values dialogues among the scouts and employees. The DVD is well regarded among both employees and other companies that have requested information about the program.

Overall, EnBW is not the same place today as it was in 2005, when the values campaign began, and it is especially not the same organization that was near failure between 1997 and 2004. Some of the visible transformations that happened include:

- EnBW now offers an environment in which people feel they can speak openly and honestly about the issues that concern them.
- Nostalgia for the past has been replaced by a forward-looking energy; instead of complaining about problems, company members have developed the reflex of seeking solutions.
- The bottom-up workshop process that launched "Our Values Take Shape" set a precedent for new kinds of interaction between EnBW employees and their employer.
- Four years after its start, the effects of the process are still palpable in the organization. Company members are now far more confident that their voices will be heard and that their opinions can have an impact on the company's culture and success.

Most important, the values campaign literally became synonymous with the idea of a bottom-up process for corporate change. For the employees who went through the process, the journey to arrive at the values changed the culture as much as the final values did. The process itself opened the door to a more inclusive, open-minded, team-oriented atmosphere.

Two events demonstrate the transformative effect that the campaign has played at EnBW. First, the heads at two of the sixteen EnBW business units have implemented their own versions of the values program in their companies to mobilize employees and improve processes. This development is a telling sign of how the academy has filtered into management thinking within EnBW. It is hoped that other managers may also adopt bottom-up campaigns as they work to implement changes in their units. Second, when EnBW's new CEO took over in 2007, he received advice from an internationally renowned consulting agency that had studied the company to abandon the ten values and redevelop new ones. He rejected that advice without hesitation, informing the consultant that he would never throw out values that had been developed from the input of more than 800 EnBW employees.

Conclusion: The Corporate Academy as a Strategic Force

The case is a great example of how a corporate academy can transcend the traditional roles prescriptions of the learning function. Whether it is values or any other topic that requires a fundamental change of perspectives, the EnBW experience shows that it is not so much about "teaching" the content in traditional settings but about designing a comprehensive organizational process.

To be able not only to design but to implement such a process, perhaps the "stars need to be aligned." In EnBW's case, this alignment included a new CEO who could play on a broad leadership clavier, balancing clear strategic direction and decisiveness while allowing and even nurturing a bottom-up process. It also included a CLO who had earned credibility and trust through her professional work and who demonstrated exceptional sensitivity to timing and the pulse of the organization's readiness for change. The circumstances also included a burning platform for cultural integration, driven in significant part by repositioning the company and the brand in the market, creating a real "pull" behind the need for a unified culture. And last but not least, it included a corporate learning unit that was closely linked to the "grass roots" of the company and not just to the senior leadership.

But even perfectly aligned stars require the creative intelligence of a design that fosters the right processes at the right time. The six phases discussed herein oscillate between executive guidance and employee empowerment, all embedded in a pervasive culture of dialogue. If learning functions have the credibility—and the power that comes with it—to design such dialogue architectures, and if they are able to solicit the support of the key stakeholders of the firm, they can become true transformers—not only catalysts but true drivers of strategic and organizational change.

About the Principal in This Case

Dagmar Woyde-Köhler holds a degree in education and German literature and history from Heidelberg University. She began her career as a secondary school teacher and moved on to train and supervise student teachers. In 1991, she participated in an eighteen-month leadership program for positions in public administration, business, and foreign affairs, during which she spent six months working for BASF (Germany) and six months for the County of San Diego, California. Upon completion of the program, she became the Head of Education, Science, and Cultural Programs for the State of Baden-Württemberg. She joined EnBW in April 1997 as the Director of Human Resources, developed the concept for EnBW Academy, and has been its director since its establishment in 2000. She was awarded the Chief Learning Officer of the Year award in 2008 by a prestigious German business magazine.

Designing Customer Centricity for Multiple Market Segments: The *perspectives* Project

BASF

This case tells the story of *perspectives*, a unique campaign by the world's leading chemical company, BASF, to transform the mindsets of its people and its corporate culture from a product- and technology-dominated company to one driven by its markets and customers. The case provides an excellent example of a comprehensive learning architecture driving major strategic and organizational change.

As an important element of implementing BASF's "Strategy 2015," the *perspectives* case sheds light on the very common challenge of opening up an organization's boundaries to the outside world. This is especially difficult for companies operating in a business that is dominated by cutthroat competition on cost and efficiency, with limited options for differentiation and little room for business model innovation. In addition, the chemical industry faces public mistrust on environmental issues, often creating a culture of defense and wariness. All this makes BASF's efforts to rethink their way of doing business and implement this philosophy on all levels of their organization more remarkable.

Customer orientation has since long been a staple of corporate learning activities. Many companies spend significant funds on the qualification of their marketing and sales force, often even extending their training efforts to customers and the supply chain. This type of learning is typically driven by the goal of improving marketing and sales skills for a fixed set of products and services. Usually these programs do not touch on the essence and nature of the company's customer relationships. They may help improve it, but they do not fundamentally change it.

The following case is very different. It tells the story of a strategic initiative that fundamentally challenges the role configuration between supplier and customer, reaching deep into all functional elements of the organization. At first glance, BASF's *perspectives* project may seem like just another effort to improve customer relationships, but as the case unfolds, we unveil the architecture of a deeper transformational learning initiative that reinvents formerly unquestioned industry routines to open up new and exciting opportunity spaces for BASF and its customers alike.

In February 2005, BASF was ranked as the number one chemical company on *Fortune* magazine's list of America's Most Admired Companies. Founded in 1865 in the German town of Ludwigshafen as a manufacturer of industrial dyes, the company has come a long way. Over the last two decades, the firm managed to grow significantly through a series of transnational acquisitions that assured industry leadership in many segments of the chemical market. Today BASF offers a broad range of products, including chemicals, plastics, agricultural solutions, oil and gas, and more. Its fourteen operating divisions and more than 95,000 employees serve a diverse portfolio of international customers from multiple industries in more than 200 countries. With revenues of $80 billion in 2008, BASF ranks first in *Fortune* magazine's list of global chemical companies.

Typical for an industry that is deeply based in natural science, BASF built its success on a strong commitment to research, innovation, and technological leadership, along with reliable product quality. The firm's ascent to global leadership has paralleled its reputational growth as an innovative and reliable supplier. But would that be enough to protect the company's global leadership position in the future—especially in a market that faces an increasing commoditization of products? The answer became very clear when, at the turn of the millennium, the chemical industry was confronted with an unexpected disruptive environment, featuring a challenging combination of new technologies, novel delivery mechanisms, and new regulations. BASF quickly recognized it was time to rethink its identity and seek out a new level of sustainable competitiveness.

Realizing that to sustain its industry leadership in a B2B market requires thinking beyond the traditional sources of competitive advantage, BASF announced in 2004 the launch of new global guidelines that aimed to drive profitable growth and competitive differentiation for the foreseeable future. The heart of the new strategy, called BASF 2015, is comprised of four cornerstones that transcend traditional product-oriented thinking and outline a new set of values (see Exhibit 5.1).

These four guidelines seem to be no-brainers and may sound trivial at first. But on closer examination they offer deep insights and major transformational challenges for a global yet traditional company that finds itself on the brink of change.

Exhibit 5.1. The Four Cornerstones of BASF 2015

We earn a premium on our cost of capital	We help our customers to be more successful
The Chemical Company	
We form the best team in industry	We ensure sustainable development

The first guideline—*We earn a premium on our cost of capital*—with its focus on profitability is a response to the firm's fast international growth, which was partly driven by the desire to gain market share and global reach. It introduces performance as a new beacon over growth and recognizes that only companies that consistently earn profits in excess of the costs of the equity and debt capital they employ can be successful and survive in the long term.

The second guideline—*We form the best team in industry*—recognizes the importance of people and talent as a critical resource in times of product commoditization. This requires a mental shift from the traditional perspective that sees the source of competitive advantage not so much in relatively easily imitable products but in relatively hard to duplicate talent. People and a great team are required for creative and innovative solutions that may be different for each customer and context. Thus this guideline also signals trust and appreciation for every individual in the company.

The third guideline—*We ensure sustainable development*—is based on the insight that ecological sensitivity, social responsibility, and striving for long-term success instead of short-sighted profitability are instrumental in building a compelling and differentiating business that fosters long-term partnerships with customers. Applying these competences authentically across the value chain can turn into a real value proposition for customers who face similar pressures; at the same time, a commitment to sustainability is an important contribution to building a brand.

The fourth guideline—*We help our customers to be more successful*—puts the customer's success at the center of all of BASF's business activities. It recognizes that creating sustainable customer relationships requires more than securing profitable economic transactions. This implies a shift to a perspective deeply rooted in innovation and a differentiated business model that serves unmet needs of markets and customers.

Each of the four guidelines of BASF 2015 may sound familiar. Profitability, people orientation, corporate responsibility, and customer focus are common mantras for mission statements and strategic cornerstones. They are not difficult to come up with. However, the challenge lies in implementing them in complex organizations that have deeply engrained practices that work against these desired values. The art of transformational learning is to bring the substance of such statements alive, building on the history and the specific context of the corporation. Our case illustrates how this leading corporation tackled one of the more challenging of the four: true customer orientation.

Creating True Customer Orientation: The *perspectives* Project

Exhibit 5.2 illustrates how the company defines this strategic guideline on its Web site.

Exhibit 5.2. BASF's Customer Orientation Strategy Statement

We Help our Customers to be more Successful

We're there where our customers are. We invested in good time in growth markets and are now active in all important markets worldwide. In order to grow profitably, we want to focus even more closely on our customers' needs in the future and develop and apply the best business models for them and us.

We want to tailor our innovations more closely to impulses from the markets: We are increasingly developing new products and services in close collaboration with key customers. We enter into research and development partnerships with such customers to find tailor-made solutions that ensure our mutual success.

In the areas of specialties and standard products, we look at the individual needs of our customers and develop the appropriate solution. We combine new products and services to yield system solutions that offer our customers a competitive advantage and create profit potential for us. With standard products, we concentrate on quality, reliable delivery and an appropriate price-to-performance ratio.

New areas of knowledge open up new market opportunities for us: Biotechnology and nanotechnology, materials science and energy management technologies will fundamentally change our customers' businesses and their expectations of us. We want to seize and shape technological change as an opportunity. We are particularly focusing on the advantages of biotechnology in order to tap into new potential through innovative solutions for the food industry, animal nutrition and agriculture.

Source: http://www.basf.com/group/corporate/en_GB/content/about-basf/strategy/customers.

The decision to dedicate one of the four strategic pillars of BASF 2015 to customer centricity ("help our customers be more successful") was driven by the insight that the health and profitability of its customers is an important fundamental of BASF's own profitability and growth. Playing a major and recognized role in the customer's value creation process radically redefines the traditional value proposition of commodity manufacturers. Done right, such an approach opens up entirely new combinations of products and services, creates a unique brand, and assures long-term, trusted relationships.

However, "done right" is the key variable in this equation. While it is easy to agree at a conceptual level on the necessity and the benefits of a dedicated customer orientation, it is extremely difficult to change the texture of a company like BASF, whose success has always been driven from the inside out: excellence in research, innovation through proprietary labs, core processes that focus on efficient manufacturing and product line optimization, flawless logistics, reliable delivery, and so on.

There is nothing wrong with such virtues—they formed the basis of BASF's success in the past, and they are certainly worth keeping in the new BASF 2015. But true customer centricity—"helping *them* to be more successful"—requires an organizational architecture that is built as strongly in the spirit of "outside-in" as it was for inside-out. It became clear that moving beyond lip service and truly implementing box 4 of the strategic guidelines would require a structural and cultural shift that could only be initiated and sustained through a wide-ranging, dedicated, and sharply focused change program.

On the basis of this insight, BASF launched in 2005 what it named *perspectives*, an organization-wide culture change initiative aimed at transforming BASF into a more customer-centric organization.[1]

Initially, the project was to be rooted within the company's existing Marketing & Sales Academy, a structure that had been set up a few years earlier to systematically develop the skill set of those employees who dealt with customers. However, BASF's Board of Executive Directors quickly realized that the traditional educational portfolio of their academy programs would not be enough to create the envisioned degree of strategic and organizational transformation required at the time. After all, the objective was to change the company's DNA, a process that would penetrate many of the company's practices and functions across the entire internal value chain—and beyond.

The *perspectives* initiative was thus conceived to be entirely something else. "We did not need another MBA school, with an academic type of learning process proposing seminars," stated Andrés Jaffé, who heads up *perspectives* today. "Rather, we were aiming for a comprehensive learning architecture where you can apply new insights, mindsets and processes immediately to a relevant customer-related project out of your own business unit."

The *perspectives* project, originally named HCS—"Help our Customers to be more Successful"—sought to create an entirely new way of looking at the company's business. It was based on using interaction and dialogue with customers as means of changing attitudes and modifying business unit behaviors. The project's objective was to teach BASF people (referred to internally as *peers*) to challenge the way they talk to and interact with customers about their needs—without prescribing or prejudging the conversation according to BASF standards. Instead, the peers must be able to acknowledge customer diversity as a value and incorporate those views into their operational business decisions.

In essence, the *perspectives* mission was to assist the business units in developing and implementing a portfolio of customer-centric business models that maximized mutual value creation and set the foundation for sustaining relationships. To achieve this, *perspectives* designed a comprehensive learning architecture that created new ideas for value creation, utilized customer focus groups, and launched a more unified marketing and sales network that would help BASF peers exchange experiences and best practices.

Applying the "Blue Ocean" Philosophy

In its quest to innovate the way BASF did business with its customers, *perspectives* drew heavily from insights and concepts of the business best-seller, *Blue Ocean Strategy.*[2] In this book, authors Kim and Mauborgne make the argument that achieving a hard-to-beat competitive position is not based so much on how to best win within the existing industry paradigm; instead, obtaining industry leadership is primarily based on creative ways to open new market spaces and play the game differently.

The reasoning goes like this: When industry boundaries are clearly defined and accepted and the competitive rules of the game are well known to everyone involved, companies try to outperform their rivals to seize as large as possible a share of the existing pie. But as a market becomes increasingly crowded, prospects for profits and growth shrink. Products become undifferentiated; competition becomes cutthroat, turning the ocean red with blood. Companies that continue to compete in such market conditions within the established rules follow a "Red Ocean" strategy—a strategy that ultimately leads to low profitability and decline.

In contrast, Blue Oceans are characterized by untapped market spaces, renewable demand creation, and the opportunity for highly profitable growth. A "Blue Ocean" strategy redefines the industry space by reinventing the dominant value equation. By rewriting the rules of the game, a company can leave the cutthroat fighting in Red Oceans behind and make traditional competition largely irrelevant.

With its new emphasis on redesigning the customer relationship, BASF was heading for the Blue Ocean. The company's leaders understood that they needed to work hard on value migration by developing different and compelling value propositions that mattered to customers and on redesigning their overall customer interaction patterns. *perspectives* would bring these theoretical and conceptual ideas to life—no trivial task in a company of over 95,000.

Understanding the Value Curve and Its Organizational Implications

"Helping customers to be more successful" requires a deep understanding, first, of how they create value themselves, and then how BASF's products and services can best enhance this process. Rather than just "selling the inventory," customer centricity requires an honest and exclusive focus on offerings (factors) that add demonstrable value *for customers* while eliminating services that are of no

Exhibit 5.3. Reinventing the Value Curve

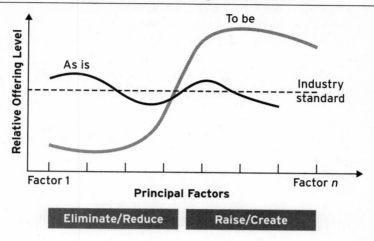

value to them. This understanding provides the foundation for redesigning the "Value Curve" and playing the game differently than industry incumbents do (see Exhibit 5.3).

Creating a new value curve requires intensive discussions with customers and noncustomers in the market. The insights gained from these allow the company to evaluate the value components of its existing services *through the eyes of the customer,* which provides the basis for eliminating low-value activities while sparking and inspiring new ideas that offer additional benefits for customers. This effort leads to a unique customer-oriented value proposition that breaks away from the constraints of the dominant business model of the industry, opening up new markets and services in the previously untapped Blue Ocean universe.

Defining Customer Interaction Models

When companies perform the value curve exercise well, they can shift themselves to a market segmentation that is based on their customers' real needs and identify the "Customer Interaction Model" (CIM) that best meets these requirements. By identifying and selecting the most profitable CIM, business units can decide how best to address their customers' needs and possibly work with them on optimizing the value equation. This then allows them to align their "back end" accordingly and tailor their product/service packages to each customer.

Understanding the customer and then redesigning the organization from an outside-in perspective is key. This is easier said than done, because we all tend to perceive customer needs through the lenses of our own capabilities and strengths, and we tend to adhere to established industry standards—"the way it's done." If there is some deeper understanding, it is usually limited to the strategic marketing function, but that seldom finds its way to other parts of the organization.

Truly turning a company's product orientation upside down, however, requires that the concept of "understanding the customer" becomes pervasive *throughout the entire organization*— not only in the sales and marketing function, but also in product development, customer service, manufacturing, logistics, research and development, accounting, and more. The best insights about what creates customer value remain useless if the "back end" of the company cannot deliver the promises or does not organize itself to optimize boundary-spanning processes across the chain. One reason so many smart consulting projects about market dynamics remain toothless is that they do not take into account the hard work of corporate learning that is required to create true impact.

The *perspectives* project would change this. In conjunction with other internal and external teams, and with a thorough analysis of all BASF businesses, a high-level customer needs-based segmentation was developed. From that, and with further development, BASF created six distinct customer interaction models that would provide the basis for all further activities (Exhibit 5.4).

1. *BASF as Trader/Transactional Supplier.* This customer interaction model is appropriate for customers who require products that meet standard specifications. Typically, price is the most important decision factor. Products are undifferentiated, and suppliers may easily be replaced. The market in many cases allows for spot buying/selling behavior; pricing is often made very transparent by index prices. Such a market is characterized by numerous anonymous or rather shallow

Exhibit 5.4. BASF's Six Customer Interaction Models

Trader/Transactional
Supplier

Learn/Reliable
Basics Supplier

Standard Package
Provider

Product/Process
Innovator

Customized Solution
Provider

Value Chain
Integrator

buyer-supplier relationships. Efficient delivery, market pricing, and risk management skills are the key to excellence for the trader/transactional supplier.

2. *BASF as Lean/Reliable Basics Supplier.* This interaction model best suits customers for whom high reliability in quality and delivery is critical. Customers acknowledge product/service differentiation to a certain degree. The products provided usually meet standardized specifications. Brands are typically used to transport reliability—"a name you can count on"—enabling such suppliers to charge a limited premium. For this model, price remains a key purchasing factor.

3. *BASF as Standard Package Supplier.* Customers who follow this interaction model want a choice but do not require (and would not pay for) a uniquely tailored solution. Customers can "mix and match" standardized product/service components to design their own packages. This allows for many different configurations of end products. The standard package is clearly defined as to what is included, which components may be added, and what each component will cost.

4. *BASF as a Product/Process Innovator.* This relationship may be the appropriate model for customers most interested in superior product performance. Here, the purchasing decision is driven by certain product functionalities rather than price. Most of the product/process innovators' business is based on new and/or highly innovative products. Such providers closely monitor the industry to locate new trends early. On the basis of their observations, they regularly develop and launch new products. Substantial investments in research and development and a full innovation pipeline are typical for these providers. One of the key skills needed to become a best-in-class product/process innovator is to understand product life cycles and to manage product launches.

5. *BASF as Customized Solutions Provider.* When a customer requires a very specific, highly customized solution that is not available "off the shelf" (even as a combination of components), the customized solutions provider is an appropriate customer interaction model. Here, the performance of the product or solution is more important to the customers than the price they pay. Customized solution providers work with their customers as partners in jointly developing a solution not offered to any other customer. These suppliers dedicate significant research and application development resources to specific customer requests. Customers typically enjoy some period of exclusivity via ownership of patents.

6. *BASF as Value Chain Integrator.* In this model, customers are looking to reduce cost or complexity by having a supplier take over part of a process. Having a value chain integrator assume responsibility for complete process steps (usually downstream) may reduce the customer's own risk and generate substantial savings in transaction costs. Value chain integrators typically provide their own staff and equipment to run operations, quite often at the customer's site. These providers usually charge per output unit delivered. This means that they bear the operational and quality risks involved— something that should be considered only if the provider indeed demonstrates superior knowledge or skills. Risks must be mitigated appropriately.

These brief profiles illustrate clearly that each CIM follows a different relationship rationale, from none to low intensity (trader/transactional supplier) to a highly interdependent one (customized solutions provider, value chain integrator). The complexity of the value propositions and the related business models grows accordingly (see Exhibit 5.5).

For BASF, segmenting its market based on customer needs meant a change in perspective that required a significant rethinking of how the company worked. As Andrés Jaffé, current head of *perspectives*, explained, "The CIM models helped reveal to us how we needed to organize ourselves to fulfill the needs of each specific segment."

Exhibit 5.5. The Six CIMs and Their Value Propositions

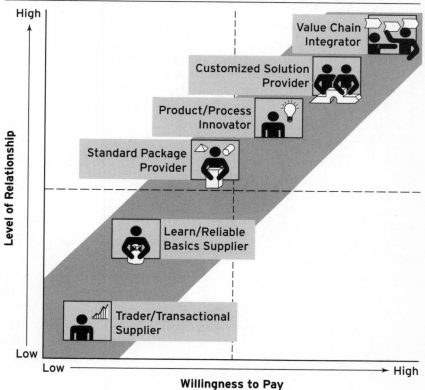

The Pathfinder Method

Once the six customer interaction models were defined, the *perspectives* team was faced with the challenge of translating this new segmentation into organizational processes that supported the models. Like most companies, BASF had organized itself by product line, with a strong inside-out orientation to its processes. The new way asked for a more flexible, responsive organization that would be able to serve six very different CIMs.

Recognizing that it would take much time and a significant cultural shift to achieve these changes, the *perspectives* team developed a methodology that enabled each business unit to identify the most suitable CIM for a customer segment based on a structured set of questions, which could then turn their enhanced understanding into a customized set of product and service offerings. They named it "Pathfinder."

The BASF Pathfinder process works as follows: First, a business unit gathers a cross-functional team to answer the questions in the Pathfinder about the customer's behaviors as the team experiences them, arriving at a preliminary perceived CIM. To validate their assumptions, the business unit next enters into a series of in-depth discovery conversations with the customer, not based on selling their product but with the honest intention of obtaining a thorough understanding of the customer's value chain as well as the market segment's value chain. This discussion either validates or challenges the business unit's internally perceived CIM and provides a reality check on the type of relationship the customers in this segment require.

However, the question for the business unit now is, Can we operate a sustainable business model that holds value for both the business unit and the customer? The enhanced understanding of the role that BASF's products and services can play within that chain as enhancers of value, and what a customer-centered business model for that customer would look like, now feeds into the creation of value curves and the business unit's value proposition. Much of this happens in a strategic dialogue between the business unit and the customer, eventually leading to a clear model that optimizes the overall value system between BASF's potential offering and the customer's needs.

Based on this new mutual understanding, a CIM is chosen that best meets the needs of the customer. Each CIM includes a *back-end* model that supports the front-end activities. The back end consists of the assets, plants, and strategic alliances required to produce the products and services the customer needs, including the entire supply chain and logistics. In addition, there are certain *enablers* needed to support the business model, such as the skills and capabilities of the staff who deal with the customer interface.

Exhibit 5.6 illustrates the interplay of the three elements that support the customer-centric business model.

Exhibit 5.6. The BASF Business Model

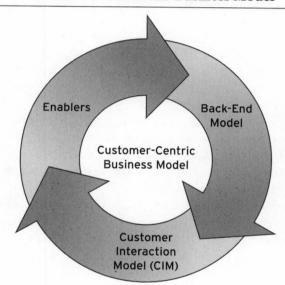

Leading Change from the Bottom Up

To make the Pathfinder methodology work, employees' behaviors and attitudes toward customer-centricity needed to be transformed, throughout the entire company, across all functions. It was time to leave the conceptual drawing board and enter the nuts-and-bolts world of organizational transformation. As its first major step, the *perspectives* team set for itself the ambitious goal of enabling 20 percent of the marketing and sales population to become effective change agents.

In Spring 2005, *perspectives* staged several big "Impact Events" across Europe, North and South America, and Asia to create awareness about the cornerstones of the program among marketing and sales employees, to awaken and challenge their cognitive maps on value, and to question whether value was being shared throughout the value chain. All marketing and sales managers were invited, and in addition to John Feldmann, board member and sponsor of the customer centricity project, at least one member of the board participated at each event to demonstrate the board's unfaltering commitment to BASF 2015. The presence of John Feldmann at all of the Impact Events enhanced identification of BASF's employees with *perspectives*.

As a next step, the most experienced and motivated people became members of "Impact Groups" whose mission was to act as change agents and spread the initiative throughout the corporation in their respective areas of influence. In a series of carefully designed "Accelerator Workshops" (AW), the teams deepened their understanding of the key concepts of the new customer-centricity and received coaching on how to apply the concepts of value curve design and CIM segmentation in their daily work. They then returned as change agents to their business units to act as multipliers of the initiative.

To help all BASF employees grasp these ideas and tools and develop a common language, the company launched "*perspectives* Key Concepts" (PKC) workshops. In 2007, PKC workshops became mandatory for all professional new hires. BASF offers two PKC workshops: PKC A workshops educate every employee about the rationale and key ideas behind *perspectives*, with case studies from real customer projects that demonstrate how the strategies are used and what tools are needed. People learn how to identify current and future customer needs, how to select the appropriate customer interaction model to work with a customer, and how to co-create new offerings for customers in the uncharted Blue Oceans. In PKC B, participants who have direct dialogue with customers receive support to advance their communication skills, build their understanding of market dynamics and customer value, and improve their ability to report their market perspective back to the organization.

By December 2008, *perspectives* has touched 7,300 participants with its program worldwide. According to Andrés Jaffé, this is just the beginning: "Our goal is, in five to ten years, that everyone in BASF not only understands the concept of CIM and Value Curves, but is also able to understand the segmentations and is willing to act accordingly."

Maintaining Momentum

The *perspectives* team was aware that passion had to play a role in such an ambitious cultural change endeavor. "We have to catch people's hearts," said Jacques Delmoitiez, President BASF Polyurethanes, the architect of *perspectives*. Consequently, the *perspectives* team designed an integrated portfolio of learning interventions to build momentum and eventually to sustain the change process. The portfolio consists of three main areas of activity (see Exhibit 5.7):

1. *Enabling activities*, which address the development of critical skills for individuals and teams who are engaged in a marketing or sales function; they are the foundation for the other two activities.
2. *Implementing activities*, which support the creation of real-life customer-centered business models through coaching.
3. *Networking activities*, which focus on sharing and leveraging experience and knowledge within the organization worldwide.

Exhibit 5.7. The *perspectives* Learning Architecture for Maintaining Momentum of Change

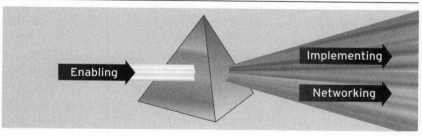

Along with the general marketing and sales workshops (AW and PKC), *enabling* is supported through a variety of topic-specific workshops called "Deep Dives," which provide an in-depth learning opportunity on issues critical to the success of the *perspectives* project. Deep Dives are offered on such topics as value pricing, product launches, and negotiation skills. Another enabling activity the company recently launched was an accreditation program on the key concepts and tools of *perspectives* in collaboration with the Mannheim Business School. Upon successful completion of a three-day program, participants earn a diploma. Additional collaborative programs in Europe have been started with INSEAD and the Louvain School of Management, at FUCaM (Les Facultés Universitaires Catholiques de Mons). The company also plans to roll out similar programs with business schools in North America and Asia in the coming years..

To assist with implementation challenges, the *perspectives* team devised a series of unique initiatives designed to achieve immediate results. One of these was the Business Model Lab, which offers intensive coaching on implementing *perspectives* concepts for specific business cases. The lab uses a highly structured approach to help participants achieve stronger business impact by working with them to understand and reveal customer needs and to develop new value propositions and innovative go-to-market solutions. Brainstorming workshops designed to boost business model innovation are another implementation initiative. In these sessions, staff from *perspectives* help facilitate and coach customer-led events that are sponsored by BASF business units. Recently, the *perspectives* team adapted brainstorming software called i2i to moderate idea creation sessions through the BASF intranet to give these events a global reach.

Finally, one of the keys to the program's success are networking activities that encourage the sharing of expertise and experiences with other BASF staff across regional and divisional boundaries. To foster this exchange, the *perspectives* team initiated Cross Divisional Impact Groups in 2007. These groups of experts with diverse BASF and professional backgrounds come together to work on a specific cross-business topic such as the implementation of a specific CIM, brand management, or a product launch, sharing experiences across business unit boundaries. After participating in this process, each Cross Divisional Impact Group develops a comprehensive reference guide that contains a synthesis of their work so that others confronted with same issue can quickly find solutions.

Upon completion of a group, the participants become members of a "Community of Excellence" for their topic. The communities are available on a regional and sometimes global basis. For instance, if a question about a product launch emerges in BASF Asia, employees do not have to call headquarters in order to find answers; they can refer to the Asian Community of Excellence, from whom they can receive support and access to the Product Launch Reference Guide. This ensures that learning is continuously transferred into the different regions. These Communities of Excellence also handle the regular updating of the reference guides with new learnings from the different regions or business units.

In addition to this supporting corporate learning portfolio, the *perspectives* team often conducts dialogues with division-level management to review the status of Impact Group projects and to exchange the marketing and sales best practices gathered from other units globally. In these forums, "good-practice owners" present their experiences to the group, and people identify other projects for which the proven methods might apply, thus preventing reinvention of the wheel. This exchange further leverages the transfer of know-how within BASF, leading to a proliferation of ideas and exposing good-practice owners who share their knowledge with peers, who can then implement the learnings in their daily business under the motto, "Copy with Pride."

Finally, BASF annually sponsors internal business forums, such as the South American Business Forum held in April 2008, in which 150 marketing and sales managers of various South American BASF organizations presented and exchanged their best practices. North American and European Business Forums followed in September and November 2008. Also under development is "Synapse," an online social network that enables BASF colleagues to find subject matter experts. Synapse will also enhance cross-learning and create communities of practice that can help avoid duplication of work and create synergies.

Challenges and Lessons Learned

In retrospect, much of what happened at BASF in the past few years seems logical and sounds like a smooth process. However, as always happens with transformational learning projects, the *perspectives* program had to overcome numerous challenges in the five years since its inauguration.

One of these was gaining commitment from BASF managers. As in any large company, many initiatives are running in parallel. When *perspectives* was launched, the project had to compete for attention as people asked, Why should this become our priority as opposed to all others? However, *perspectives* was able to build on the strong support of BASF's board, in particular of John Feldmann, who wanted to see this pillar of the strategic guidelines come to life, and the team was able to communicate a compelling conceptual framework that hit the nerve of BASF's strategic challenge. Finally, the corporate learning architecture was not lofty but addressed the bottom line (with its focus on customer-driven business modeling), and it provided support through its enabling, implementing, and networking activities. This combination proved successful.

Still, despite all these mechanisms, it remains a major challenge to keep both the momentum going and the quality of the process high. The same key questions—"How can we help our customers be more successful?" "Is our business model still appropriate and are we implementing it consistently?" "How can we make sure that we obtain a fair share of the jointly created value?"—have to be asked and answered time and again. This will not stop in the future, since the pace of external change is even more likely to accelerate than to slow down.

All in all, the reaction to *perspectives* among BASF employees has been extremely positive. In particular, the project created a new sense of self-esteem among employees, who are proud to work for the world's leading chemical company, and it established a common language for marketing and sales within BASF Group. Andrés Jaffé attributes the success of *perspectives* to its ability to solve concrete problems: "The project is tailored to solving challenges while managing existing tasks." The continuous exchange of information and experience throughout the company, along with the willingness to learn from each other, is fast becoming part of BASF's corporate culture—a decisive advantage in an ever-faster changing world.

Future Outlook of *perspectives*

A measure of success for *perspectives* today is that hardly any board member gives a speech that does not mention *perspectives*, Blue Oceans, or CIMs several times. Feedback from external observers has also been excellent. Global customers frequently comment on the common language and unified processes they experience while working with BASF. "It's not rocket science, but it is probably a benchmark for the chemical industry," Jaffé remarks. He cites these factors as contributing to the success of the project:

1. The *perspectives* project reports directly to John Feldmann, member of the Board of Executive Directors, demonstrating strong board commitment and support—a key factor in pushing it through the culture. Jaffé states, "*perspectives* is a global initiative which is not linked to any division or department within the company. Leading a project directly reporting to the board with its total support makes a big difference; it opens doors necessary for success."
2. The people within the *perspectives* team and the twenty professional trainers responsible for the workshops that ensure the implementation of the *perspectives* guidelines combine excellent sales skills, coaching skills, and business understanding—important prerequisites for a project of this magnitude.
3. The fact that the team was able to create a buzz around the program's early successes and build a passion for the program throughout its implementation. "Motivation was at the heart of the change success. From day one and the big kick-off events, we tried to keep people on board with constant experience-sharing initiatives."
4. Probably the key factor for the high acceptance of this initiative is that the *perspectives* team never took credit for successful projects. The credit always went to the good-practice owners. In so doing, the team achieved a high degree of penetration by shifting their emphasis from pushing concepts

into the organization to requesting support by the Regional Business Units after only a few years.

The real sign of the program's success is to be found in the texture of the corporate culture at BASF, which today shows detectable signs of change. Today, no one is asking, "What is *perspectives?*" any more. The project has become part of BASF's organizational routine. In a group of more than 95,000 employees, that is an outstanding achievement.

Finally, the *perspectives* team has set up mechanisms to continuously monitor the impact of the initiative on the market through a variety of methods. BASF's public relations department regularly asks customers for their opinion through surveys that assess the level of customer satisfaction as well as BASF's customer orientation. In addition, Conjoint Analysis is conducted to determine how different features of a given product or service offerings are valued. A third measure of customer perceptions is provided through a control division set up to track internal performance; it analyzes the performance of the business units that have implemented a new CIM and compares them to other units.

Conclusion: Using Learning to Transcend the Value Chain

The *perspectives* project is a great example of a corporate learning initiative that reaches far beyond conventional understandings of learning. It encompasses virtually all elements of the corporation and transcends the value chain by including customers in the creative process of developing customized business models. In complexity and ambition of the learning architecture, the project represents Level 4, sometimes Level 5 of the five-level model presented in Chapter Three of this book. Let us take a look at some key elements of the architecture that have helped drive the transformation at BASF.

For one, the project was established for the purpose of implementing an important strategic cornerstone that has been perceived as critical for the long-term maintenance of BASF's leading position. As such, it had—and still enjoys—the full commitment of the CEO and the board. Senior management commitment is always one of the most important elements for the viability of corporate learning initiatives.

In addition, the board elevated the initiative beyond the established learning function (in this case the existing Marketing and Sales Academy, which would have intuitively been the place to put it). Instead it created a dedicated project organization independent from traditional functional or divisional structures and staffed it with leaders who had reputations as successful line managers. Jacques Delmoitiez, who launched *perspectives*, came from the helm of a business unit where he had successfully managed a $1.8 billion business. His successor, Andrés Jaffé, had a global procurement responsibility before talking over the lead at the project in 2007. The direct line to the board and the résumés of the persons representing the initiative lent a great deal of credibility in the organization.

Branding also played a role. Although *perspectives* is a major corporate learning project, it was not and has not been labeled as such. While the *perspectives* team draws significantly from the expertise of BASF's dedicated learning function—especially in the area of enabling activities—the project does not come with the traditional connotation of "learning." *perspectives* transforms not only people's skills and mindsets, but *organizational* capabilities and routine, resulting in a strategic repositioning of the firm.

Furthermore, by using Kim's Blue Ocean Strategy metaphor and the related frameworks (such as value curve and CIM), BASF management chose a conceptual model that is relatively easy to communicate and that makes intuitive sense. Reinforced through an easily applicable toolbox for analysis and business model development, this metaphor helped create a common language for the initiative across the entire corporation.

Finally, the combination of expeditionary inquiry (that is, customer dialogues and research) with the triangle of enabling, implementing, and networking tools has had a powerful effect on leveraging experiences and carrying the project forward toward a sustainable, institutionalized practice.

It would be interesting to learn more about the variety of customer-centric business models that emerge in this process and to apply an economic value analysis on the direct and indirect impact of *perspectives* on the value chain cluster of BASF in terms of industry innovation and the related profitability gains. At any rate it is safe to assume that the company will enjoy a significant return on its investment in this learning initiative, both in terms of business results and the quality of its customer relationships.

About the Principal of This Case

Andrés Jaffé, Group Vice President *perspectives*, took over as head of the *perspectives* project in January 2007. He formerly worked as a Director in Procurement in charge of global purchase activities for all organic chemicals and renewable raw materials. He studied electrical engineering at Simón Bolívar University (Caracas, Venezuela) and attended the International Trade Techniques Program at the Wirtschaftsuniversität in Vienna. He completed a Master of International Management at the American Graduate School of International Management (Phoenix, Arizona) in 1988.

Notes

1. The pioneering team responsible for the founding of the project includes Jacques Delmoitiez, the architect of *perspectives*, and Wilfried Hänsel, Group Vice President and representative for the operating business, as well as the regional representatives Frank Jungmann (Europe), Alyson Emanuel and Jacqueline Saunders (North America), Chris Meyer (Asia), and Sean Jones (internal business consulting).
2. Kim, W. Ch., and Mauborgne, R. *Blue Ocean Strategy: How to Create Uncontested Market Space and Make Competition Irrelevant.* Cambridge, MA: Harvard Business School Press, 2005.

Transforming the U.S. Army Through an Informal Leadership Learning Network

U.S. Army

Much has been written about communities of practice as spaces for peer-to-peer knowledge exchange that lead to a participatory culture of "situated" learning. Self-organized lateral discourse and information flow across functional and geographical boundaries are known for their power to promote learning and collaborative sense making and to harvest the knowledge potential of organizations. However, the concept can be hard to implement as a truly self-organized and informal learning infrastructure, especially in large and complex organizations that typically suffer from an overkill of formal structures and regulations. Often communities are launched only to dry out after initial excitement, or they exist in the shadow of mainstream formal processes without much managed impact on the organization's performance. Successfully anchored communities of practice are quite a rare phenomenon in the world of large corporations.

The more striking is the following case. It exemplifies how the U.S. Army, often perceived as the symbol of a hierarchical, doctrine-driven institution, came to adopt a radical change in the way it learns and disseminates knowledge among its military leaders. The story originated as a grassroots effort by a small team of company commanders who set up an informal virtual platform for their peers to share ideas and learn from each other in order to improve their leadership capabilities. As the informal network grew in popularity, the Army took note of its strategic value and has now adopted it as a key learning strategy for other key leadership positions in the organization.

What makes the case particularly interesting is that the CompanyCommand project is much more than just another example of how communities of practice work. The initiative is not only extremely well designed; it also unfolds on the very unique background of an extremely hierarchical and rigidly structured organization, and it evolves into a comprehensive learning architecture that showcases the cross-fertilizing interplay of informal grassroots processes and formal routines. Today CompanyCommand touches thousands of Army leaders across the globe who are in the strategically sensitive position of executing the Army's strategy on the field. As such, the learning project has become a major transformational force toward a military organization of the twenty-first century.

———

While they were commanding companies in separate units of the U.S. Army, Nate Allen and Tony Burgess were friends and neighbors. For several years, each evening after work they would spend countless hours sitting on their front porches, talking about what was working for them in their jobs and what wasn't, sharing lessons learned, and brainstorming different approaches to the challenges they encountered in their profession as company commanders. They would tell each other how they were developing key relationships among their troops and how they were nurturing the junior leaders they were responsible for. They would discuss books they were reading and ponder ideas for implementing new practices in their commands.

Company commanders like Nate and Tony play a key role in the Army. They are the last line of direct command, the interface between the strategic intent of the organization and its operational execution. Company commanders put strategy into practice; they enact policy and carry out the tactical implementation of strategies. As such, they carry an incredible amount of responsibility, and their performance can make or break any military campaign they are involved in. Company commanders are typically responsible for approximately 120 soldiers, and they usually have five to eight years prior experience. Within the U.S. Army's force of 500,000 soldiers, there are a total of approximately 3,600 company commanders.

In the complex and rapidly changing environment of the modern battlefield, company commanders are continuously tasked with learning on the fly and "figuring it out" on the ground. There is a lot at stake in how these young leaders enact their responsibilities; the ultimate success of any operation depends very much on their judgment. Generals might craft a brilliant strategy, but if company commanders and their teams do not execute it effectively, the strategy will fail.

On the other hand, strategies for operating in unpredictable environments are seldom perfect, often incomplete, and sometimes even flawed. If company commanders can figure out something better on the ground and act in accordance with the demands of situation, the results can often be very effective, especially if the information can be passed around quickly to other commanders who can use it with their own troops. The on-the-spot creation of new insights on how to deal with novel challenges and the rapid movement of information is what contributes to the ever-more important adaptability and flexibility of a modern Army. It can also inform and affect the overall strategy that relies on continuous intelligence from the ground.

Over the years, Nate and Tony had many front-porch conversations and shared a wide array of ideas with each other that they would apply to their own commands. Without their personal relationship, they never would have been able to cross-fertilize their leadership practice in a timely or efficient enough manner to be useful to each other. Under the Army's hierarchical knowledge management system, the best ideas the two men shared on their porches would have taken months, if not years, to get approved and disseminated. First, they would have been passed vertically up the chain of command to be reviewed by senior officers and identified as effective. Then the ideas would have to be validated by the organization's "owner" of functional knowledge and packaged in a way that would ultimately not include rich context, reducing the idea to a set of principles. Then—maybe—they would be finally distributed back out to the field.

Furthermore, for one of Nate's and Tony's ideas to be passed on to future generations of company commanders, it would require structured communication with the Army headquarters staff responsible for capturing and categorizing the organization's codified knowledge. The new idea would then have to be validated as one of the Army's "best practices," in its "doctrine." Once vetted, validated, and approved, the idea might be stored in the Army's Center for Lessons Learned repository. If it were an extremely good and broadly applicable idea, it might be written about in a field manual and embedded in the institution's training curriculum. The entire process might easily take eighteen to twenty-four months from idea inception to incorporation in a field manual or training syllabus.

An example of the time lag is what occurred in Somalia in the years between 1992 and 1994. After the Army's initial experiences with peace enforcement operations there, it took about eighteen months to publish the white paper written on these types of operations. By then, however, several follow-on unit rotations had already been completed, none of which had had access to valuable lessons learned. It simply took too long to harness the experiences and collective know-how of the initial units who served in the country and make their insights accessible for those who prepared for the same experience set.

Creating a Virtual Front Porch

Nate and Tony recognized the critical importance of timely management of relevant knowledge, not only in terms of its impact on their own performance, but also as a contribution to the overall strategic and operational effectiveness of the Army. Their front-porch experiences had taught them that informally sharing their insights and professional issues without relying on the formal flow of communication was personally gratifying, and it helped them to be better company commanders. Wouldn't it be great if they could move their private front-porch conversations to a *virtual front porch* that would enable their peers across the world to engage in a similar experience? Together with some of their friends, Nate and Tony came up with the vision of a Web-based resource that would provide lateral connections and real-time learning and collaboration opportunities, an online space in which seasoned and current company commanders could share experiences, lessons learned, management systems, and helpful planning aids with current and future commanders.

With entrepreneurial spirit, and without formal approval from their superiors, the founding team began working out the details of their idea. They teamed up with others to create an "e-zine" on the Internet, which they called "CompanyCommand." They solicited ideas, stories, and helpful tools from other commanders and would post these once a month for others to read and access. They also featured themed first-person articles, monthly profiles of commanders, ongoing message threads, and specialty subgroups devoted to exploring specific topics of value to segments of their audience. And, they facilitated an online discussion forum in which members could post questions and provide feedback. The site's original design was modeled on an outdoorsman Web "forum" that allowed hunters and fishermen to ask questions and get immediate answers from others.

Everything in the online space was targeted toward the effective practice of company command and organized around its main functions, such as leadership, combat, training, fitness, marksmanship, and more. If commanders did these well, they would be effective. To populate the new forum, they recruited a team of volunteers who acted as "topic leads" for the different content sections of the community space. The volunteers were selected for their passion and experience in the topic area they were responsible for. For example, the *marksmanship training* section of the community was facilitated by an experienced commander who had deep expertise in and a passion for this aspect of training.

In the first month, the site had 400 hits (the founding team and all of their friends), but word of mouth spread quickly, and readership began to take off. To further expand the number of engaged community members, Nate, Tony, and their team worked on creating a social architecture that would foster a bigger grassroots movement. They recruited "point men" from across the ranks of company commanders through their personal network of relationships. The point men, located at Army posts around the world, spread the word and generated participation at the local level. The founding team reasoned that if they could create a network that added value to each member's work, other company commanders would be attracted to the forum, without having their involvement mandated by the Army. Their logic proved to be true.

Becoming a Community of Practice

Etienne Wenger is credited with coining the term *community of practice*. He defined the term to mean "groups of people who share a concern, a set of problems, or a passion about a topic, and who deepen their knowledge and expertise in this area by interacting on an ongoing basis."[1] By definition, communities of practice engage practitioners in meaningful conversation, which could involve connecting either in face-to-face and/or virtual dialogue.

As CompanyCommand expanded its membership among U.S. Army commanders, it became a widely used informal community of practice. During its first two years, the site still remained largely under the radar as an unsanctioned Army resource, although the founding team's superiors were aware of its existence and tacitly allowed it to operate. As the popularity and usage of the platform grew, the initiative's value became more and more evident. The online space was succeeding at connecting disparate leaders in synchronous and asynchronous discussions, suspending many of the knowledge-sharing limitations associated with the usual Army protocols, as well as time and geolocation. The forum enabled its participants to create new knowledge for novel challenges as they arose unexpectedly in the Army's environment over time.

Two examples illustrate the effectiveness of the CompanyCommand online forum in fulfilling these needs:

1. Greg, a commander in Germany, wrote to the forum with a question about how to best support his team logistically in combat. A Gulf War I company commander, Hal, responded

to him with his firsthand advice, as did Patrick, who had recently commanded a company. Other forum members soon added more sharing from their experience, all providing Greg with extensive high-value content as he prepared his team for Iraq. Without CompanyCommand, Greg would have spent hours researching through the Army's doctrine, and he would have never found the amount of timely, contextually relevant, and down-to-earth practical wisdom of experience he received from Hal, Patrick, and others who as fellow professionals responded to his question from their own experience.

2. Stan went to Iraq intending to be a staff officer throughout his deployment—and not expecting to command a company. However, when a company commander in his unit was killed in action, he was told to prepare to take command immediately. He checked in with the CompanyCommand team and was able to connect with three seasoned commanders who had had the exact same experience of needing to quickly take command in Iraq following a previous commander's death. As can be imagined, this unique circumstance is filled with complexities that a traditional approach to taking charge isn't equipped for. The challenge of helping a unit grieve its past commander while at the same time getting back on its feet to accomplish its missions is overwhelming. Stan was able to get advice, support, and encouragement from many experienced leaders in a way that he could have never found by any other means or timing.

Gaining Formal Acceptance

After two years of operation, and sporting several thousand members, the senior ranks of the Army took serious note of CompanyCommand. The success stories from the field, the excitement of company commanders who used the platform, and a growing insight into the necessity of increased organizational adaptability and responsiveness convinced them that the forum represented a unique and indispensable value. They approved a plan to formally adopt, resource, and host the CompanyCommand platform behind the Army's firewall.

The founders formally transferred all rights to the Army, even though to them, as fellow members of the community, the initiative had always been from the outset owned by and for the profession.

Today, CompanyCommand is fully resourced by the Army and is used extensively throughout the organization, not only among junior officers in the field but also by Army training facilities tasked with developing junior officers. The Army lets CompanyCommand remain an "informal" community of practice. It trusts the self-organizing dynamic of the platform and does not mandate its usage. Members can determine on their own the content of the site, how it is used relative to the formal trainings received, and what value the information provides to them in their professional leadership development.

The founding team now plays both an operational and an enabling role. Similar to the philosophy of the Red Cross, the full-time team members view themselves in service to the true heroes of the organization—the members and volunteers who drive different elements of the community of practice. The Army supplements their work with a full-time service staff that includes an operating officer who focuses on the day-to-day operations of the forum, and a chief technology officer who focuses on continuous development of the online forum experience using emergent technology, such as the capability to tag content and upload video entries. The team also has a full-time facilitator who seeks to recruit and train volunteer topic leaders for subgroups and topics within the forum.

Army leaders continue to be committed to the essence of the founding team's idea—creating countless real-time virtual front-porch conversations that increase the effectiveness of individual company commanders and improve the overall corporate practice of company command across the organization. The forum remains dedicated to connecting past, present, and future company commanders in an ongoing and vibrant conversation on how they can enact their responsibilities to lead and build combat-ready teams and how to deal with challenging and ambiguous leadership situations. And, the platform still operates in a way that allows its members to own and drive the community's direction and learning agenda. With ongoing U.S. Army deployments to the Middle East, participation has continued to escalate. Not surprisingly, the most popular content areas today are those that deal with unit deployments to Iraq and Afghanistan.

Blending the Virtual Platform with Face-to-Face Activities

After it had caught on virtually, CompanyCommand expanded into sponsoring face-to-face meetings to connect leaders on a local basis where they could discuss issues relevant to their practice of command. One of the key initiatives the team created is called "Leader to Leader" (L2L), in which the CompanyCommand team conducts in-person meetings with commanders located in a specific distant location.

The face-to-face sessions serve a dual function. On one hand, they actively reach out to local company commanders and inform them about ideas being discovered and lessons learned by their peers across the organization via the online platform. At the same time, they are designed to build trust and informally connect the otherwise isolated learnings of those disparate leaders back into the greater community. The knowledge flows two ways, as the forum learns from leaders located at the edges of the organization, and these leaders gain familiarity with the rich opportunities the platform provides. This blending of localized face-to-face gatherings with online community content has proven to be a powerful and effective approach for fostering learning and knowledge sharing in the context of a large borderless community of practice with members who are scattered throughout the globe.

An example of the effectiveness of the blended approach was an L2L meeting conducted in Iraq with a group of new company commanders. The facilitator of the session began by introducing carefully selected content from the community online space that was highly relevant to the Iraq context; he actively shared it with the commanders to stimulate dialogue. To complement the virtual platform "knowledge" with real peer-to-peer encounters, the CompanyCommand team invited several company commanders who had spent time in Iraq to attend the meeting. Combining platform content with the rich background of the experienced fellow commanders, they engaged in small-group discussions around a variety of topics that were relevant for new commanders, like how to build strong relationships with their first sergeants and how to develop a ninety-day on-boarding plan.

The sessions were successful in providing critical knowledge and useful tools to the newly minted company commanders who were about to begin their command responsibilities in Iraq. The model is highly effective, and the team has used this blended approach for many other L2L meetings.

Turning the Social Infrastructure of Learning Upside Down

Overall, the CompanyCommand initiative has not only revolutionized an important element of leadership learning in the Army, it is also changing established routines of organizational communication. Emphasizing self-organized, just-in-time horizontal discourse about the essence of the profession, it has created an entirely new perspective for how military training and battle preparation can be accomplished effectively. This perspective is very different from the conventional approach to learning and knowledge management. It differs particularly in three important aspects that constitute much of the social and organizational texture of learning in complex organizations, namely:

1. Who decides what is relevant?
2. Who controls access to information?
3. Where is relevant knowledge located?

The answers to these questions determine not only the organizational culture of transmitting and sharing knowledge; as this case clearly demonstrates, they also determine the degree of agility, flexibility, and responsiveness of large-scale systems. The traditional approach to learning is a mirror of the mechanistic and hierarchical approach to organization and communication: knowledge resides in the expert (or teacher, superior, and so on), who decides what knowledge is relevant and who controls access to the relevant information. The CompanyCommand approach turned this logic upside down. Let's have a closer look on how the project dealt with the three questions.

People Decide for Themselves What Is Relevant

The first principle the CompanyCommand team learned about building a successful community of practice stems from a deep conviction that people learn best when they can decide for themselves what information is relevant to them. This principle revolves around "three Cs"—content, connection, and conversation.[2] The platform must be designed so that every member of the community can easily find quality content relevant to their particular need, interest, or challenge; connect with other members of the community who might be relevant to them; and develop meaningful conversations with those who have relevant experiences to offer (Exhibit 6.1). At any time, it is up to each member to determine what information is most useful to them within their specific context, and it is up to them what they will learn.

For example, if a member comes into the community space looking for advice on how to conduct a memorial service for a

Exhibit 6.1. The 3 Cs: Empowering People to Decide the Relevance of Information

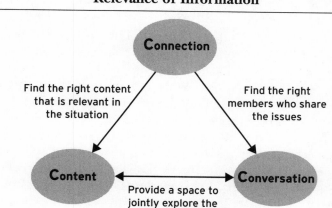

lost soldier, he can find related content on the community's online space, which could be a story, a model service program, a video interview, or another relevant knowledge object. He can connect in meaningful conversation with other members who have either lost a soldier and experienced grieving or planned a service memorializing a soldier.

A good example of the power of the 3C model is a special initiative the CompanyCommand team accomplished to support some new commanders and their troops who were preparing to deploy to Afghanistan. To bolster the commanders' knowledge and confidence, the team created a Web-based survey and sent it out to every officer in the Army who had commanded a company in Afghanistan. The survey asked questions like:

- If a company commander could read only one book on Afghanistan before deploying, what book should it be, and why?
- What is one thing that surprised you when you got to Afghanistan? Explain.
- Describe one or two innovations you implemented and how they made a difference.

They collated the survey answers and organized them according to the questions and the respondent's rotation date in Afghanistan. They then published a hard-copy book containing the responses so that the commanders preparing to deploy to Afghanistan could easily carry the content with them and access it whenever they wanted. The content of the book was also made available on the online space. In addition, the CompanyCommand team also purchased the commercial book that was rated as the most highly recommended in the survey and provided a copy to each leader preparing to deploy.

To make the learning intervention a truly blended approach, the CompanyCommand team then organized an L2L session in which they invited six leaders who had commanded companies on the ground in Afghanistan to spend three days in face-to-face small-group discussions with the commanders who were about to deploy, a sort of front-porch meeting of the minds. The experienced leaders shared their combat stories and passed on their hard-earned knowledge to those about to depart on the mission. The relevant, down-to-earth know-how exchanged in the face-to-face sessions could not have been as powerfully experienced in any other format. The team found that the in-person sessions contributed to forming deeply trusting relationships among the participants, which translated into ongoing connections between many of the participants on the online forum. At that time, the meetings also inspired a new subcommunity on the CompanyCommand online space, the "virtual front porch," created solely for the company commanders in Afghanistan.

The sum total of information and opportunities to learn generated by this initiative is extensive. CompanyCommand provided the content, the connections, and the conversation, but at all times the commanders made their own choices on the relevancy of the information to their own experience—an approach diametrically opposed, but complementary, to the traditional Army training deploying commanders receive.

People Control the Access to Knowledge

The second principle that determines the dynamics of a learning solution relates to the control of knowledge. The team discovered that people have more willingness to be engaged in learning when it is created following the rule, "If *they* build it, *they* will come," than the opposite, "If *we* build it, *they* will come." Applying this principle is revolutionary compared to the Army's traditional knowledge management paradigm, in which the institution creates the knowledge necessary for deployment and determines when and how it is distributed to commanders.

How access to information and knowledge is designed is a major enabler—or disabler—of any community of practice. Some organizations realize the power of peer-to-peer exchange and create an online platform thinking they can foster a community of practice. Then they send out a memo essentially commanding people to use it—only to become disappointed by the lack of response. In not recognizing the principle of self-organization, these organizations destroy the inherent opportunity of the system by applying a traditional top-down management approach. Contributing to the platform becomes a duty and part of the job description, and access and usage become regulated according to the logic of hierarchical control.

As CompanyCommand demonstrates, it's the opposite approach that yields engagement. Communities need to grow organically, and they can only do so when organizations limit themselves to being facilitators and enablers of the process, allowing the practitioners themselves to invent and create their own community space, the content, and the suite of resources most relevant to their needs. Ownership creates commitment, and communities thrive best when the essential democratic mantra is applied—a community *by* and *for* the people.

Knowledge Resides in Both the Organization and the People

This third principle addresses one of the deepest issues of any organizational learning initiative: where the knowledge resides. Like most organizations, the Army traditionally has taken a strictly hierarchical approach to knowledge management. They often assume that the institution's knowledge systems, subject matter experts, and appointed senior leaders are the ones who possess the expertise of sufficient value and accuracy needed for effective practice. They distill best practices from those sources and transform that knowledge into policies and doctrines. They then train and direct field practitioners to teach and implement the work in those ways.

This model might be effective in a stable, reliable, incrementally changing environment in which linear processes can be codified and the future is predictable. During the comparatively stable environment of the Cold War, a top general in the Army could stand in the Fulda Gap in Germany and talk to a company commander on the ground about the way that he defended that same piece of terrain against a potential Russian attack twenty years ago. The combat model and the best practices for a commander at that time were codified and clear, and they could count that it would more or less stay this way.

But this static and top-down approach to knowledge is not in sync any more with today's dynamic and constantly changing military context, nor is it appropriate for most of today's business organizations. Change has become too fast and unpredictable, and traditional knowledge cannot keep up with the interdependencies under which we now operate. Also, taking into account the dynamic nature of the context, an organization's interventions change the conditions under which it acts, often in unpredictable ways. Like in a chess game, each move creates a new strategic situation, forcing the player to reevaluate the game and possibly come up with a new strategy.

Karl Weick calls the loss of stability today a *vu jade* experience—referring to the opposite of *déjà vu*. He uses the term to describe the sinking feeling one gets from the sense that "I've never been here before, I have no idea where I am, and I have no idea who can help me."[3] A perspective that relies only on previously codified and tested knowledge often leads exactly to this sense of *vu jade*, in which everything you've ever learned before seems useless.

Recognizing this problem, some organizations have turned to a more emergent approach to learning in which expertise and knowledge of best practices is seen as residing with the workers at the touchpoints or edges of the organization—the interface of the organization and the environment. In this perspective, senior leaders can see themselves more as *chief learners* than as *chief experts* whose job is to act as facilitators of an ongoing organizational learning process. They provide support by connecting those leaders on the edges of the organization, enabling them to collaborate.

This approach, while fostering agility, has its own set of limitations. It runs the risk that learning veers off from the organization's interests or that decisions made will not be aligned with the organization's overarching strategic goals. Lessons learned can become so highly contextual that they cannot be generalized into relevant knowledge everyone can use. In the military, for example, a lesson learned on the ground in Kosovo may not be relevant in Iraq. Lessons can be so diverse that even something learned in an outlying region of Iraq may not be applicable in Baghdad.

Given the limitation of both the hierarchical and emergent approaches to organizational learning, the CompanyCommand team sought to develop a model that blends the two approaches to where knowledge resides and draw from the best of both. This approach seeks to align or balance both the informal (emergent) and the formal (hierarchical) aspects of organizational knowledge, creating a healthy tension that keeps strategic learning at the top of everyone's mind. It is important to feel this tension; its absence is an indicator that something has gone too far in one direction. For example, if the learning becomes too hierarchical, it easily becomes the latest corporate bulletin and loses the immediacy and relevance that drives involvement of the community members. But if the learning becomes too emergent and localized, it won't connect with the broad array of leaders who also need to acquire the organizational resources.

The aligned approach has the potential to bring organizational leaders and field practitioners into the same conversation. Through this structured encounter between formal organization and informal networks, both worlds benefit. The field is seen to be immediate, trustworthy, and having a significant voice in the organization's learning agenda. The institution is viewed as in touch, adding value to the practitioners through its backbone of knowledge and resources.

For example, institutional training system leaders who are tasked with training the next generation of leaders have the potential to add a strategic perspective to conversations while drawing emergent lessons from the field and offering them to novice leaders. This dynamic increases the relevance of the standard training schoolhouses while providing the otherwise detached senior leaders a broad view of what is being learned and applied across the peripheries of organization, where change happens on a daily basis.

Aligning the formal and informal is how organizations become highly adaptive. Conducting continuous conversations around current practices enables new challenges to be unearthed and identified as they arise, heightening the organization's ability to sense and respond quickly. As leaders scan the trends and themes across the community space, they are better able to anticipate emergent opportunities, needs, and threats. They can then shape the future with these in mind (Exhibit 6.2).

Exhibit 6.2. Aligning Formal and Informal Knowledge Domains

The power to transform the organization happens
when the formal and the informal are aligned

Emergent Knowledge
Informal, Tacit

Assumption:
The "touch points" of the
organization know what the
most effective practice is

**Community
of Practice**

Hierarchical Knowledge
Formal, Explicit

Assumption:
The leader/organization know
what the most effective practice
is and tell the field to implement

Source: CompanyCommand Team.

Further Enhancements

Today, the Army is working with the founders and current
staff to further enhance the value of CompanyCommand for
self-organized lateral learning. New features are continuously
being added to provide an even richer experience and further
strengthen the unique architecture of the learning space. For
instance, users can not only tag content themselves by using a
community developed taxonomy, which makes it easier for everybody to find content; in a new feature, members can also create
their own "folksonomy" of personal tags, which builds up a new
vocabulary that commanders can share and adds a new richness
to the traditional tagging. This practice-based linguistic differentiation provides distinctions that might prove useful in the continued advancement of the corporate practice of command.

Another attractive feature is a dedicated online forum
in which seasoned commanders present a real-life leadership dilemma they experienced, and members can "vote" on a
multiple-choice form which solution they would have chosen.
Next, the results of the votes are made available to the community, illustrating the distribution of voting along with information
about how the seasoned commander had handled it. Members
can then join an online conversation with their peers about the
pros and cons of the commander's solution versus the various

alternatives, thus improving their own decision-making skills and knowledge.

CompanyCommand has also implemented a social network-like feature, called iLink, which was developed by the Defense Advanced Research Projects Agency (DARPA). When members log into the forum, they receive recommendations about new people to meet and new information to read, based on iLink's scanning their profiles and page views, then matching each user's interests to other people and pages. The forum is making every effort as well to innovate new technology as quickly as it comes out. They have explored, for example, technology that scans videos and interprets and translates speech to text so that videos could also be tagged and text searched.

To keep the platform alive in the minds of the company commanders, the team sends a monthly newsletter to all forum members. The newsletter features new content and is designed to attract them back online to the forum, thus strengthening the value of the network by increasing participation. Blending traditional media with the online platform, the team submits articles from members to a regularly printed Army magazine, thus "weaving" the forum into other Army communication efforts and encouraging those readers to come into the forum.

Inspired by the success of CompanyCommand, Army leaders have established another program that leverages the model as a key part of a new learning strategy. Called the "Battle Command Knowledge System," the program supports the development of networked communities of practice like CompanyCommand for key jobs at other hierarchical levels. Throughout a leader's professional career, he or she will be able to tap into a community of fellow practitioners, learning from peers in an ongoing and highly adaptive manner as he or she rotates through jobs.

Conclusion: Creating a Learning Architecture That Enables

Communities of practice have been around for more than a decade, but few organizations have captured their strategic value as well as the founders of CompanyCommand and the U.S. Army. The evolution of CompanyCommand is a great example of how to merge the informal and the formal, the emergent and the hierarchical, the adaptable and the controlled. The success of CompanyCommand in drawing members into the network, inspiring sharing across distance and function, and encouraging face-to-face meetings is impressive testimony to the value of innovative learning architectures.

But this case is also special for another reason: it takes place in the unique organizational structure and culture of the military. No other organization is built as much on discipline and a clear chain of command. For many, the Army is the very symbol of a hierarchical, authoritarian system. And justifiably so—there is little time for debate, pondering, and reluctance in the heat of combat.

So how could the CompanyCommand initiative—a "radically democratic" grassroots project—unfold so successfully in this context? After all, the logic of informal, self-organized, horizontal networks is arguably diametrically opposed to authoritarian control. Informal communities are voluntary, they are self-determined, they treat all members as equals, and they are about discourse and an interactive creation of meaning. But, ironically, it is exactly the military culture that may have been the most important factor in making the project so successful and sustainable that it has become a global benchmark.

Discipline and commitment to the profession—key values of the Army—played an important role in getting this venture off the ground. The founders and their team were highly dedicated to understanding the impact of their initiative and to continuously improving and fine-tuning the design of the learning universe they created. Speaking to members of the team, you can feel their passion and their very personal commitment to make the community work. They did it not because they were told so, or for an abstract cause of improving the practice of knowledge management and learning; they did it because they sincerely wanted to help their fellow commanders be better soldiers. This deep sense of community and belonging that characterizes members of the military goes hand in glove with the requirements of the social architecture of networks. Speaking with members of the CompanyCommand team, you can feel the deeply embedded service attitude that is typical of the Army profession. This attitude made it natural for them to have a truly enabling (rather than controlling) mindset toward the project—one of the most important success criteria for informal network management. And finally, if there is any organization that requires teamwork, shared knowledge, and trust to survive and thrive, it is the military.

In other words—it is the very DNA of the Army that assures the robustness of the initiative. The tenets of the institution— discipline, service attitude, trust, a sense of community and belonging, and high standards of excellence—provide a powerful context for successfully anchoring an initiative based on emergence and self-determination.

The case illustrates with impressive clarity that informal networks that are based on voluntary participation and a free and self-determined flow of information thrive only if they are embedded in a solid organizational architecture—but it must be an architecture that is designed to enable, not to control. This requires a skillful management of the dialectic tension between the formal and the informal, something at which the CompanyCommand team excelled. After only a few years, the initiative has changed the culture of the Army, enhancing the organization's adaptability, flexibility, and responsiveness. It has become an important contribution for creating a "Learning Army," enabling it to better cope with the challenges of the twenty-first century.

About the Principal of This Case

Nate Allen is an officer in the U.S. Army and is currently on faculty at the National Defense University. As representatives of the CompanyCommand and PlatoonLeader founding team, Nate and project cofounder Tony Burgess were recognized among *FastCompany* magazine's Top 50 Innovators in 2002. Nate's most recent paper, "Leader Development in Dynamic and Hazardous Environments: Company Commander Learning in Combat," received an American Educational Research Association's (AERA) Best Paper by a New Investigator Award in 2007. Nate Allen has a PhD in management and technology from George Washington University's business school. He also has an MA in industrial/organizational psychology and an MBA.

Notes

1. Wenger, E., McDermott, R., and Snyder, W. *Cultivating Communities of Practice*. Boston, MA: Harvard Business School Press, 2002, p. 4.
2. Dixon, N., Allen, N., Burgess, T., Kilner, P., and Schweitzer, S. *Company Command: Unleashing the Power of the Army Profession*. West Point, NY: Center for the Advancement of Leader Development & Organizational Learning, 2005.
3. Weick, K. E. "The Collapse of Sensemaking in Organizations: The Mann Gulch Disaster." *Administrative Science Quarterly*, 1993, *38*, 628–652.

The Executive Hero's Journey: Going Places Where Corporate Learning Never Went Before

PricewaterhouseCoopers

PricewaterhouseCoopers originated in 1998 when Price Water-house merged with Coopers & Lybrand. The union created the largest global professional services organization in the world, pro-viding industry-focused assurance, tax, and advisory services for public and private sector clients. Given the size of the company and the breadth of its operations, the merger upped the stakes for PwC to be sure it had the right leadership for the twenty-first century.

This case tells the story how PwC started to address this lead-ership challenge through its Ulysses program, a very unortho-dox but now famous initiative, in which teams of PwC partners accept a three-month leadership challenge, taking them out of their comfort zone and business environment to go on a field assignment in a developing country. Their objective is to learn by making a sustainable positive impact on a complex economic, social, or environmental issue. As part of a carefully crafted five-step leadership journey, participants work with nongovernmen-tal organizations (NGOs), community-based organizations, and intergovernmental agencies; the executives donate their professional skills on a pro bono basis to advance a specific project in a local community struggling with the effects of poverty, conflict, or environmental degradation.

But the Ulysses program is about much more than just building leadership skills for the future. Participating in the program changes not only the participants, it also changes the conditions in developing countries, and it helps brand PwC as an authentic corporate citizen. As such, the program is an outstanding example of a large-scale learning intervention that includes stakeholders way beyond the immediate relevant value chain. The Ulysses initiative is a major step toward fulfilling the social contract organizations ultimately have with society, a contract that today few businesses understand and even less fulfill.

In this context, the case belongs to the avant-garde of learning architectures, connecting a deep personal leadership learning experience with values-based organizational transformation and authentic corporate citizenship. As such, it is not only a strategic but also a highly political corporate learning initiative.

> Tell me, O muse, of that ingenious hero who travelled far and wide after he had sacked the famous town of Troy. Many cities did he visit, and many were the nations with whose manners and customs he was acquainted; moreover he suffered much by sea while trying to save his own life and bring his men safely home; but do what he might he could not save his men, for they perished through their own sheer folly. . . . Tell me, too, about all these things, O daughter of Jove, from whatsoever source you may know them.

So begins the opening day of a leadership experience unlike any other conducted in the corporate world. Twenty-five PwC partners sit in a circle on the floor, listening intently to a facilitator—who might be more appropriately called their guide—reciting a synopsis of the classical Greek epic, the *Odyssey*.

The *Odyssey* is attributed to Homer and is thought to be written in the late eighth century BC. It relates the heroic voyage of Ulysses (the Roman name for the Greek "Odysseus") as he sails home to his wife on the island of Ithaca, following ten years of brutal fighting in the Trojan War and the defeat of Troy.

Ulysses's journey takes yet another ten years to complete as he and his twelve ships of warriors encounter many calamities along the way. Among these are landing on the island of the Lotus-Eaters, where his men eat leaves that cause them to lose their desire to return home until Ulysses forcibly removes them; the warriors all becoming prisoners in the cave of the one-eyed Cyclops, who eats a pair of men every day until Ulysses cons the monster into drinking a potent wine to fall asleep, after which the men blind him in the eye and escape tied to the underbellies of his sheep; and Ulysses himself becoming a prisoner of the beautiful nymph Calypso, who forces him to remain on her island for seven years. Ulysses finally arrives home, the lone survivor from among all his men, where he reunites with his wife Penelope, who has waited faithfully during the twenty years of his absence.

Sitting around the circle listening intently to the narrative, the PwC leaders try to make sense of how the epic relates to their work as accountants, tax advisors, and consultants to some of the most famous companies in the world. It's easy enough to recognize the metaphor of the "hero" in the story, and how Ulysses's heroism might relate to them as role models within PwC. Just as the Greeks admired that leader for his courage and resourcefulness, Western business culture expects modern leaders to share those same heroic traits, even if they will never meet up with man-eating monsters or nymphs who hold them captive.

But the Ulysses program is not aimed at teaching warrior skills and heroics. It's about a transformational journey of self-discovery, a challenging quest during which the travelers get to know themselves more deeply and put themselves up against real-world tests that will cause them to reexamine all their values and assumptions. The voyage is a deep dive into their identity and sense of Self, so that they can come home a different kind of PwC leader. As the program's slogan pointedly states, this is a journey to "come back changed." The participants don't yet understand exactly how their inner transformation will happen, but they've committed to going. They notified their clients that they'll be away on a three-month absence, and their families are prepared to miss them for the duration.

The Origins of Ulysses

The Ulysses program is the brainchild of Ralf Schneider and a group of PwC's young high professionals who together were interested in exploring the concept of leadership in the twenty-first century. Ralf served as Head of Global Talent Management for all of PricewaterhouseCoopers between 1999 and 2008 (he is now Head of HR for Leadership, Talent, Resourcing and Organizational Development for HSBC). Soon after Ralf joined the company, he sat down with his managing partner to reflect on the nature of PwC's leadership needs in the future. They were looking far off in time, ten or twenty years ahead, foreseeing that PwC would ultimately need to redefine its understanding and practice of leadership. They would have to develop a new breed of leaders—global citizens, committed to the firm, with excellent networking skills, able to lead across boundaries, understanding and harvesting multicultural diversity, and acting in a highly ethical and responsible way as ambassadors of the premium accounting and advisory firm of the world. They were not exactly clear how to achieve these objectives, but they knew that a rapidly changing business environment would require these skills from their best people. The managing partner gave Ralf $200,000 to move forward in developing a program—and then he retired and left the company.

That may have been serendipity for Schneider, who relates what happened next. "I took my interns down to a basement office for a couple of meetings over two months where, under the radar, we put together the first draft of the Ulysses program. It was a co-creative effort between all of us, and actually it was a young Italian intern who came up with the name *Ulysses*. In our minds, *Ulysses* was not originally intended to be a program, but rather an experimental laboratory where we could test out ideas about a new framework for leadership."

The thinking behind the Ulysses program was based on four elements that Schneider and his team saw as important next-generation leadership requirements.

1. Leading within PwC's Networked Structure

Following the merger with Coopers & Lybrand, PwC found itself with 150,000 people, 9,000 partners, and offices in 769 cities in 144 countries. Typical for global consulting firms, the company's organization was a vast network of highly skilled professionals, structured along territories and regions, core practices, and industry expertise. In such a decentralized networked environment, effective leadership cannot be based on hierarchical authority and positional power; it needs to be based on relationship rooted in trust and talent. Ralf was convinced that the next generation of leaders would come from those who could attract followers based on their values and their ability to bring in clients, work with the diversity of people now composing PwC's ranks, and create respect through their knowledge and expertise, not their titles. Leaders at PwC would have to be less like commanders and more like Hollywood producers, constantly assembling the most talented crew for each new project based on the skills needed, the location, and the timing. As Schneider wrote in an article on the Ulysses program, "The mentality of *power over subordinates* is replaced by *power through others* requiring leaders to mobilize people and release energy through purpose and meaning, good reasoning, and addressing the collective imagination."[1] In his view all this was possible only if leaders understood and lived their values in a responsible and authentic way. Leadership is attributed to people based on who they are as human beings.

2. Leading in an Emerging World

Schneider took stock of what was happening not only inside PwC but also outside of it. It was an emerging world increasingly full of disruptive market changes, technological advancement, and global shrinking. In such a world, leadership would need to emphasize qualities like creativity, innovation, adaptability, and quick thinking to manage projects in an increasingly complex environment. The next generation of leaders not only had to be problem solvers; they also had to become visionaries and meaning makers, able to interpret trends and innovate new ideas that inspired people to crave working with them—and also motivated customers to seek them out.

3. Leading in a Global Stakeholder Environment

As an advisory and accounting firm, PwC banks its reputation on public trust. Not only must clients trust the integrity of the firm, but the firm itself has to have the highest degree of trust, since it attests to the financial statements of its clients and makes pronouncements on their valuations. If the firm lacked integrity and public trust, of what value would its valuations be? As Schneider put it, "PwC essentially sells trust by the hour." In the emerging world, however, creating public trust was becoming a larger and more complex endeavor. To create trust, people need to really know you—something you can achieve quite well locally. But how do you develop and nurture trust if you are a global company with clients and employees from every culture and a complex stakeholder universe? How do you secure a globally sustainable "license for doing business," as Schneider called it? You could do it only by taking corporate social responsibility to the next level, through embedding authentic ethical behavior into the very DNA of the firm, creating a brand that would earn a maximum of public trust. All this suggested that PwC would need leaders who were more sensitive to a wider range of stakeholders, who understood the significance of diversity and corporate citizenship, and who could fathom the changing role of business in society to act with empathy and social responsibility.

4. Leading in a Highly Competitive World

Schneider and his team were also concerned with a very practical issue: competitive advantage. How might PwC's leadership of the future help distinguish the firm from among its peers and competitors? Despite PwC's dominance in the industry, it was clear that winning and keeping clients would become increasingly difficult in the future. What was the core competence of PwC that might give them an edge over others? It could be a new type of leadership. While qualities like expertise, responsiveness, speed, and attention are critical in the professional services business, they are relatively easy to replicate. But distinctive leadership could be a branding quality that sets PwC apart. To achieve this, it was critical that the next generation of PwC leaders have a strong sense of their identity and depth of character, personal integrity, and values that would help build long-lasting relationships with employees, clients, and other stakeholders.

The *Aha!* Moment

Such were the foundations of analysis that drove Schneider and his team to seek out a new kind of leadership program that could result in building a new generation of leaders. But the more they considered how to create such a program, the more they realized not only that such an animal did not exist in any business school or off-the-shelf executive development program, but that they were dealing with issues that could not be taught by a teacher. How does a teacher teach qualities like creativity, innovation, adaptability, self-identity, values, respect, appreciation for diversity, vision building, sense making, and sensitivity to community? How does one teach the unteachable, and how can you learn what cannot be taught?[2]

The breakthrough idea to create a program based on a journey of self-discovery must have been an *Aha!* moment for Schneider. He says they were not basing the program on the American scholar Joseph Campbell's recently rediscovered ideas on universal myths and archetypes of human experience that popularized the idea of a hero's journey, though the Ulysses challenge is a modern example of Campbell's paradigm of heroes and self-discovery. Their concept of sending potential leaders into a Third World country to work on aid projects was related to the need to take people out of their familiar contexts and expose them to a world of significant difference to trigger learning experiences on a deep personal level that could not be achieved otherwise.

Depriving people of their ordinary daily routines and taking them out of their comfort zones provides them with a powerful stimulus to reassess their values, examine their assumptions, seek ways to build new relationship, and find solutions to complex problems using their creativity and innovation. A key ingredient in the experience, in fact, must be adversity. As Schneider explains it, "Challenge is a feature of the developmental experience, which provides a chance to experiment, to practice and grow while working with others and being exposed to different perspectives and unfamiliar settings."[3] To build the leadership skills Schneider envisioned, people had to be given opportunities to lead in a meaningful and socially productive enterprise.

Designing the Program

In 2001, nearly two years after the idea emerged, the first Ulysses program was launched. The long period of planning speaks to the complexity of working out the details and logistics of the ambitious program. It was not easy to convince the organization to allow a group of their best partners to leave the business for months, possibly jeopardizing client relationships and losing millions of dollars in billable time. It was not easy to find the Third World projects and to negotiate the relationships with the partnering NGOs. And it was not easy to identify the candidates who would carry the pilot. But Schneider and his team were convinced that testing the idea at least once was worthwhile.

The objectives for the program were clear. The Ulysses journey should address the four leadership challenges mentioned previously and help participants improve in three personal values:

1. *Responsible leadership.* Ulysses would help PwC partners evolve into responsible leaders who could foster values-based behaviors and ethical responsibility.
2. *Diversity.* Ulysses would help PwC partners work with a multiplicity of stakeholders to learn how to tolerate different value structures, break down cultural barriers, and actively embrace the diversity within the PwC organization as a source of innovation.
3. *Sustainability.* Ulysses would help PwC partners enlarge their vision of the role of business in the world and understand how to achieve sustainable relationships with stakeholders.

Finding organizations who would agree to partner with the program was next. PwC had a number of cross-sector relationships with nongovernmental and international organizations and social entrepreneurs; Schneider contacted some of them to explore their potential involvement. The NGOs understood how they too would benefit, receiving the free expertise of PwC professionals to improve the effectiveness of their projects. Ulysses would be a win-win for both PwC and the NGOs, and several agreed to accept PwC groups as soon as the program was fully designed.

It was clear that people could not simply be sent away without good preparation and support for the challenges they would encounter. The program required careful pre- and postjourney work. Extensive thinking went into how to best prepare people for leaving their families and clients, how to help them through the cultural shock they would undoubtedly feel in a strange land, how to find the right types of challenges for them without overstretching them in a way that would hinder learning, and how best to reintegrate them into their jobs and use the learning they would come back with.

In the end, the full Ulysses program was designed to consist of five phases of activity and support. Each phase is a critical element in the entire experience.

1. Preparation and Selection

The program seeks to have twenty to twenty-five participants each year. To get a diversity of participants, each PwC country organization is allowed to send only one high-potential future leader from its ranks each year. The countries can use their own process for selecting their finalists, but the candidate has to be approved by senior management. Selecting the right candidate is critical, because the person must have the ability to tolerate the conditions under which they may find themselves and be open to the challenging experience that Ulysses would present to them. To further assure diversity, the expertise of the participants varies across accounting and finance, strategy, tax advisory, and management consultancy. And, to qualify as a candidate, the PwC partner must be in his or her first ten years of partnership, with the potential to become a globally influential leader in the firm.

After the participants are selected, they are briefed on the program in general. While still in their jobs, they begin working with a personal coach to collect 360-degree feedback to assess their current leadership styles and build the teams with whom they will be going into the field.

2. Foundation

Next, all participants convene to attend a one-week foundation workshop in which they meet their fellow group members, most of whom they don't know in advance since they all come from the many PwC offices around the world. They hear the Ulysses story told and begin reacting and discussing their own concepts of leadership and the hero's journey. During these days, the participants continue working with their coaches, who attend the sessions so they can better evaluate their leadership strengths and weaknesses and uncover their hidden values. To capture the unfolding personal learning process, participants begin writing personal leadership stories in which they imagine themselves growing as leaders. The program uses storytelling extensively as a technique to delve into the unconscious and inspire self-reflection.

In this phase, participants also learn to do meditation and yoga so they can de-stress when they are out in the field and maintain self-confidence, courage, and strength. They devote time to working in their teams, which consist of the same three people who will eventually work on the NGO projects together. The purpose of the teamwork is not just about getting to know each other, but more important, to learn how to coach each other, since team members will need to support each other once they are out in the field.

3. Assignment

The heart of the Ulysses program is the two-month project assignment in a trying environment. The twenty to twenty-five participants split up in groups of three to work with the NGO project they have been matched with. The matches have been carefully made based on the professional skills of the teams and the type of expertise the project requires. The teams live and work at their assigned locations, which may be in any of twenty-three countries situated in central or southern Africa, South America, Central

America, Central Europe, Eastern Europe, Australasia, or Asia. Their projects will involve a human, social, or environmental issue to which the team must apply its professional expertise to make a sustainable impact. They have to analyze the challenge, develop plans and solutions, and implement these in a complex and unfamiliar political and social context. The projects are usually highly challenging because of the lack of resources and infrastructure, as well as harsh conditions such as poverty, conflict, tropical heat, a lack of transportation, ignorance, or just an abundance of insects. Most participants have to deal with a foreign language and culture and with locals who often lack education or have a different set of values.

By the end of 2008, Ulysses teams have influenced more than forty projects, targeting a broad range of issues. The following examples illustrate the level of challenge and complexity the teams face when asked to bring on their expertise.

- *Tajikistan (2001).* Working with the United Nations Office for Project Services (UNOPS), the Ulysses team assisted in building a rehabilitation, reconstruction, and development program. Their work focused primarily on proposing ways to achieve sustainable economic development. The team had to find ways to bring peace and stability into the country by supporting local governance, strengthening the decision-making mechanisms, and supporting conflict prevention activities.
- *Namibia (2003).* The Ulysses team spent two months developing a project management system for the Alliance of Mayors' Initiative against HIV/AIDS in Africa (AMICAALL). In their first weeks, the team traveled thousands of kilometers to visit villages devastated by AIDS to meet with mayors, youth groups, businesses, religious leaders, and schools to understand the programs in place. They discovered a lack of coordination and an insufficient leadership structure to guide the initiatives. Their project management system helped organize political commitment, leadership, and knowledge for better impact analysis and action planning. The system was also designed to manage any other community-based type of projects in Africa.
- *Zambia (2003).* The Ulysses team was asked to assess and develop the Elias Mutale Training Center for Sustainable

Development, which trains unemployed youth in organic agroprocessing to grow crops and raise animals. One of the poorest countries of the world, Zambia suffers from a mix of economic, climactic, and social conditions that have left its population without adequate water, food, and shelter. The team worked at the center's farm, assisting in raising poultry and rabbits to teach people small business financial management and how to become sustainable. They taught a class in accounting and identified new activities through which the center could raise funding. In a second phase of their journey, they traveled to another part of the island and taught laid-off mine workers small business management.

- *Belize (2003).* Working with NGO Fauna and Flora International, the Ulysses team produced a professional evaluation of the growth and income-generation potential of the ecotourism sector in the country. The result of the project was a professional evaluation of the full scope, implications, and marketing linkages of ecotourism in Toledo. Secondary results focused on the adoption of conservation-friendly policies and development plans for Toledo by government, NGO, and private sector agents.

- *Uganda (2004).* The Ulysses team was charged with compiling and publishing a resource directory of all HIV/AIDS services available in Uganda, which had been severely affected with more than 1 million people dying from AIDS and leaving 1.8 million orphans. Without a communications infrastructure for mobile phones and faxes, the team had to spend several weeks traveling the country to meet with service providers, village leaders, and small agencies, often under a tree or in a simple schoolhouse. They organized a meeting for many of the NGOs at which they taught leadership and time management skills. Their directory of services was the first in Uganda and provided a critical element in the fight against AIDS: knowledge.

- *Timor-Leste (2004).* The Ulysses team was tasked with reviewing and finding ways to enhance the Recovery, Employment and Stability Program for Ex-Combatants and Communities (RESPECT), which provided education and job training to East Timor. A Babel of languages and cultures, the island had been occupied by Indonesia and war had ravaged the country, destroying 85 percent of its infrastructures in buildings and homes. The team visited seven of the country's thirteen districts and provided advice and technical support, working with UN Development Programme leaders to assess small business development through microloans that funded simple projects such as road building, sanitation, irrigation, and factories.

- *India (2005).* Working with NGO Gram Vikas, the Ulysses team developed a strategic business plan to enable the NGO to empower hundreds of thousands of impoverished individuals by applying strategic networking concepts. In 2007, a second Ulysses team built on this work and helped Gram Vikas to forge strategic alliances with other organizations.
- *China (2006).* Working with the NGO Save the Children, the Ulysses team provided support to the Yunnan Minority Basic Education Project (YMBEP) by reviewing the project's income-generation elements, which help provide scholarships for poor children and allow them to continue basic education. The team made recommendations and helped develop models and methodologies to appraise their income-generation projects.

Throughout the assignment phase, the participants receive coaching support, both from their teammates and from their coaches via regular phone calls and sometimes an onsite visit. If possible, the teams have access to an online PwC platform on which they can exchange photos, advice, and feedback with other teams. Some teams capture their experience in a video documentary that later gets posted on the company's intranet and becomes a powerful tool for spreading the Ulysses experience throughout the firm.

4. Debriefing

After eight weeks away, the participants return from their assignments and are allowed to spend a few weeks with their families. They then reconvene as a group for a week to debrief the Ulysses leaders and staff and to share experiences with the other teams. They evaluate their learnings systematically against the Ulysses objectives and mission. Tapping once again into the power of storytelling, each team is asked to develop a story that synthesizes its experience so that team members can transfer the learnings back to their own organizations and to build an archive of Ulysses stories. The debriefing phase is intended to boost the transformative learning process intellectually, emotionally, normatively, and practically. The objective is to help participants make sense of their experience in terms of both the learning dimensions of Ulysses and understanding their own new leadership identity.

5. Networking

As participants return to their jobs and share their experiences with others, they disseminate some of the program's experience throughout the PwC organization. Their conversations and role modeling contribute to positive change by inspiring leadership and cultivating interest in community engagement. Ulysses alumni also continue to network among themselves, supported by a dedicated intranet platform, which also contributes to building the new leadership culture throughout PwC. After eighteen to twenty-four months, the program managers conduct interviews with the participants to further stimulate reflection, dialogue, and networking. These interviews also serve as a feedback loop to continuously improve the program.

Exhibit 7.1 summarizes the five phases of the learning journey.

Exhibit 7.1. The Ulysses Journey Time Frame

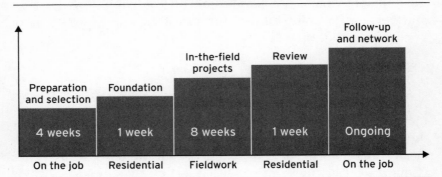

Source: www.pwc.com/Ulysses.

The Multistakeholder Significance of Ulysses

The Ulysses program has captured international attention, not just in the human resource and leadership learning communities, but also in the public eye and the international business press. The compelling human interest element and the innovative approach the program takes to the twin challenges of leadership development and corporate social responsibility are unique. The initiative deserves all the accolades it has received, given the valuable contributions of the PwC Ulysses teams during the past seven years in twenty-three countries have improved the lives of millions of people.

But what makes this case especially interesting and valuable is the multilayered impact of the learning architecture. Ulysses is an ingenious multistakeholder learning intervention that reaches beyond the individual hero's journey, affecting virtually everything it touches. Those affected include the PwC partner on the journey, his or her family and friends, the Ulysses staff, the PwC organization, PwC clients, the entire professional services industry, the NGOs and other partner organizations, and finally the villages and countries that host the teams. The intention behind Ulysses was to build leadership competences for the twenty-first century and to engage the company in mutually beneficial, socially responsible activities around the globe for purposes of authentic branding. This in itself is bold and innovative. However, Ulysses is much more. By affecting all these stakeholders, it creates a large-scale systems learning impact that goes beyond the boundaries of the firm. It is a paragon of a comprehensive learning architecture that drives political, social, economic, and cultural change. Let's have a look at how the various stakeholders are affected.

The Learning Impact on Ulysses Participants

The design of the program targets a deep personal learning experience. The main focus of Ulysses is on personal growth and social responsibility, on thoroughly questioning fundamental assumptions and reshaping values and attitudes. The exposure to radical context difference in combination with meaningful, tangible project work adds an emotionally formative element that other types of leadership programs simply don't provide. As the Ulysses participants come back to share their story with their partners and staff, there is a key change in their day-to-day interactions. It is not about being a hero; it is about being a responsible leader who relates in a more meaningful way. The mantra is: Don't try to be interesting; be interested.

On the professional side, the participants learn to sharpen their skills by applying them in an unusually challenging environment. As one Ulysses participant who was part of a team that went to Uganda to coordinate local AIDS projects put it, "Back home in Australia we would have solved the problem in two or three weeks. Here it takes months. But what we learn here helps us to be much more effective in our familiar environment." In other words, if you can make it there, you'll make it everywhere.

While PwC has not yet measured the direct impact of the Ulysses program on the participants' capabilities to lead, PwC recognizes three types of professional growth that the participants are likely to experience:

1. *Personal leadership development.* They heighten their self-awareness of their values, beliefs, and world knowledge that drives their sense of personal leadership.
2. *Integrative development.* They learn to deal with people from all over the world, which helps to build shared vision and understanding.
3. *Strategic development.* They practice long-range anticipatory thinking, learn to cope with complexity, and learn to translate their vision into sustainable action and commitment.

The Learning Impact on Friends and Family

Having a loved one or close friend away for three months on a project to benefit an abject village, city, or country thousands of miles away would make most people think twice about their own lives and values. Many of the families become eyewitnesses to the action and hardships of life in Third World countries when participants have access to the Internet and post their blogs and photos. When participants return, they are eager to share their stories with their families and friends, further raising awareness about the trying conditions and harsh realities of life they have seen. It is not often easy for their environments to digest the sometimes severe changes in attitude and values Ulysses alumni bring back from their journeys. The mutual adaptation process that follows a life-changing experience is often emotionally difficult for all parties concerned. However, when the process is well managed—and possibly supported by coaching—it is a rewarding learning experience for everyone involved.

The Learning Impact on the Ulysses Staff

Each Ulysses team has different story to tell, so there is an ongoing cycle of learning for the staff. The intense debriefing sessions provide opportunities for input about how to run the program, choose a different NGO, change locations, or add a new element to the way the program is run. Furthermore, the interviews conducted eighteen and twenty-four months following the journey continue to educate the staff as they see how the participants change over time, which allows them to witness and learn the more long-range personal and professional repercussions of the experience.

The Learning Impact on PwC as a Company

By the end of 2008, 120 partners representing thirty-five territories had gone through the Ulysses experience. Although this is only a small fraction of PwC's 9,000 partners, they comprise a powerful cross-cultural network of responsible leaders. Each and every one of the Ulysses alumni has gained an understanding of the responsibilities that business has to collaborate with a diverse range of stakeholders and create sustainable solutions for communities and markets across the world. To maximize their leverage within the global PwC organization, the alumni are organized as a community with explicit objectives. They commit publicly on the company's Ulysses Web site to:

- Live the Ulysses spirit, enabling behaviors that can change lives
- Challenge and support the firm's leadership with a variety of perspectives on the firm's development

- Connect PwC and its people to the broader society
- Connect PwC's local, territory, regional, and global levels with one another

These commitments are designed to have organizational impact. And they are not only a paper commitment. According to Schneider, the project has yielded significant awareness and cultural change within PwC. Ulysses alumni are highly regarded in their units, and their stories are well known throughout the company. Ulysses has become a source of inspiration for many leadership programs across the PwC network, which have picked up the message of responsible leadership and the impact that Ulysses has touched hundreds of participants and key talent around the globe.

The Learning Impact on PwC's Clients

Ulysses transforms not just the partner who went on the journey, but his or her clients as well. Like family and friends, clients become fully aware of the partner's absence because a substitute PwC partner must work with them during the three months. Ulysses participants discuss the purpose and objectives of their leaves at length with their clients, who usually appreciate the initiative once they learn about its implications. It is not usual for clients to become personally involved in the partner's progress. Schneider relates that many Ulysses travelers write blogs while on assignment, and many clients were reading those blogs, vicariously living the journey with the PwC partner. Rather than being annoyed or upset that their consultants were gone for three months, the clients often demonstrated unconditional support for the partner and eagerness for the project to succeed. On more than one occasion, clients even shared the PwC partner's Ulysses story with their own executives and staff.

There is also a residual learning impact on PwC's clients in that, when the partner returns from Ulysses, the client will be dealing with a "changed" person who has gained leadership qualities that will benefit the client. In Schneider's words, the partner "will be able to deliver against the things that clients really care about." To understand how Ulysses does this, Schneider explains the model of creating a PwC experience for a client and shows how Ulysses alumni become more authentically customer oriented than other consultants. The model progresses in three steps:

1. *We invest in relationships.* Ulysses teaches participants how to build trust-based relationships. Through the challenges of the program, they learn who they are as individuals and what they stand for. This enables them to create authentic relationships with others.

2. *We share and collaborate.* Ulysses transforms people who know how to build relationships into people who can share and collaborate at a very deep personal level. This then allows them to transform business relationships with clients, relationships that go beyond just a business transaction.

3. *We walk in each others' shoes.* Ulysses provides participants with the ability to understand the core of the clients' needs. By sharing and collaborating at a very deep level, the partners learn to walk in the clients' shoes, seeing the world from their perspective. This helps them relate to clients not from the position of what PwC has to sell, but from the point of view of what the clients want PwC to accomplish for them. In Schneider's words, "This is probably the biggest learning that Ulysses has to offer those involved in the project. Working at the grassroots level and living outside of your comfort zone requires you to open up, to connect at a human level and really listen to understand how the community wants to and can learn from what you have to offer. This opens up a space of co-creatives that is meaningful and produces value."

In short, Ulysses creates a learning dynamic between PwC's partners and its clients that continuously deepens their relationship and allows PwC to provide clients with a depth of service that meets their real needs, even if unstated. The partners learn from each other and become a very tight team to accomplish what the clients want done. The clients win because they now have a consultant who delights and satisfies them far beyond the level of service they received before. PwC wins because they now have loyal clients. This is not only mutually beneficial learning but the creation of the most valuable asset of an advisory firm: a sustainable trusted client relationship.

The Learning Impact on the Professional Services Industry

There is no doubt that Ulysses has a learning effect on the entire professional services industry. The program is practically a trademark for the PwC brand, and it garners them wide press coverage and publicity. By making values-based leadership and ethical behavior cornerstones of their competitive advantage, PwC redefines the rules of the game by "outbehaving the competition," pushing *all* the players upward toward greater social responsibility and ethical conduct.[4]

The Learning Impact on the NGOs

Obviously the NGOs are major beneficiaries of the program, not only because they receive free support but because they themselves learn in the process. The Ulysses assignment—making an NGO project sustainably effective—requires an approach that addresses the ecosystem of which the NGO is an important part. By working closely with the NGO, the Ulysses team also strives to optimize the processes, mechanisms, and capabilities of the NGO's organization. This is critical, because after all it is the NGO that remains with the local project long after the PwC partners are gone. Working with experienced PwC partners, the NGOs learn to be more effective organizations, which in turn will make their projects more effective. By transferring some of the toolkit of a leading professional services firm, the NGOs become smarter and more professional. While they may never achieve the same level of expertise as a PwC partner, they build up knowledge to improve their own problem-solving skills, which then might help them on another challenge in another city or country of activity for the NGO. In this way the learning is mutual, meaningful, and sustainable for both parties, involving exposure to new knowledge for the NGO and the infection of passion and purpose of a bigger cause for the consultant. As a result, a new space of opportunity for understanding and a possible future opens up for both.

The Learning Impact on the Communities

The villages, cities, and countries that the Ulysses teams help are among the neediest in the world. In some of them, the average income is less than $1.00 per day. Poverty, hunger, social conflict, AIDS, illness, and ignorance control the lives of the people living there. The Ulysses program is a learning intervention for these communities.

The PwC teams come into daily contact with indigenous people, creating a mutual clash of cultures. Dialogues with the local population foster knowledge transfer and mutual understanding. The intervention of the Ulysses participants becomes the blueprint for future actions that can transform the lives of the inhabitants. Whether it's finding microfunding, creating a sustainable economic plan to eradicate poverty, or writing a proposal to help the NGO get sponsors to support their programs for the blind or for basic education for children, the Ulysses project introduces a new level of competence and confidence into people who now have better means at hand to solve their own problems in the long term. The behavior and code of ethics of the teams may also showcase new ways of doing business and new ways of governance to the locals, especially when their business structures and governments are ineffective, inefficient, or corrupt. PwC's global expertise helps breed local expertise and brings change to where it is needed most. And as Ulysses is building for sustainability, many organizations offer more than one project, so a real partnership can be created over time.

Creating a Value-Oriented Community

The Ulysses program is unique in its forceful design and purpose to transform PwC into a value-oriented community, redefining the essential value contribution of business organizations. It is no coincidence that the initiative was created within a professional services firm. Few other businesses are so strongly based on brand and trust to sustain customer relationships, and few depend so much on attracting and retaining the best talent to provide services at a consistently high and reliable standard. PwC decided to fight the war for talent and customer loyalty by striving to become the most ethical and responsible company in its field—and the Ulysses program is a centerpiece of this effort.

There is deep business reasoning behind this decision. Today the business world is under increasing pressure to justify its behavior and provide meaningful contributions to solving the mounting societal and environmental challenges. The recent economic meltdown has made it very clear that the exclusive focus on short-term profit and shareholder value is a shortsighted business proposition that ultimately leads to disaster, not only socially and environmentally, but also economically. Unethical corporate behavior may provide short-term returns, but it damages the all-important brand in the long term. The creation of sustainable business value requires a holistic stakeholder orientation together with a deep understanding of the interdependencies of financial, human, societal, and environmental values.

Managing a corporation as a value-oriented community creates over time a positive loop, linking business performance with talent attraction and retention. By authentically contributing to the health of society and environment, companies earn their license to operate. By providing meaning and opportunities for people to contribute to a greater good, they become attractive workplaces for knowledge workers who seek more than just financial success. Credible corporate citizenship creates a brand of trust that attracts and retains customers as well as professional talent—the most important assets of consulting firms. Exhibit 7.2 illustrates this dynamic.

It is easy to see the contribution of Ulysses in this context. By actively addressing real issues in developing countries, the program has a strong impact on local societies, catering to their social and environmental needs. By sending high-potential partners on a meaningful and emotionally challenging journey, the program affects the personality and the value system of its most critical resource. By providing an architecture for disseminating the Ulysses experience on an organizational level, it elevates the personal experience into organizational ethical learning.

Ulysses was designed to create the next generation of leaders at PwC, but it is also transforming PwC into a next-generation organization that is truly a value-oriented community. It puts PwC on track to become a benchmark responsible organization of the

Exhibit 7.2. Organization as Value-Oriented Community

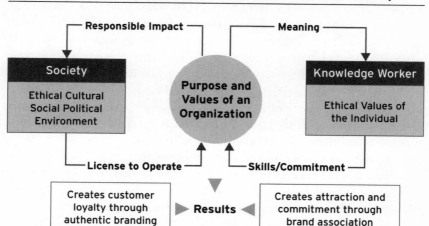

twenty-first century, a company that makes a true difference in the world and one that people are proud to work for.

Conclusion: Final Thoughts and Outlook

As a corporate learning architecture, Ulysses is a remarkable case and deserves the recognition it enjoys in the leadership development community. It is one of very few examples in which learning reaches not only beyond the boundaries of the firm to include customers or suppliers. It is more than just a learning initiative that aims to transform the industry; it aims to transform society. As such, it also aims to reframe more than just the way the consulting industry works; it intends to move the entire business world toward a more comprehensive paradigm of value creation.

As the world's leading auditor, PwC is ideally positioned to drive this process. In 2008, more than 80 percent of the world's 1,000 largest companies were in one or another way clients of the firm. In many cases, PwC is a trusted auditor and tax advisor, with potentially significant impact on client companies. Leveraging these relationships in the spirit of Ulysses could have significant impact on the overall role of business in today's world.

Ulysses was launched as a talent management effort. Ralf Schneider, its architect, brought with him the guts of a former Air Force officer and the brain of a former lecturer of Organizational Behavior. He realized his vision in a consulting firm—a company without tangible products, depending entirely on talent and customer trust. Many marvel about the boldness of Ulysses, but if there was a context in which it could have been realized, it was the combination of a number of factors and a bold innovative team at PwC. A successful one-to-one transfer of the concept to other businesses is highly unlikely, because to be effective in other environments the concept may require significant design modifications. Few companies are able to afford having their key people take a three-month absence, and their abilities to contribute to Ulysses-like projects may be different depending on the core competence of the firms. However, the idea of putting important talent into a very alien context in which they give their best to bring sustainable success to worthy social or environmental projects, thus shaping an increasingly value-oriented community, is worth exploring for every organization.

The case illustrates the many levels of learning the Ulysses initiative addresses, creating a ripple effect beyond the participants in the project. However, the explicit learning design of today's Ulysses project includes only the PwC participants and their roles as alumni. It does not deliberately address the effects on the context, such as the families, NGOs, or the local social and political infrastructure. As a next step in developing Ulysses, the design could be enlarged into a managed architecture that includes the context in the same way the team manages the participants and the impact on PwC. Applying the design spirit of Ulysses to the NGOs and the local communities would elevate them from contextual stakeholders to active participants in a transformational learning universe.

About the Principal in This Case

Ralf Schneider is currently Group Head of HR for Leadership, Talent, Resourcing and Organizational Development for HSBC. Before joining HSBC, Ralf served as Global Head of Talent Management for PricewaterhouseCoopers. Prior to that he was a Managing Director of an independent German training and HRD consultancy, specializing in international management development with a network in Europe, U.S.A., and Asia, where he has worked extensively. His work as a consultant and senior human capital executive has focused on the areas of human capital strategy, leadership development, organizational learning and change, corporate social responsibility, cultural diversity, and knowledge management.

Notes

1. Pless, Nicola M., and Schneider, R. "Towards Developing Responsible Global Leaders." In *Responsible Leadership*, ed. Thomas Mark and Nicole M. Pless. London: Routledge, 2006, p. 214.
2. "How does one teach the unteachable?" and "How can you learn what cannot be taught?" are questions asked by Ulysses advisor Peter Pruzan, Professor Emeritus of Copenhagen Business School.
3. Pless and Schneider, "Towards Developing Responsible Global Leaders," p. 219.
4. An expression coined by Dov Seidman, author of *HOW: Why How We Do Anything Means Everything in Business (and in Life)*. Hoboken, NJ: John Wiley & Sons, 2007.

Managing the Strategic Asset of Cutting-Edge Technological Expertise

EADS

Attracting, developing, and retaining professional talent is a critical success factor for every corporation. It is a particularly important challenge for companies in knowledge-intensive industries, where expertise in research, design, and engineering constitutes the core of a company's competitive advantage. But it is a matter of sheer survival for a company like EADS, (the European Aeronautic Defence and Space Corporation), whose entire existence depends on continuously creating, advancing, and applying some of the world's most sophisticated and complex technologies.

EADS is Europe's largest and the world's second-largest aerospace company, probably best known for its flagship product, the Airbus. Among its total staff of 116,000 people are more than 42,000 researchers, engineers, and technical specialists, many of them among the brightest in the world. The critical role of this immense brain power reaches beyond the task of getting today's work done. In the aerospace and defense industry, which literally requires rocket science, major projects may take years, if not decades. Innovation and invention in the fields of engineering, materials science, design, and manufacturing demand constant research, experimentation, trial and error, and coordination among thousands of people across the globe. Producing the next-generation airplane, helicopter, satellite, rocket, missile, or communication system requires an army of technical experts from many disciplines who not only have to excel in their work but also to invest in continuous learning. They must be dedicated to staying on their projects for years at a time and committed to remaining with EADS.

This case tells the story of how EADS addresses the strategic challenge of managing its core asset: expert talent. It highlights the development and implementation of a dedicated "experts policy" that acknowledges the company's technical professionals and rewards them with a promotional track equal to that of management. It illustrates the focused effort of a global technology leader to maximize the creation, development, and nurturing of scientific and technical value by encouraging communication, networking, innovation, and knowledge sharing among a large population of highly skilled individuals who are usually noted for an individualistic approach to their work that limits a high-tech company from fully capitalizing on its human assets.

Despite its global reach and reputation, EADS is a young company. It was established in 2000, through a merger of France's Aerospatial Matra, Spain's Construcciones Aeronauticas (CASA), and Germany's DaimlerChrysler Aerospace (DASA). The new firm subsequently formed partnerships with several other companies in Great Britain and Italy, which created a European multi-country organization.

Today, EADS is divided into five divisions that represent its product range: Airbus, Military Aircraft, Eurocopter, Defense and Security Systems, and Astrium, which itself is broken into three divisions, Space Transportation, Satellites, and Services. EADS's head offices are in Munich and Paris. In 2008, its revenue exceeded EU42 billion (US$55 billion).

To digest its politically delicate transnational mergers, EADS leadership found it vital to integrate the diverse and independent organizations that had sprung from several European countries. The first goal was to create a unified entity, one that would share a common vision and sense of collective destiny.

EADS decided to approach this goal through its Corporate Business Academy (CBA), a learning platform that was a combination of the original member companies' learning units. Hervé Borensztejn, who had ample experience as former Head of Corporate Learning of Vivendi and Moët-Hennessey Louis Vuitton (LVMH), was appointed as the new CLO and Head of CBA. His first task was to foster a unified perspective and identity among the company's senior management. He developed a series of integrated leadership learning programs, crowned by the Executive Forum, an annual event during which the group's 200 top executives explore strategic issues.

Waiting in the wings were the company's 40,000 engineers and 2,000 researchers, who received no special attention in the early years following the merger. While a few of the original pre-merger companies such as Astrium and Airbus had programs and practices to recognize and reward their top experts, EADS had not taken any steps to create a corporate-wide initiative aimed at the preservation of its top scientific talent. Repercussions were showing up in several areas. For example, the company began experiencing a technology gap as they needed to quickly integrate new technologies such as composite materials, without having sufficient expertise in this area. Also, because of the increasing number of new programs EADS was running—such as the new Airbus models A350, A380, and A400M as well as the Tiger and NH90 models from Eurocopter—the company also found itself with a shortage of experts. Compounding the draught of talent, some of the firm's very experienced engineers were retiring without any successors.

Then-CTO Jean Marc Thomas (who is now a director of Airbus) was not happy with this situation. He was convinced that the management of technical expertise was of such strategic importance that it could not be left to the business units alone—it needed corporate attention and orchestration. He knew that quite a few technology companies in France had attractive programs that catered to experts. It was clear that EADS could not afford to neglect its experts, especially given the diminishing interest in scientific careers throughout Europe that would make it more difficult for the company to attract new talent and retain its current crop of experts in the face of increasing competition for their expertise. Also, a strategic approach to addressing the "experts pipeline" was critical, as EADS's experts population was aging, with more than half being more than fifty years old and eligible for retirement within a decade.

In early 2003, Jean Marc approached the Corporate Business Academy with a request to arrange a corporate learning solution for all the company's technical experts. Hervé Borensztejn knew that such an initiative would significantly broaden the scope of CBA beyond the executive development activities they had focused on so far. He recognized the strategic importance of the project and wholeheartedly agreed with Jean Marc's perspective. With the emphatic backing of the corporation's top technology officer, Hervé embraced the opportunity to get involved and dove into the job of designing a program that would redefine not only the role of experts but also the role of the learning division as a key strategic player in the future of EADS. He put together a small team and began designing a policy for managing expertise as a strategic asset—a policy that would not only sustain a high level of technological sophistication but also enhance the status of technical experts throughout the group, increase the firm's attractiveness, and ensure solid links between scientific and business initiatives.

Assessing Expert Practices Inside and Out

The team's first steps were to investigate the experts management practices already in use among the Group's divisions and to benchmark experts policies at other high-tech corporations. They visited several firms and found one of the longest-running and most successful experts programs was at Thalès, a French-based producer of mission-critical information systems for aerospace, defense, and security with whom EADS enjoyed a close business relationship. Thalès had put in place an experts policy nearly two decades prior and had established a solid reputation among graduates from France's best universities. Other companies they visited were Alcatel—a major telecom infrastructure provider that had merged with Lucent in 2006—as well as Daimler, BMW, and Siemens. The benchmark visits were inspiring and created an even stronger passion to develop a world-class solution at home.

Inside EADS, the team found that France's Aerospatiale and Germany's DASA had a tradition of rewarding their best engineers with promotions to senior management positions. However, this practice was counterproductive in several ways. First, there is little connection, if not even a negative correlation, between high-level subject matter expertise and the ability to manage and lead. Not surprisingly, quite a few exceptional technical experts turned out to be poor managers, a waste of valuable human capital. Second, many scientists were not interested in becoming managers, as their passions were first and foremost focused on their technical work. For them a "promotion" to senior management was no reward— on the contrary. Finally, promoting top engineers to administrative positions ultimately backfired, because the company would end up losing a significant percentage of its high-level operational expertise, people who were very difficult to replace. These issues made it clear that it would be more valuable to create a promotion process that rewarded technical specialists within their own domain.

Through discussions with the divisions, Borensztejn also realized that the long-term nature of many EADS projects required special consideration. The company needed a system that could identify the right experts as early as possible and that would incentivize them to stay on the teams throughout the entire project. A space program, for instance, might last more than twenty years, so someone joining such a project team needed to have not only the right technical background but also the willingness to commit to a long-term work effort. The length of its projects also meant that the experts management system had to include a robust knowledge-sharing mechanism that would mitigate the unavoidable attrition of expertise over time.

Finally, after countless conversations between senior executives and senior experts, Borensztejn believed that the new experts management system needed one more criterion to make a difference. He had discovered that expert titles were often being awarded to recognize pure technical skills without consideration for the person's contribution to the company's business interests. In Borensztejn's view, a sensible solution had to make sure that those who were able to link outstanding technical accomplishments with tangible business contributions would be nurtured and rewarded most.

Launching the Experts Policy

Based on the insights from a nearly one-year investigation, Borensztejn and his team worked to develop a corporatewide system for managing technological expertise that was launched in mid-2004. The solution was comprehensive and contained guidelines for experts identification, recognition, development, career advancement, and compensation. Its main features are summarized in Exhibit 8.1.

Prior to launch of the system, the Corporate Business Academy published articles about the policy in the in-house newspaper and made announcements to publicize its commencement. Once the program was announced, it took nearly two years to fully implement it. One of the reasons for the slow implementation was the cross-functional nature of the project, which required collaboration between HR and technology management. While both departments agreed that the project was important, neither of

Exhibit 8.1. Key Features of EADS's Experts Policy

Objectives	Means	Expert Responsibilities
• Attract, develop, and retain experts through recognition, career management, and compensation schemes • Secure EADS portfolio of technical competences • Offer equivalent career opportunities to technical and management experts	• Assessment of individual expertise/specific accountabilities • Expert training • Same compensation for experts and managers • Internal communication and promotion initiatives	• Knowledge development • Operational advising • Networking • Knowledge sharing and transmission • Intellectual property protection

them "owned" the process, so it ranked lower on their respective priority lists. Moreover, corporatewide policies have to deal with the usual resistance from the divisions, which would have to alter their individual systems and agree to a common standard. Still, EADS's large experts community was enthusiastic, and so were the labor unions, which appreciated the positive recognition the policy granted to their stakeholder group.

The First Challenge: Defining a Common Meaning for "Expert"

One of the first challenges the team faced in designing the policy was the apparently simple task of defining the word *expert*—which turned out to be not so simple after all. It was important that everyone have a common understanding of what EADS meant by the term. But arriving at a common definition was both a linguistic and a cultural challenge, given that EADS was composed from a wide range of companies, with many nationalities, languages, educational systems, and cultural values merged into the global company. The French, for instance, believed the title *expert* referred to a graduate of a top engineering school. The Germans understood the term to refer to a person's organizational rank. Each culture and nationality seemed to have its own meaning for the term.

Eventually the team decided that the term *expert* would refer plain and simply to "people possessing high-level technical expertise" without regard to the level of degree attained or the stature or prestige of the person's university background. The EADS corporate documentation stated simply, "Experts use their high level technical skills each and every day in one of the aerospace and defense fields that are of importance to the Group."

Creating the Expert Ladder

Next, the team addressed the issue of different levels of seniority within the experts community. To avoid the syndrome of losing good experts by promoting them into leadership positions where they might be unhappy and not very effective, any hierarchical differentiation had to stay within the domain of expertise. The solution was to establish three levels that would distinguish technical professionals in the future: Expert, Senior Expert, and Executive Expert. The titles and responsibilities were consciously chosen to mimic the management hierarchy, emphasizing an equality of recognition between scientific and business roles.

The three levels are summarized as follows:

1. *Experts* must have at least five years experience in their technical fields. The title is awarded to individuals for having made a strong local contribution to their departments or project teams.
2. *Senior Experts* must present a minimum of ten years experience in their fields. They must have earned a compelling reputation throughout their entire EADS division, and, as a general rule, they must have participated in several product development programs.
3. *Executive Experts* are "the best of the best." As with executive managers, the title is awarded to individuals who not only have top technical expertise but also show leadership skills and behaviors. In addition to having twenty years of engineering accomplishments, Executive Experts must be renowned throughout the EADS Group and beyond.

To further reinforce equality between the management and expert career tracks, the new policy abolished separate remuneration scales. Experts would be compensated like managers, Senior Experts like senior managers, and Executive Experts would receive stock options as part of their compensation whenever executive managers did.

In consideration of the decreasing shelf life of scientific knowledge and the changing business needs of the corporation, the titles and all the benefits that came with them were not awarded in perpetuity. Appointments would be valid only for a three-year period, after which each expert would need to undergo a review process to renew his or her title. This element of the policy encouraged continuous learning and assured that the technical capability portfolio remained in sync with the evolving business requirements of EADS. This stipulation was no different than any managerial title; either you have to stay at the "top of your art" and the company has a need for you in that area of expertise, or you need to move to another job or lose your title.

Nevertheless, it was the company's intention that the experts title would be a true career ladder for most people who qualified. They were not planning on downgrading someone who had become an expert at one of the levels; the more likely scenario would be that an expert no longer needed in one role would find a way to shift to another job. However, it did happen in one division that dozens of experts lost their titles because their field of expertise or their level of expertise was no longer key to the business. As a result, there is now an annual expert's portfolio review by the divisions' CTO to ensure the division fits the company's business needs.

Building Flexibility into the Experts Career Path

One of the characteristics specific to EADS's business is that some elements of the company's projects change with the award of different contracts across its business units. This peculiarity of large-scale technology projects requires a high degree of flexibility in the deployment and the use of technical expertise. Expert engineers needed to understand that their titles did not automatically remove them from certain types of roles. On occasion, they may need to become project managers or laboratory directors and then shift back to purely operational positions once the project is completed.

In the long run, Borensztejn strongly believed that blurring the lines between pure managerial or pure technical activities was critical to the company's sustainability. Rather than promoting a single-line career path, the experts policy had to be designed like a path with multiple branches. The concept is illustrated in a fan-shaped diagram in which the left and right lines demarcate the traditional career paths—either managerial or technical (see Exhibit 8.2). A line in the middle that branches out to various roles depicts how the learning team wanted their experts to view the journey at EADS, which would call for venturing into both management and technical territory as an individual moved forward in time.

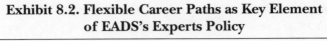

**Exhibit 8.2. Flexible Career Paths as Key Element
of EADS's Experts Policy**

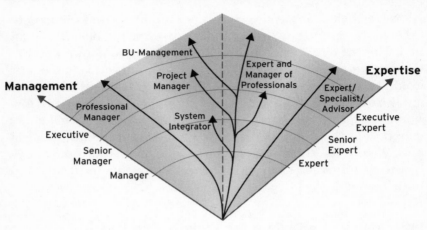

The Experts Appointment Process

The experts policy established a clear process for appointing experts. Each of the five EADS divisions, through its divisional HR department and divisional CTO, could appoint its own expert and Senior Expert titles. Executive Experts had to be named at the corporate level by the Group HR department and the Group CTO.

All appointments, however, use a standardized nomination and evaluation process throughout the group to ensure that awards would encompass both technical expertise and ability to meet strategic business objectives. In the process, expert candidates for any category would be asked to submit an application, completed through the combined contributions of the applicant, his or her manager and/or division leader, and a career management advisor. This application consists of three sections that cover different areas of performance:

1. *Person.* Along with personal information and references, this section assesses the candidate's knowledge, experience, and potential. The individual must have earned recognition for

extraordinary competence within his or her team, division, and, in the case of Executive Experts, throughout the group and even beyond company boarders.

2. *Position.* This section assesses how well the individual fits with EADS's strategic orientation. What is the value of the person's area of expertise for the company's business? How pertinent are the links between the person's expertise, research and development strategy, and overall business strategy?

3. *Performance.* This section examines the candidate's contributions to the group. How many patents does the applicant have to his or her name? Has the person given internal and/or external conferences? Has the person taken steps to transfer his or her knowledge? The section specifically uses Hay methodology indicators to measure a technical expert's performance.

The process for appointing Executive Experts goes through additional scrutiny and involves the senior management of EADS. After all, Executive Expert is a corporate-level title and gives its holders a voice that will and should be heard at the top of the company. Candidates are nominated on the divisional level, but they need the approval of the Executive Technical Committee (ETC), which reviews the candidate's file and votes. Founded in 2006 by EADS CTO Jean Botti, the ETC is the company's most senior technical decision-making body and includes Botti and the CTOs from the five divisions. The ETC uses a competence map that outlines the company's short and mid-term needs to determine where it is critical to name an Executive Expert.

Once the ETC has voted on who should become an Executive Expert, the candidates are assessed by the corporate head of HR, who focuses on applicants' nontechnical qualities and evaluates them in accordance with standards for senior leadership skills and behaviors, just as for any other executive appointment.

An Early Dilemma: Can a Company Have Too Many Experts?

One of the key objectives of the new experts policy was to align the technological competence portfolio with the overall strategic goals of EADS. This sounds simpler than it is, as engineers and scientists tend to value technical accomplishments in themselves, without regard to whether they add value in a strategic business environment. Scientists and engineers believe it should be their specific expertise as such that counts, whereas a strategic perspective needs to assess the usefulness of an expertise in a specific business context.

Reconciling this tension between expertise and business context is one of the most difficult challenges of technological competence management, because as the context changes, previously valuable expertise can quickly become irrelevant. What good is a deep expertise in chemical film processing when the industry goes digital? Unfortunately, the nature of expertise is such that it grows with depth, but the deeper it is, the harder it is to adapt to new contexts. Experts by definition tend to stay within their fields of expertise; business by definition evolves by creative destruction.

In EADS's project-driven business environment, the need for certain types of expertise varies according to the current project portfolio and the firm's development plans. However, when the new experts policy was first implemented, the divisions named experts primarily for their technical accomplishments rather than in consideration of strategic needs. This led not only to the promotion of potentially less useful competences, but also to a proliferation of expert titles, rising at more than 20 percent per year, which ultimately caused rancor among the management population, who became concerned about being outnumbered.

In response to these concerns, Borensztejn and his team reemphasized the importance of naming experts where the business needed them. Although no ratios or quotas had been defined, they urged the five business divisions to attribute titles only in direct relation to the needs of their business strategy. The divisions got the message, examined their needs more closely, and started to award titles more frugally. In particular, the highest-level Executive Expert appointments now average only three or four per year per division.

As of today, from the total population of more than 42,000 engineers and researchers, 1,100 professionals (about 2.6 percent) have been awarded with one of the expert titles, of which 80 percent (880 individuals) are Experts, 18 percent (198 individuals) are Senior Experts, and 2 percent (22 individuals) are Executive Experts. The greatest number of experts is found among the engineers and technicians working in the five business divisions. They develop new products or enhance old ones, and they are typically involved in specific programs like the Airbus 350 aircraft. Their work is the one most clearly driven by business interests, and they generally have little trouble incorporating a business perspective into their technical approach.

There are also technical experts found throughout the corporate value chain, in research, development, and support functions. (All research activities within EADS are structured with regard to the firm's twenty principle areas of expertise—that is, electronics, aerodynamics, image treatment, composites, and so on—and the same categories are referred to in the expert policy.) There are also people who are experts in the areas of maintenance, certification, testing, and production. And at Innovation Works, the corporate research unit, there are research engineers who work for all the business divisions, focusing on technologies to be used within the coming five to ten years.

Recognizing That Experts Need "People" Training

Another key objective of the experts policy was to maximize the value of the intellectual and creative capital that rested in the talent of the company's researchers, engineers, and technicians. To achieve this, Borensztejn knew that it would be critical to make that capital visible and sharable throughout the organization. The more visible experts are, he reasoned, the easier it would be for others to access their expertise and the greater a contribution they could ultimately make to the company. The policy therefore laid out a series of duties that experts were expected to fulfill above and beyond their regular jobs. These duties focused on five principle areas of impact:

1. Knowledge application and development
2. Operational advice
3. Expert network participation
4. Knowledge management and transfer
5. Intellectual property rights

As the learning team monitored how well the expert population began applying these principles, it became quickly apparent that the experts needed support in the form of training. The issue was not the need for continuous education in their respective fields of knowledge, but rather how to make them better comprehend the implications and responsibilities of the new, larger role that came with their expert title. The learning team decided to create a dedicated program that would explain to the experts their overall duties to the company and provide methodologies to accomplish them. The program consisted of two three-day learning modules.

Module 1: EADS Strategy and Policies; Influencing Through Communication and Negotiation

This module addressed the issue of linking technical expertise with strategic business objectives. Engineers are sometimes so focused on their technology that they are only superficially familiar with what is going on beyond their worlds. The module sought to help them locate their expertise in the context of the company's business applications. Also, experts are often positioned at the heart of complex networks or are called upon to represent their divisions in a customer or supplier relationship. As such, they must be able to influence the decisions of people from outside of their technical sphere, which requires business rather than technical arguments. This is a challenging yet highly relevant shift in focus of the role of experts, which the program addressed by working with the participants on the art of effective communication.

Module 2: Innovation; Industrial Property; Knowledge Transfer

The second module was designed to more deeply examine the importance of expertise to EADS's business applications. Experts looked at real cases of innovation and analyzed how preparation and leadership contributed to the process. They also reviewed the steps necessary to protect discoveries and technologies. Finally, the module devoted attention to how experts needed to contribute to internal and external knowledge transfer using the methods and tools available to them.

To date, the company has trained roughly 500 out of the 1,100 total population of experts, with very positive results. The main impact of the training has been that the experts have better understood their roles and have been able to identify concrete actions to implement their responsibilities in their organizations. The training has also been a driver for cultural change, helping to break down the silos that generally enclose these highly specialized engineers. The experts cherished the opportunity to interact and share knowledge. In the past, EADS had been reluctant to mix engineers from different divisions due to concerns about information leaks, and perhaps some interdivisional rivalry. But the new program provided an environment conducive to having the experts transcend their usual comfort zones and enter into a spirit of collaboration and knowledge sharing, which led to innovative synergies between the company's top specialists across many areas of expertise. The learning team has seen a number of results linked to the topics addressed during the training, such as:

- An increased number of knowledge management initiatives, conferences, and exchange of practices between divisions
- An increased number of patents, and
- A rise in experts' involvement in program reviews and innovation processes

The training also proved to be an excellent way for the learning team to gain a better understanding and knowledge of this population so that they can plan future initiatives for them.

Getting Experts to Network

Another important element in EADS's experts policy was encouraging experts to network among themselves. Borensztejn and his team believed that the more opportunities they could create for high-level engineers to interact—even for those working in unrelated fields—the greater the chances were that they would produce new insights.

Technical experts tend to work in isolation and often have a limited set of social skills or desire to communicate their research with others. To address this issue, the learning team made it a requirement that experts had to participate in networking if they wanted to get and keep their titles; to help them, they launched several initiatives to promote expert interactions.

For instance, Borensztejn's team sponsors an annual "Experts Day," where experts from various divisions meet to explore their common role as technical references for others. They also organize monthly expert lunches as a simple, low-cost initiative that merely requires reserving a table in the company cafeteria and communicating the date.

In 2007, a "Knowledge Management Day" was organized at the EADS Executive Education Center in Villepreux, France, that was attended by fifty Senior and Executive Experts, each an indispensable knowledge asset of the firm. They took part in a "marketplace of perspectives," where they described problems to each other, explored solutions, and exchanged best practices. One Executive Expert, Isabelle Terrasse, praised the initiative, considering the networking potential generated by the expert policy its most valuable feature. She believes that encounters between experts are the most promising means to stimulate sustainable innovation, which is a key challenge for a company like EADS that has already achieved a high level of technological leadership.

These initiatives have successfully generated both a greater sense of community among the experts and some new initiatives. The value of networking attracted so many experts that Alain Hensgen, who is in charge of the project, relates that he has become the central "operator" in a new "expert communication system." Whenever an expert is unable to find an answer to a technical question within his or her division, he or she can e-mail the question to Hensgen, who then forwards it to the entire expert community. An expert intranet portal is now being implemented to further facilitate this role.

The benefits of enabling experts to interact are increasingly apparent, stimulating EADS corporate management to allow them more freedom to circulate, which does not happen easily in the highly confidential culture of a defense corporation.

Hensgen hopes that experts will eventually be able to shift in and out of various divisions and projects and serve the company's needs by applying their skills across a wide range of areas.

To further assure the sustainability of the new system, an Experts Committee has been created, chaired by Hensgen. Each division is represented by two experts: one HR representative, and one person from the technical department, generally the person in charge of knowledge management. The committee meets twice a year to examine matters including communication about experts, special training, and expert positioning and gaps. It offers experts the opportunity to voice the concerns of their community and actively participate in the continuous development of the system.

The EADS Hall of Fame

In 2007, EADS also introduced the "EADS Hall of Fame," an initiative that was sponsored by the company's CTO Jean Botti and managed by Hensgen, who reports to Borensztejn. The Hall of Fame is intended to be a powerful tool to build EADS' reputation as the source of some of the world's greatest technology innovations and inventions, and to communicate EADS's technological leadership to stakeholders inside and outside the firm.

The Hall of Fame annually attributes awards in four categories: greatest inventor, innovator, craftsman, and lean manufacturer. Each of EADS's five divisions nominates individuals to the Executive Technical Committee or to the "lean council" for the nominees in that category. Any EADS employee can be nominated, not just experts. In the first year of the awards, twenty candidates were reviewed, from which the four winners were chosen.

To announce the awards, EADS held its First Annual EADS Hall of Fame awards ceremony on November 1, 2007. At the event, 150 EADS members, their spouses, and celebrity soccer players gathered at the appropriately chosen Parc de La Villette Science Center in Paris. The sports theme and presence of the athletes was intended to reinforce the sense of team spirit at EADS. It also contributed to a fun, relaxing, enjoyable atmosphere. When the winners and first members of the EADS Hall of Fame were announced, the results showed that superlative talent was well distributed throughout the EADS Group. Each of the four winners came from a different division, and, perhaps not surprisingly, two of the four winners were from among the experts population! (The other two winners were a worker who had an invention to repair blades and a team who had improved their plant.)

Problems and Pitfalls for Managers of Experts

Managing experts is not a trivial task. Keep in mind that only 1,100 of the more than 42,000 engineers and researchers carry that title. Representing the essence of EADS's intellectual capital, they tend to be strong-minded individuals who are highly motivated to follow their calling and who are highly employable at competing companies. Managing these individuals requires supporting their motivation while assuring at the same time that their callings remains in sync with the business requirements.

When the new system was first implemented, the managers would decide where experts should devote their energy, whether or not they should attend trainings or conferences, and how large of a budget they should be granted to carry out their work. However, many experts soon expressed frustration over receiving insufficient time or resources to pursue what they considered worthwhile subjects. In addition, it turned out that the managers were not always fully aware of the views of their experts, and there were often serious gaps between the divergent perspectives and a general lack of mutual understanding.

Consequently, Hensgen composed and addressed an e-mail to all managers of experts to review and clarify their duties. He stressed the importance for managers to set clear objectives with experts and to follow up on established action plans. Such objectives might include defining a number of patents to file in the coming year or getting more actively involved in knowledge transfer. Concrete goals provided both parties with clear guidelines. This system has proven beneficial, as the experts' objectives become directly linked to their expertise. Hensgen now reinforces this policy for managers by discussing the role of experts at the annual meeting of the Executive Forum.

One other challenge repeatedly raised among management is how to make the best use of experts. Experts are often called in as emergency technicians to solve problems encountered in a project, but those assignments detract from the individual's time. As a result, the learning team has urged program directors to consult and plan for the use of expert time as early as possible, so deployments can be better planned in advance. Soliciting an expert's participation early, during project conception and development phases, also makes better business sense, because the expert can highlight the pros and cons of various concepts and thus enable program managers to make more reliable decisions and plans.

Conclusion: Learning as a Strategic Force at EADS

The power of EADS's approach to expert competence management lies in the comprehensive architecture that has been put in place by Borensztejn and his team, which creates learning processes on a variety of levels. First and foremost, the initiative is about securing and improving the strategic effectiveness of the company's most important asset—technological capability. Its emphasis on identifying the best and promoting them within a transparent system of career steps within their own domain is a powerful symbolic act with very tangible impact. On one hand, it provides motivation and attractive career perspectives for professionals, who hitherto could only advance by becoming managers. On the other hand, by creating a development model that is parallel to management careers, the project puts its finger very visibly on the important relationship between business context and technical expertise. The program's attention to managing this tension is reflected in many principles of the policy: it plays a role in the appointment process, it gets addressed in Module 1 of the expert training program, and it gets reinforced in the leadership guidelines managers receive for how to deal with their experts.

The experts policy has helped ensure that the company has a continuing supply of the right people in the right places at the right time. It has helped EADS to develop a more robust tracking system to examine its expert talent, which allows the firm to quickly draw a strategic capability map by answering questions about where it possesses the most and least expertise, where it is in danger of losing knowledge and know-how due to retirement, and what competences that are likely to be needed in the future are missing from the group's portfolio.

If Hervé Borensztejn had followed the traditional, narrow role definition of corporate learning, he would have addressed the issue of building expert competences through traditional training programs, probably along technical content domains (making experts better experts), maybe also along the technology/business axis (making them relevant experts). However, without the holistic and overarching policy that introduced a new title hierarchy and an integrated system of accompanying mechanisms, the traditional learning intervention of the two training modules would not have been as effective. It was important to create the cornerstones of an overall capability management system first,

Exhibit 8.3. The Evolution of Learning and Development at EADS

2000	• Combination of 3 training departments of merged companies to form the Corporate Business Academy (CBA) • Focus: Facilitate the merger and develop leadership • 50 programs, 28 staff members, 40 million euro budget
2002	• Combination of arrival of Hervê Borensztejn and strategic reductions throughout the unit • Retained 2 of previous programs • 5 staff members, 4 million euro budget
2003	• Launch of FAST program for high-potential managers • Executive forum for top 200 managers
2004	• Expert policy marks CU's move beyond domain of leadership and into technical arena
2007	• CBA becomes Leadership Development and Learning (LDL) • Focus: Talent pipeline, competency management, and learning • 15 people, 15 million euro budget • 75% global skill management (technical + business), 25% leadership development • Model: Shared service provider (program design) for all "customer" divisions

so the learning programs would not only make more sense but would also be anchored and reinforced.

This is why the EADS case is an outstanding example of how to extend the role of learning toward a strategic talent management architecture that is not embedded in an HR paradigm, but in a solid understanding of organizational capability management. It comes as no surprise that as we are writing this case, Borensztejn's portfolio of responsibilities has expanded from the original task of providing leadership development through the Corporate Business Academy. The department he heads today is now called Leadership Development and Learning (LDL), and it has become a key player in the strategic and organizational development of EADS (see Exhibit 8.3).

About the Principals in This Case

Hervé Borensztejn is Senior Vice President, Deputy Global Head of HR, and CLO at EADS. As CLO, Borensztejn leads the Learning Shared Services division (130 people in four countries, 200 M€ turnover), drives competence management, and is in charge of the development of the company's top 1,000 executives and top 2,000 high potentials. He also runs the P&L EADS Executive Education Center, located in Villepreux, close to Bordeaux, France. Prior to joining EADS in 2002, he worked as an HR consultant, recruiting for high-tech industries, and held HR and competence management positions at companies including LVMH, the Vivendi Group, and Générale des Eaux. Borensztejn holds a degree in mining engineering as well as a PhD from Paris' École des Mines.

Alain Hensgen is Vice President of Learning, Competency, and Knowledge Management at EADS. He is a member of both the corporate HR and technical departments; his responsibilities include competence management, senior executive development, change management, and design and implementation of EADS learning, knowledge management, and expert policies. Hensgen is a graduate of the Sorbonne and of Sciences Po (Paris), where he now lectures on management. Prior to joining EADS, Hensgen was Director of the Human Capital Practice at PricewaterhouseCoopers, Paris.

Leadership Learning as Competitive Strategy in the Chinese Market

Novartis

Over the past decade, China has become one of the most, if not the most, important market for nearly every global corporation, and many companies have established substantial operations there. Global companies are used to adapting to local market conditions, but in this case the sheer scale and breathtaking dynamic of the Chinese market, together with its proverbial cultural differences from the West, make issues of intercultural management a particularly critical success factor.

One of the major challenges Western companies face is how to attract, develop, and retain Chinese leadership talent that is not only anchored in the local culture but also able and willing to adapt to the standards and culture of a global corporation. Many Western corporations address this issue unilaterally by pushing large-scale uniformity and standardization throughout the organization into all regions and countries. But such an approach succeeds typically only on the surface; it leads to continuous systemic conflicts between corporate and regional interests, and it creates high opportunity costs in terms of local effectiveness. A standardization approach is particularly problematic for China, with its significant political, legal, social, and cultural differences that cannot be easily integrated into the mainstream paradigms of European or American business practices.

This case tells the story of how Novartis—one of the world's leading pharmaceutical companies, with a significant presence in China—dealt with one of the key challenges in the Chinese market: the shortage of management talent that meets the high standards of a global corporation. The case focuses on how the creation of a dedicated Novartis China Learning Center became the platform for a locally customized, yet still globally integrated leadership learning system that created positive repercussions beyond building management skills and retaining talent.

As a result of this sophisticated strategic learning initiative, Novartis today enjoys not only a growing pool of Chinese executives of international calibre but also enhanced brand recognition in China as an employer of choice and an exemplary corporate citizen—both critical factors for local competitive advantage. In addition, Novartis has become an even more international corporation by actively capitalizing on the interplay of cultural differences. As such, the case is not only an interesting lesson about the power of a leadership learning solution, it also offers a prime illustration of how flexibility, adaptability, and sensitivity can be vital to provide an effective response to challenging global leadership circumstances.

The Emergence of a Global Industry Leader

Headquartered in Basel, Switzerland, Novartis is one of the world's leading pharmaceutical companies and one of the world's fastest-growing health care corporations, with 2008 revenues totalling $42.6 billion. The company was created in 1996 through the merger of Swiss pharmaceutical companies Ciba-Geigy and Sandoz, both of which were 150-year-old organizations at the time. With the merger, Novartis became the world's second largest health care corporation.

Over the next years, a new company took shape. Novartis restructured its business portfolio, and the company aggressively approached the U.S. market as well as the emerging markets of China, India, and Latin America. At the same time, Novartis introduced a stronger performance-based compensation system and standardized processes and behavioral policies throughout the workforce. By fostering intense cross-functional collaboration between the two major empires of every pharmaceutical company—research and development, and marketing and sales—Novartis strived to shorten development time and gain more agility in the marketplace.

The changes created a major transformation process that left few stones unturned. But the efforts soon paid off—Novartis rose quickly to become a key player in the global pharmaceutical industry, and in 2004 the *Financial Times* named the company's CEO Daniel Vasella the most influential business leader in Europe of the past twenty-five years.

Reshaping Novartis from the heritage of two traditional Swiss companies to an agile global leader posed significant learning challenges across the entire organization, especially in creating a leadership culture that would sustain the transformation. The company needed new leadership development programs that would enhance business performance and enable it to respond to market challenges more effectively. The task to create and implement new learning initiatives fell to Frank Waltmann, who was named Novartis's Global Head of Learning in 2002, after he had been with the firm for three years in various management learning capacities. Frank immediately started designing Novartis's global learning activities to meet the requirements of the future: growth, globalization, and high performance. He was dedicated to transforming learning into a strategic force that would make a difference, and he was pleased that he had top executive support behind him.

He needed this support. At the time of the merger, little attention had been given to the integration of the various training departments from the original companies. They had merely been combined without putting much effort into formulating a compelling common strategy. They largely continued to provide in-house skill training, together with a few uncoordinated leadership development programs.

It is not uncommon that the learning and development function gets neglected in the heat of post-merger integration. It is indicative of the marginal role that learning plays in the mind of the architects who design newly combined structures. We know that post-merger integration is not the forte of many corporations; mergers and acquisitions are usually about buying market share or complementing the business portfolio, so the focus is on realizing economies of scale or scope. Few realize the power that a strategic learning platform can bring to the process as an enabler of integration, as a developer and orchestrator of the new capability portfolio, and as a catalyst for strategic and organizational discourse that can help make sense of the new post-merger context.

To create a more unified learning strategy, Waltmann stayed in continuous touch with top executives to learn about their perspectives; he shut down superfluous training departments, placed people elsewhere in the company, assessed program relevance, eliminated duplication, and renegotiated responsibilities and relationships with the divisions. The idea was to craft a consistent, centralized, world-class learning division that would become a veritable brand within the organization, so people would grasp a vision of learning that was exciting, different, and new.

Over the next five years, his corporate learning team shed its reputation of being "just a training department." While basic training, such as languages or information technology, remained decentralized, corporate learning took the responsibility for driving all management learning on a global scale, with an emphasis on building leadership capabilities in four areas that were regarded as critical for long-term success: external focus (customers, supply chain, regulators), innovation, people, and performance. Today, each of the twenty-five leadership development programs that are currently offered by corporate learning fits into one of these categories.

Novartis China

In the meantime, Novartis continued to become more global. The company's research and development headquarters was moved from Basel, Switzerland, to Cambridge, Massachusetts, to take advantage of the Boston area's heavy concentration of medical researchers—a bold move for a traditional Swiss company. New and more focused attention was given to emerging markets such as China, Russia, and Latin America, with an eye to rapidly growing their organizations and improving bottom-line results. China, as largest and most dynamic emerging market, ranked especially high on the company's agenda.

China presented one of the world's fastest-growing and most competitive pharmaceutical markets. There were already more than 3,500 pharmaceutical manufacturers in the country, the top ten of which controlled 15 percent of the overall market. But Novartis was not new to the country; Geigy, its pre-merger company, had been present in China since 1886. Geigy's long-standing reputation as a responsible and reliable business gave Novartis China an early advantage over other foreign multinationals. From the beginning, the company was recognized for its ethical and compliance standards, which were deemed higher than elsewhere. In addition, a serendipitous circumstance benefited the newly merged entity: *Novartis China* in Chinese translates as "commitment to China"—a coincidence that contributed to an almost reverent belief that the company would be a positive force for the country. Novartis quickly became the sixth-largest foreign pharmaceutical corporation in the country, with a 3,000-people-strong workforce that included 150 scientists and more than 500 managers.

The rapid growth and success created a challenge—the same challenge facing most other global players that operate in China: how to cope with the lack of adequate local management talent. Like most other Western companies, Novartis preferred to have locals rather than expatriates run their China businesses. Local talent was not only less expensive; more important, it was embedded in the culture, which is invaluable in a country where *guanxi*—personalized networks of influence and social relationships—remain at the heart of doing business.

But few Chinese individuals were qualified for middle or senior management positions—at least according to Novartis's high standards. They called it the "Chinese paradox": a "shortage among plenty." Although China was annually producing five million university graduates, including roughly 650,000 engineers, only a very small percentage of them had the skills to work for a foreign company. There were more than enough young people capable of entry-level jobs, but candidates who could run a business the Novartis way were more than scarce.

To add to this challenge, Novartis's reputation as a top company made its talent a constant target for actively solicitous competitors and headhunters. In fact, turnover among the company's skilled Chinese managers was approximately 30 percent per year. Managers rarely stayed with the company more than two years and often as little as six to eight months. And it were not only foreign companies who competed for this talent: There was also a significant amount of "reverse brain drain," as Chinese executives who gained experience with Western multinationals would often leave to work for Chinese companies that had an exploding need for good people. Novartis would have to address the two issues at once: how to grow new leaders and how to retain those who were already there.

A task force at Novartis began studying the situation. They discovered that when Chinese people leave a company, they are rarely motivated by the desire for just a salary increase. Their core motives for departure are career development and the maintenance of interpersonal relationships. If such factors encourage people leave a company, Novartis reasoned, finding ways to satisfy those needs might convince them to stay.

Launching the Novartis China Learning Center

The company's global leadership development programs had been going on for two years and had gained a reputation as important elements for driving strategic change through the corporation. Why not use a leadership learning initiative as a response to the Chinese talent pool challenge? Emphasizing people development would resonate especially well in China, because the Chinese not only had a culturally embedded respect for learning and education, but they were also eager to absorb knowledge and concepts from the West—although they usually picked and chose what best served their needs.

In September 2004, Frank Waltmann received a mandate from the corporate executive committee to launch Novartis Learning in China. Excited about the challenging assignment, he thought about the best way to utilize the experiences he'd had so far. It was clear that a simple one-to-one translation of the current global leadership programs would not work; they needed something more specific, tailored to the challenge at hand. Maybe Novartis could develop a specialized China Learning Center that would cater to the local context while at the same time meet the global standards of Novartis Global Learning, which had become a companywide trademark.

To explore this idea in more detail, Waltmann investigated corporate learning centers of other global companies. What he saw made him think twice. In some instances, a learning center had been a pet project of a CEO who had moved on and had been replaced by someone less passionate who abandoned the idea. In other cases, a wave of enthusiasm had led to the creation of a large-scale executive training center in a foreign territory, but eventually the financial and organizational support died down, leaving an unsustainable and orphaned enterprise. In some companies, the demand for executive development was not high enough to continuously fill the centers' capacity, so the centers were opened up to outsiders, diminishing their prestige and brand identity for the corporate executives. Maybe a center was not the best solution after all.

On the other hand, Waltmann knew Novartis needed something that would create a visible brand in this highly competitive market. Based on what he had seen, and careful to avoid too-high fixed costs that could jeopardize the project in the long run, he decided that they would create a Novartis China Learning Center, but it would not be a physical place, with the tail of infrastructure costs that are usually attached to it. The new center would be virtual, a lean and flexible organization, driven by a set of highly visible activities. Unencumbered by the constraints of a building, Novartis would have a greater flexibility to offer the leadership programs as needed, and it could form outside partnerships for providing them in a customized fashion for the Chinese talent.

The Lure of a Local Mini-MBA

One of the first initiatives Waltmann undertook on behalf of the Novartis China Learning Center was a partnership with Beijing University to create a mini-MBA program, to be known as BiMBA. Given the Chinese reverence for education, he believed that one of the best ways to attract and retain Novartis's talent was to offer people the opportunity to earn an advanced degree.

A proprietary Novartis MBA program that would be accessible only for selected company employees would pay off by helping build the company's brand as a leading employer, which could further help ease its recruiting and retention issues. It would also add an element of corporate citizenship to Novartis's record in this field, enhancing the company's reputation as a contributor to the overall educational quality of professionals in an emerging country.

Waltmann selected Beijing University because, compared to other Chinese schools of higher education, it was thought to have the best combination of Western business understanding and knowledge of the Chinese market realities. It also had experience working with other pharmaceutical companies, which was important if programs were to be customized. After agreeing on the overall purpose of the program and the cornerstones of their future partnership, local HR Director Jennifer Jin and several Peking University professors worked together to design an eighteen-month mini-MBA program that would be delivered at the university's China Center for Economic Research (CCER) facilities.

Linking the program as tightly as possible to the specific needs of Novartis was critical—after all, it was not supposed to be just another MBA program but a tool to attract, develop, and retain local talent. The faculty selected to teach in the program had to be introduced to Novartis's specific issues and language before they could start delivery. While Chinese professors are generally familiar with Western business and management theories (Western management books are translated into Chinese very quickly), they often lack connections between the theories and the real business world, especially when challenged with managing in the complex environment of a global organization. The BiMBA program would make a difference if the local faculty were not only familiar with the latest management theories but with the very specifics of Novartis business, strategy, and markets. Only a thorough knowledge of these internal issues would enable them to enter into relevant discussions with Novartis managers, who would then emerge from these courses with immediately applicable insights.

In Fall 2005, the first forty-seven-person BiMBA class got under way. Every six weeks, participants spent one weekend at the Peking University campus, taking the classes and working together on project assignments. In the following year, another group of fifty-four students got started. In 2007, eighty-two managers enrolled in the program, and in 2008, one hundred got started, enough for two classes per year.

To boost the prestige of the program and heighten the perception that the opportunity is a reward for outstanding achievement, the company introduced a transparent and thorough nomination process and made performance an important selection criterion. In January of each year, Novartis China supervising managers engage with each manager in a personal development planning discussion during which they discuss the candidate's qualifications to enter BiMBA. In March, all supervising managers gather for a "Talking Talents" session to rank their high achievers. Only managers who achieve a rating of at least 2.2 on a 3-point matrix can be nominated. In June, supervising managers then create division-level ratings and nominate the final candidates.

The nominations are passed on to Novartis China President Jeffrey Li, who reviews them to confirm or deny each candidate's status. This lends additional prestige to the program; it also encourages young managers to work hard for the opportunity to get nominated for a prestigious company-paid career development program, and it sends a message to Novartis workers that the company cares about their development.

Today, the program has become a compellingly effective employee retention tool, guaranteeing Novartis at least five and a half years of employee commitment from each participant. Apart from personal motivation, this commitment is a result of the policies associated with the program: People must work for Novartis for two years to be nominated for BiMBA, and—as with many corporate-sponsored MBA programs—they must sign a contract to stay with the company for at least two years after completing the eighteen-month studies. While it is too early to predict how long people will ultimately stay with the firm, five years is a vast improvement over the average tenure of Chinese managers, which is less than one year.

Localizing the Success of Global Programs

The BiMBA project became a clear success, and it put the Novartis China Learning Center on the map. But the mini-MBA alone would not be sufficient to address the more complex leadership issues of Novartis China. To groom Chinese executives so they would meet international standards of senior leadership at Novartis, they had to become part of the strategically focused global leadership programs. The easy way would have been to just invite the Chinese executives to participate in these programs. But would that accommodate the very specific context of doing business in China? Certainly not.

Waltmann had worked hard to create a globally aligned strategic leadership learning architecture, and he was not willing to jeopardize it. But he also knew that bending the rules of global consistency made sense, because given the idiosyncrasies of the Chinese environment, customization to the culture was critical to success. He decided therefore that the Novartis China Learning Center would specially adapt ten of Novartis's corporate leadership development programs, and he would make sure to optimize the interplay between local and global requirements.

The challenge was of course to keep the cornerstones of the global programs consistent, while at the same time inserting a Chinese flavor into the standards. The adaptations had to be strong enough to cater to the local context, but they needed to fit with the overall spirit of the global concept. Adapting the programs involved managing the unavoidable tension between corporate alignment and regional differentiation, but Frank and his Chinese counterpart Felix Li, Novartis China's CLO, approached the task with creativity and perceived it as a great opportunity for mutual intercultural learning.

Localization had to be visible, for example, so Waltmann and Li incorporated notions from Chinese philosophy into the leadership concepts. The approach to leadership had to demonstrate sensitivity toward Chinese cultural ideals such as the reverence for people of older generations. In one program, Novartis's leadership and assessment practices would be presented in the context of Chinese business scenarios, not Western situations. Another program had to make changes to account for the fact that formal authority is a recent import in China, as are assessment tools like 360-degree feedback. As a result, it featured additional executive coaches and senior executive mentors to help managers in training become more accustomed to implementing these methods and feeling comfortable using them with their reports.

Novartis also bent its language policy by making the courses bilingual, to ensure that all Chinese participants fully understood the content. Materials were provided in both English and Chinese, and depending on the program, classes were delivered in either of the two languages. The peculiarities of Chinese demographics were also addressed, for instance, through a segment that discussed how Chinese managers should lead their Generation Y workers. In China, this generation is a product of the government-mandated "one child per family" policy, and so these young workers are psychologically quite different from the same generation in the United States or Europe.

Much of these localization efforts have been led by the Novartis China CLO, Felix Li, who reports directly to the head of Novartis China, Jeffrey Li, with a dotted line to Waltmann. China is so far the only region at Novartis that has its own CLO, which is not only an indication of the importance of the market but also recognizes the cultural and political differences between China and the West. Felix Li joined Novartis in November 2006 to take the lead in adapting the existing global learning programs to Chinese needs. Waltmann was pleased with his local counterpart; Waltmann had everything to learn about China, and having a local expert executive with cultural credibility was a critical success factor for his ambitious project. Back at headquarters, Waltmann added a Chinese national to his already international learning team, who would support the development and implementation of the Novartis China Learning Center and act as operational interface between Beijing and Basel.

Since joining Novartis, Li had been attending the global executive programs at a rate of one per year, with the goal of getting to know the programs inside out so he could localize them for China. He also spent six months at corporate headquarters in Basel to build a solid relationship with the Novartis learning group and enhance his perspectives and experience. His responsibilities have evolved from talent retention to integrated leadership training, with talent management next on his agenda. With this holistic background, he can act effectively as a broker between Novartis's global strategic objectives and the requirements of the local idiosyncrasies of the Chinese market.

Taking the Locals Global

At the same time as Novartis was localizing its global programs, the company was putting more emphasis on "globalizing" its Chinese locals. Increasingly, Chinese executives have had the opportunity to engage in a globally conducted program to better integrate them into the organization, widen their horizons, and inspire them to adopt a more international attitude. Until 2006, only about forty Chinese leaders attended a global executive learning program each year. But by 2008, participation had increased to 100, and it is expected to continue rising. Much of this increase can be attributed to the impact of the adapted global programs, as these programs started to expose a critical mass of Chinese executives to a corporate strategic perspective, preparing them to become qualified participants in the regular global programs.

While the costs of travel have previously limited participation in such global programs, this constraint is being overcome as Novartis has launched programs in locations that are more easily accessible to China. Today, Shanghai, Bangkok, and Kuala Lumpur are utilized for learning locations, in addition to Beijing. These locations also provide an opportunity for the company to send its Westerners to Asia. Felix Li points out that these Asia-based global programs help Europeans and Americans become better acquainted with Eastern ways of doing business, adding that Western courses that simply explain Asian cultural differences may be enlightening but they don't enable people to interact closely. "Working with your peers from other countries is at least half of the learning experience," he stresses. As a result, when orchestrating these global programs, Novartis has found that creating cross-cultural groups is the best formula, with the ideal combination of people at a ratio of 1 foreigner to 2 locals.

The global programs are not only great learning opportunities for Chinese executives; they also generate a sense of organizational belonging that helps counter the "reverse brain drain." Being sent to a distant locale to take part in a global leadership development program is understood as a reward for a Chinese manager's achievements. In turn, the increased Chinese participation in global programs benefits the entire Novartis executive community, because it fosters intercultural understanding and learning. In a nutshell, the Novartis China Learning initiative has spawned a positive loop of ever-stronger interaction between different cultural perspectives, creating a truly international texture of discourse on Novartis' four strategic issues: external focus, innovation, people, and performance.

The Impact of the China Learning Center on Novartis

From exit interviews conducted with managers who left Novartis, the company had learned that the primary reason for changing jobs was career development. Now, the offering of high-level in-house learning opportunities has proven to be a strong incentive for people to remain. To this extent, the China Learning Center has helped achieve significant results. While average turnover in the pharmaceutical industry in China is 30 percent, the Novartis rate is just 14 percent. As of 2008, 40 percent of Novartis China managers have gone through or are involved in the BiMBA program, and since 2005, an average of 800 people a year have participated in one of the China learning programs.

The boost to Novartis's reputation as an employer and a contributor to Chinese professional education is evident. Chinese business managers report that Novartis training is better than elsewhere—"better" because it genuinely raises people's management levels. Sales representatives from other companies confirm that they applied for jobs at Novartis because of the opportunities for training and continuing education. Novartis was distinguished as "Best Employer in China" by Hewitt Associates, with the company's learning offer specifically cited as a major criterion for the award.

When Waltmann and Li are asked to identify the success factors for the Novartis China Learning Center, they refer to the following:

1. *Customization.* Learning is delivered by speakers and professors who know both the Chinese market and the particularities of Novartis's local business units. This has provided pertinent, immediately applicable learning. Simultaneously, Novartis standards about assessment tools and leadership behaviors are scrupulously reinforced.
2. *Corporate + local commitment.* Having a local CLO in addition to a corporate CLO demonstrates the company's commitment to a culturally based Chinese leadership development.
3. *Communication.* Ongoing communication and coordination among learning, HR, and business leaders on local and global levels assures the relevance of the programs and their integration into the global architecture.
4. *Continuous improvement.* Feedback from participants and instructors is directly applied to prevent stagnation and meet the evolving needs of Chinese managers. Continuous improvement includes adapting and adding global leadership development programs to the Chinese offer at the rate of one program per year.

Novartis learning in China is headed in the right direction, and today's market is too tough to envisage any lessening of its efforts. Felix Li explained that quality management principles are closely applied to the learning center, forcing it to assess what works and what doesn't. At the end of 2007, for example, he and his team surveyed key talent, asking them to evaluate the programs and vendors. Action learning was revealed to be the most appreciated learning method. Li also discovered that people were appreciative of having corporate support, even from afar. He has also pursued the quality investigation to review programs with instructors, gathering their input on where improvements were needed.

On the corporate level, the learning team discovered that programs delivered with a mixture of methodologies are the most effective and build the greatest long-term impact. The winning formula for courses combines theory and case studies, with tool-based assessment and coaching. This is a costly endeavor, but in December 2008, Novartis deployed this strategy in China for their thirty senior managers.

And the initiative continues to grow. As we are writing this case, the learning center is about to be transformed into a full-blown local corporate university that is designed to include all management levels of Novartis China. Reaching out to a larger management population and doubling the number of programs will have an even bigger impact on the quality of the workforce and the market standing of the company. At the same time, the top programs will get a more international focus and prestige by involving some the world's leading business schools, such as Harvard, as partners.

Copying China's Success

The Novartis experience with the China Learning Center has set an example. Now Waltmann is about to duplicate the model in Russia. Christened the Novartis Business Academy, the Russian learning platform has launched a mini-MBA program similar to BiMBA under a collaboration agreement with the Stockholm School of Economics. The quality and effectiveness of the Russian program content and delivery are continuously reviewed using a focus group of participants that meets with the school's faculty on a quarterly basis. As in China, Waltmann's team has set the goal of customizing one global corporate program a year for Novartis's Russian managers to ensure their local leadership development. After Russia, Latin America is likely to be a next focus of his team's attention. Customized learning may also be deployed to address the special challenges of the Japanese market.

The Novartis learning success in China has not gone unnoticed by other global corporations. Some of Novartis's competitors, such as Pfizer and Novo Nordisk, are known to have launched learning centers in collaboration with Beijing University based on the Novartis model. While this may fuel the war for local talent, it is a great indicator of the power of learning as a tool for corporate branding and its strategic importance in emerging markets.

Conclusion: A Lesson of Many Dimensions

What started as an effort to address the paradox of China's "shortage among plenty" has developed in just four years into a showcase of how to drive internationalization and intercultural learning. As we are writing this case, Novartis is reaching out to other emerging markets to further grow their network of local learning centers that are embedded in a global strategy.

The amazing lesson from this experience is that the creation of an international culture that harvests the diversity of cultural perspectives was not the result of pushing alignment from the corporate level. It was created using the opposite approach: recognizing the importance of cultural differences, Novartis global learning was able to let go of its policy of alignment, which they just had achieved in a tedious process. But they did not succumb to difference by leaving Novartis China alone. In a painstaking process of squaring the circle between corporate and regional interests, Felix Li and Frank Waltmann were able to build the best of both worlds into the localized offering. The customization allowed local executives to get in touch with a globally concerted effort, which eventually enabled them to play a more prominent role in other international programs. The stronger presence of the Chinese perspective in such programs, on the other hand, leads to a more international, intercultural exposure of *all* Novartis executives.

This probably would not have been achieved without creating the Novartis China Learning Center. The institutional commitment—setting up a dedicated structure with a Chinese CLO reporting to the Chinese CEO—sends an important symbolic message to the Chinese stakeholders about the significance of learning and the investment the company is prepared to make. It not only contributes to the all-important branding in a highly competitive environment; it also creates a strong anchor of cultural competence within the region—a critical condition for developing the balance with corporate learning that was required to create the localized solution.

It is also clear that the project boosted Novartis's reputation as a responsible corporate citizen. As an emerging country with a university system that has yet to reach Western standards of business education and research, China was not in a position to provide the leadership qualification needed to excel in a complex global business context. While Novartis was acting in its own self-interest to attract, develop, and retain its own leadership, it has made a large contribution to China in sponsoring an MBA program that has raised standards and that could produce thousands of Chinese managers during the coming decades. As such, the case is a perfect example of marrying the strategic interests of a corporation with authentic contributions to the educational system of an emerging economy.

About the Principals in This Case

Frank Waltmann is CLO at Novartis International. He holds a PhD in economics, business administration, and international relations from Albert-Ludwig University in Freiberg, Germany. Previous professional experience includes marketing, finance, and HR positions at Puma Sports, management consulting for Ernst & Young, and personal assistant to the German minister of transportation and aviation. Waltmann joined Novartis in 1999, and under his leadership, Novartis became the first pharmaceutical company to be accredited for its management learning programs by the European Foundation for Management Development (EFMD).

Felix Li is CLO at Novartis China and the head of the Novartis China Leadership Development Center. He joined the company in November 2006, having held positions in learning, people development, and talent management at Schneider Electric China, Century 21, and Novo Nordisk.

First Choice: The World's Largest Customer Focus Initiative

Deutsche Post DHL

Customer focus is on nearly every short list of strategic initiatives of large corporations. All companies face the challenge of market responsiveness and seek ways to assure consistent service quality to create a loyal customer base. After all, loyal customers reduce the cost of marketing, and flawless products and services reduce the maintenance costs of customer relationships. Creating customer loyalty is the cheapest and most satisfying way to ensure sustainable business.

So great customer service is a no-brainer—or is it? Unfortunately, delivering a great service experience is not as easy as it might seem. We all witness poor service every day, despite the undeniable efforts of companies to keep us loyal. Every company wrestles with the challenge of emphatic customer focus. But the challenge grows exponentially with size: as the distance between the center and the periphery grows, it becomes more difficult to respond quickly and flexibly to an increasingly diverse environment, and the tendency to treat customers as anonymous numbers grows. Add in a global dimension, which requires adaptation to local market conditions, and it is easy to see why the management of customer loyalty needs continuous improvement in most firms.

The following case presents the story of *First Choice*, a broad customer loyalty management initiative by Deutsche Post DHL (DP DHL), known in the United States under its international brand DHL. But this is not your usual customer focus effort. With more than 500,000 people in more than 220 countries, DP DHL is the world's largest logistics group and one of the top ten largest employers in the world. *First Choice* is one of the most ambitious organizational learning interventions ever undertaken—just by virtue of the sheer number of people involved. More important, the story of *First Choice* is ultimately about building organizational capability, not just about training people in customer service. It offers worthy lessons in designing an architecture for very large-scale change management, what anchors are required, what didactical tools are vital for success, and how to measure results. It's a lesson about the power of process and simplicity when it comes to dealing with scale.

———

> Welcome to *First Choice*, our new way of doing business; our new working culture. We can only truly become *First Choice* and the best in the industry by consistently keeping our promises and delighting our customers. *First Choice* is aimed at embedding a customer-centric culture throughout our organization. Everyone's contribution at every customer interaction is critical to our success.

So begins a letter from Deutsche Post DHL CEO Frank Appel to the company's roughly 55,000 managers who oversee a workforce of more than 450,000 people. His letter opens a forty-page booklet directed at front-line leaders, because they are the critical link in the chain to introduce the *First Choice* initiative and its loyalty management approach to every employee in the company. The goal of *First Choice* is ambitious: it strives to engage the company's workforce of more than half a million people in creating a customer interface that makes each and every interaction a driver for customer loyalty.

Combining employee engagement with improving customer service is a sweet spot for cultural transformation in an enormous organization like DP DHL. Holger Winklbauer, one of the original members of the executive team responsible for creating *First Choice* and currently Executive Vice President in charge of driving its sustainable worldwide implementation, points out that the company's front-line employees have more than *100 million interactions per week* with customers. Direct interface happens with the company's parcel delivery drivers, customer service representatives in call centers, behind-the-counter workers, mail carriers, retail employees, advertising consultants, and many more. As a logistics provider, DP DHL manages sensitive—if not mission critical—segments of the document and goods value chain for millions of customers around the world. In this environment, shortfalls in meeting customer expectations can be the beginning of an ultimately disastrous spiral that starts with customer complaints, leads to publicly aired critiques, and ends with canceled contracts, lost business, and a damaged reputation.

Efficient processes are vital in the logistics business. Freight and parcel services are highly process intensive, with many hands and transit locations involved in the pickup, shipping, and delivery of items across large distances—creating many opportunities for mix-ups, glitches, and human error. Sensitizing front-line employees to the accuracy and quality of their work has a potentially large payoff in fewer problems and customer satisfaction. Front-line employees are right there at the customer "touchpoints," so they can see if customers are satisfied or if something is not being done right—and they can correct it immediately. Each employee is also the "expert" at his or her own line of work and is in the best position to have insight into improving inefficient transactions.

A regular part of Frank Appel's agenda is to encourage his managers to become role models in this initiative, inciting them to continuous commitment, involvement, improvement, and alignment. Managers need to maintain an open dialogue with their employees, conduct regular feedback sessions, and follow up continuously to be sure customer satisfaction is vigorously pursued. They need to get to know their employees individually so that they can help motivate them to perform better at the customer interface. Most important, managers must become familiar with the *First Choice* methodology so that they can become enablers of change.

But a booklet is easily written, and ambitious goals are easily pronounced. The challenge is, how do you get 55,000 managers to buy into the idea, and how do you enable them to deliver the message to their employees? How do you train and sensitize hundreds of thousands of employees in more than 220 countries and territories so they will make every effort to delight customers in each and every one of their encounters? Getting a workforce of such size to adopt the same set of values about customer service and enact them in their daily routines is a mindboggling organizational challenge.

DP DHL was not completely new at efficiency improvement. In 2006, the company completed a program called STAR, a value enhancement and integration effort that sought to implement measurable improvements. The program was a success, but it was a very narrow initiative performed in a limited time frame. *First Choice* was intended to be completely different: designed as a key enabler of the evolution of DP DHL, *First Choice* is nothing less than a large-scale organizational learning process seeking to embed customer-focused thinking in the heart of the company culture by building the capability to systematically improve the business throughout the group. CEO Frank Appel dispenses with calling *First Choice* a "program"; in his words, it's a "philosophy." He states, "*First Choice* is a journey that will change our company entirely. It will transform our culture and the way we do business."

The History of Deutsche Post DHL

First Choice is a natural result of the enormous growth DP DHL experienced during the past decade. Originating as the successor to the German state-owned mail monopoly that transports letters and parcels within the country, Deutsche Post was privatized in 1995. Early on, the new company recognized the vast opportunities for global delivery services and logistics and launched its growth into three areas of service: management and transport of goods, information, and financial services. In 1998, the company began acquiring shares of the U.S.-based package delivery service DHL, completing the purchase in 2002 and absorbing DHL into its Express Division.

The DHL name is now used as the umbrella brand for all of the comapny's logistics services, including some of the services in the Deutsche Post business units. DHL services over 220 countries and territories worldwide, with three main divisions. The Express Division transports domestic and international courier, express, and parcel shipments globally using air and ground transport; the Forwarding/Freight Division carries goods by rail, road, air, and sea; and the DHL Supply Chain Division offers warehousing and information solutions. The last also offers Corporate Information Solutions, which is the collection, digitalization, printing, and storage of documents of all types.

DP DHL's second brand is Deutsche Post, the ongoing operation of the German mail delivery service. Deutsche Post handles approximately 70 million letters in Germany six days a week, but it has also branched into other services in the mail value chain through five other business units: Press Services, which handles domestic (Germany) distribution of print products such as newspapers and magazines; Retail Outlets, which operates domestic retail outlets for an array of letter mail, parcel, and Postbank services;[1] Dialogue Marketing, which provides services to assist businesses in direct marketing such as market research and address verification as well as mailings; Parcel Germany for domestic, nonexpress parcel service, including the Packstation network; and Global Mail, which contracts to perform the domestic and international mail delivery in other countries under the DHL umbrella brand.

When *First Choice* originated, pressure from competitors—particularly Federal Express and United Parcel Service—was mounting. The impetus for *First Choice* had more to do with the need to enable DP DHL to meet the rapid global changes in service and markets. DP DHL was also seeking to achieve organic customer growth by creating satisfied customers who would be so pleased with the quality of service received that they would naturally recommend the company to others. Increasing the number of referrals could translate into hundreds of millions of Euros in increased revenues and would be far less costly than growth achieved through marketing and advertising efforts. Focusing on the customer interface was clearly a smart move for DP DHL.

After all, between DHL's package delivery and freight services and Deutsche Post's extensive mail businesses, the company's employees come into contact with millions of customers each day. As Holger Winklbauer stated, "We face permanent change of our customers' demands, so we need to position ourselves to grow along with it. The idea is not just to fix things for tomorrow, but to change for the better on a continuous basis. It is clear that our people who are closest to our customers are in the best position to understand not only what customers want but also to improve our processes and do things better."

Designing the *First Choice* Architecture

The idea for *First Choice* originated at the end of 2005 when then-CEO Klaus Zumwinkel decided that the company needed a complete review of its processes to improve its services and motivate employees to customer service excellence. He turned to the company's in-house consultancy, which was part of Corporate Shared Services Division and at that time led by Holger Winklbauer. To achieve quick buy-in from business operations, DP DHL created a steering committee by appointing eight *First Choice* Sponsors from the company's divisions. They were selected on the basis of their reputations and their ability to become opinion leaders and drivers of the effort.

Creating a program that affects more than 550,000 people is an enormous endeavor, a task that seemed overwhelming at the outset. The *First Choice* team forged ahead rapidly by setting up eight pilot tests in the respective divisions by early 2006. Within six months they came up with the critical design decisions that eventually became the framework of the *First Choice* architecture. Exhibit 10.1 illustrates the framework of the *First Choice* architecture.

A fundamental decision was that *First Choice* had to be designed around a standardized set of methodologies and tools to support the envisioned architecture. Methodological consistency and easy-to-apply toolkits were a condition for the intended large-scale roll-out.

Exhibit 10.1. Framework of *First Choice* Architecture

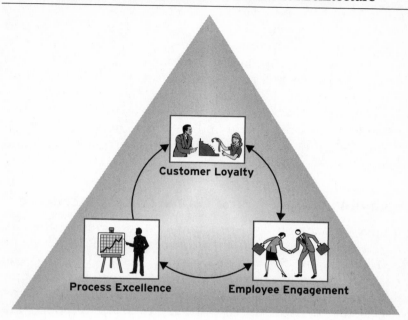

The Process Excellence Framework

With regard to driving process excellence, the team determined that it would adapt the Six Sigma approach plus Lean for the service industry. Six Sigma is a proven methodology whose five steps—the DMAIC process of Define, Measure, Analyze, Improve, and Control—would provide the rigor and scalability the company needed. Implementing Six Sigma plus Lean would require creating a group of Lean Work-Out specialists, called "Process Improvement Advisors," to run local process improvement workshops, plus a group of Black Belt experts, called "Senior Advisors," who would be able to guide the Six Sigma reviews. In addition, the project would need a large number of Green Belt experts, called "Initiative Champions," who were on the ground and knew the internal structures of their organization.

Although the *First Choice* architecture would be centrally designed, the program gave the business units the responsibility for determining which of their customer service areas required attention and what performance standards should be set in the context of their specific customer needs. The managers and employees at the periphery of the organization are in the best position to understand what their customers value most, evaluate their own processes accordingly, and assess which interventions would have the most impact in achieving customer satisfaction. This meant that *First Choice* had to empower the local business units and, at the same time, build an overarching "macro structure" to guide the units in evaluating customer touchpoints and choosing the key areas of concern.

Preparation to Launch *First Choice* Process Excellence

A proper preparation lays the foundation for bringing the *First Choice* process excellence element into each of DP DHL's countries in the various divisions und business units (BUs). It sets up in each organization a *First Choice* Office and Steering Committee composed of representatives from sales, marketing, operations, and customer service, whose tasks are to select, support, and coach the improvement area teams.

Other design requirements were that *First Choice* had to be performance driven, sustainable, and lead to continuous improvement throughout the global operations of the company. The program design had to include market research and customer surveys to help identify areas needing improvement along the touchpoints of major business processes. An integral part of the framework was to develop Key Performance Indicators (KPIs) that indicate whether the company would meet or exceed customer expectations. Similarly, *First Choice* had to incorporate methods that allowed the units to accurately measure their results in terms of their own performance improvements and their performance relative to key competitors. And, finally, *First Choice* had to create mechanisms that allowed an easy sharing of learnings among the units and create a cycle of continuous improvement.

Using these requirements—scalability, local empowerment, central enabling architecture, and market feedback—the *First Choice* team designed a five-phase program. It put the business units in charge of conducting initial research on customer

Exhibit 10.2. Five Phases of *First Choice*

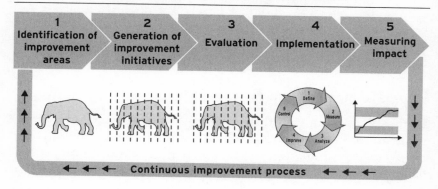

interactions, which they then used to identify and prioritize their unit's hot spots. The definition of the hot spots would pave the way for the formal Six Sigma projects on those processes that needed in-depth work-overs. Once the project was completed, the business units would again control the results. Exhibit 10.2 illustrates the five *First Choice* phases.

The *First Choice* methodology takes the teams step by step through a series of actions that increasingly drill down into those processes that pose customer satisfaction problems. It is useful to review the phases in some detail to see how each builds upon the prior one and guides each business unit's systematic process to achieve satisfaction at every customer touchpoint.

Phase 1: Identifying and Monitoring Improvement Areas

The local *First Choice* office collects any existing surveys about customer perception on the market. It may also initiate new research to understand how customers rate the country's performance relative to competitors. Under the guidance of the local Senior Advisors (Black Belts), the extended *First Choice* team identifies improvement areas by defining at a high level the core business processes of the unit. After evaluating each of the core processes and reviewing how customers perceive the unit's performance, the first phase of the Six Sigma process seeks to narrow the focus to those touchpoints that are most relevant to customers. Once these are identified, the unit checks to see if any other initiatives are already in place to address one or the other touchpoint. For relevant processes that are not being addressed, the team breaks each one down into its finer steps. This way they can be sure to target the key elements of the customer touchpoint that cause problems.

Phase 2: Generating Improvement Initiatives

In this phase, the team drills down into the selected problem(s) in detail to identify more precisely potential improvement initiatives. For each initiative, the team writes an "Improvement Area Charter" that specifies the problem and creates a work plan. Some improvement areas have to be further broken down into smaller pieces by location, product, or subprocess to spot where the bottleneck or flaw originates. Next, the team uses market surveys, internal KPIs, and knowledge gathered from team experts to help point the way to solutions.

Phase 3: Evaluating Improvement Initiatives

Having identified specific areas for improvement, the local *First Choice* steering committee narrows down which solutions will have the most effect on customer satisfaction, given the time and resources available. The team prioritizes a set of improvement initiatives according to their feasibility and impact value. The team also decides on the appropriate approach for the improvement initiative (90-Day Initiative or Process Improvement Workshop, depending on the complexity of the initial problem) and ensures that relevant employees receive appropriate training to develop the skills and expertise to manage the initiative. An Initiative Champion (a trained Green Belt) is chosen to lead the 90-Day Initiative team; Process Improvement Advisors are selected to run the process improvement workshops. Finally, they set the standards that will allow them to measure the impact of each initiative.

Phase 4: Implementing Improvement Initiatives: Six Sigma (DMAIC$^{+\text{Lean}}$)

This phase introduces the Six Sigma approach, which DP DHL adopted for the service industry, into each selected initiative. In Phase 4 the availability of skilled resources is critical—it is

Exhibit 10.3. Six Sigma DMAIC Cycle

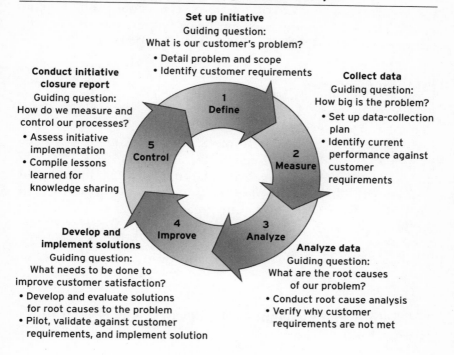

Set up initiative
Guiding question:
What is our customer's problem?
• Detail problem and scope
• Identify customer requirements

Conduct initiative closure report
Guiding question:
How do we measure and control our processes?
• Assess initiative implementation
• Compile lessons learned for knowledge sharing

Collect data
Guiding question:
How big is the problem?
• Set up data-collection plan
• Identify current performance against customer requirements

1 Define

5 Control

2 Measure

4 Improve

3 Analyze

Develop and implement solutions
Guiding question:
What needs to be done to improve customer satisfaction?
• Develop and evaluate solutions for root causes to the problem
• Pilot, validate against customer requirements, and implement solution

Analyze data
Guiding question:
What are the root causes of our problem?
• Conduct root cause analysis
• Verify why customer requirements are not met

fundamental to applying the rigor and precision of the DMAIC cycle evaluation to the problem. To ensure a professional application of the methodology, the company's full-time trained Six Sigma Black Belt experts (Senior Advisors) come into play again; together with the trained local Green Belts (Initiative Champions) they analyze the initiative in detail, get to the root of the problem, and develop an optimal solution. Process improvement workshops conducted in this phase follow the same logic, but focus more on application of the Lean tools. Exhibit 10.3 illustrates the steps of the DMAIC cycle.

Phase 5: Controlling Impact, Sharing Knowledge, and Reiterating *First Choice*

In this phase, the teams wrap up the initiatives completed and document the lessons learned to ensure sustainability of the solutions.

They track all initiatives over a period of twelve months to assess their full impact and recommend any necessary follow-up to maintain continuous improvement. They may also revisit any other critical issues identified in the first round.

Piloting *First Choice*

Following the design of the *First Choice* architecture, the steering committee decided to test the five-phase approach to validate it before launching it on a companywide basis. They proposed eight pilots, located in different countries and continents of the DP DHL's network, so that the committee could assess any differences in cultural reactions. The pilots began in early 2006, with nearly the entire year set aside to validate the methodology and provide a proof of concept for *First Choice*. The eight pilots were successful, and at the end of the year, the company's Executive Committee approved a full rollout for the start of 2007.

The Employee Engagement Framework: Engaging a Half-Million Employees

The most staggering element in this case is its scale. To leverage *First Choice*, the team had to:

- Set up a worldwide communication campaign addressing the goals of *First Choice* and highlight successes along the way, in line with the implementation plan.
- Address the 55,000 line managers responsible for driving the continuous improvement process and make them familiar with the methodological approach and their role within *First Choice*
- Deliver standard tools and intervention formats that would allow managers to engage their respective teams

With a communication campaign aimed at managers, and the training of the Advisors and Initiative Champions, *First Choice* got connected with more than 60,000 employees, but even that represented only about 12 percent of the company's workforce. As Winklbauer points out, "We still had to wrap our hands around how to communicate with the other 90 percent—nearly 500,000 people—our front-line employees." The company clearly recognizes their key role: they are the face of the company to the customer. All the Six Sigma process improvements in the world cannot repair the damage from a grumpy employee who doesn't treat a customer with respect or demonstrate a commitment to service excellence. Frank Appel wrote, "Our frontline employees are the key to this change process. They are the people with the power to make a difference—the driving force that executes on our improvements. It is vital that we engage them at every level. Our people need to feel that our objectives are their objectives, and *First Choice* needs to really matter to them."

Again, the insight is clear, but how do you make several hundred thousand people not only listen but also reflect and possibly change their behavior? The company needed something scalable, easy to use and comprehend, but with impact. The solution was to create a teaching organization of thousands of front-line managers. Instead of cascading lengthy and expensive training programs, the *First Choice* team decided to develop several toolkits that put managers directly in charge of presenting *First Choice* to their employees and begin discussing with them how to deliver customer satisfaction. The toolkits included the following.

The Dialogue Maps

The *Standard Dialogue Map* was developed for the start of the rollout. It was one of the most important tools for spreading the *First Choice* message on a large scale with consistent messages. The Standard Dialogue Map is a two- to three-hour workshop format. Managers receive a detailed facilitation guide as well as a set of materials—information on *First Choice* and various facilitation material such as posters—to run the session. The workshop ends with a concrete action plan to improve the customer experience created by the respective team's service. The *Dialogue Map Compact* allows the team to follow up in their efforts to improve the customer experience in a one-hour workshop. As with the Standard

Dialogue Map, managers are provided with all relevant materials to run the session without a lot of individual preparation.

The Meeting Toolkit

The *Meeting Toolkit* is a special aid that managers can use to engage with their employees and improve *First Choice* behavior and customer orientation within their team. In a series of twenty- to thirty-minute meetings, managers and their teams brainstorm simple things they can do together and as individuals to improve the customer experience. Each meeting is supported by posters highlighting *First Choice* behavior. The Meeting Toolkit helps managers to ensure that DP DHL becomes and remains *First Choice* for its customers. Predefined themes for the action meetings on *First Choice* behavior are:

- Acknowledging and fixing our mistakes
- Always taking extra care
- Achieving best quality standards
- Always giving a smile to colleagues and customers
- Sharing knowledge to enhance quality

Managers are provided with all relevant materials, such as a facilitator's guide, session material, and tips for effective discussions.

The Manager's Toolkit

This toolkit allows managers to work with their teams to learn more about customer-related issues. To design and write the elements of this tool, DP DHL hired getAbstract, a global leader in the business of publishing business book summaries. The company's core competence is taking complex business issues and distilling them down to the bare essentials in a clear, understandable, easily digested format—exactly what *First Choice* needed. Thomas Bergen, CEO of getAbstract, stated, "If you want to roll something out to 500,000 people, you cannot use complex architectures. You have to say what you expect people to do. If a customer complains, the employee should know what to do and say. At the end of each session, you want people to be able to relate to specific action items in their head."

The toolkit had to be designed in a way that encouraged managers to lead, not to explain. The sessions had to create a context that demonstrated to employees that their leaders were personally involved in *First Choice*, not simply lecturing them about changing their attitudes. The format of the sessions had to give managers a platform to act as role models. In terms of content, the rather complex issue of customer service excellence was broken down into ten core themes (presented in Exhibit 10.4). To make the material highly approachable, each theme was presented in the form of a typical real-life story that employees could relate to and identify with. Managers and employees themselves were asked to contribute their own personal stories of times when they have experienced good or bad service. This interactivity invited employees to look at customer service on a very personal level, making the sessions concrete and colorful, not abstract or theoretical.

Exhibit 10.4. Manager's Toolkit: Customer Service Themes

You Count: We can't succeed without you

Understanding Great Service: Five good reasons to give it

Giving Great Service: How to thrill your customers

Know Your Customers: Internal and external

Complaints: Deal well with grievances

Internal Customers: How to be a good one

Difficult Colleagues: Build civil relationships

Mistakes: How to learn from them

Get Effective: Manage your time, your work, and yourself

Continuous Improvement: Get better day by day

Following the principle of simplicity and efficiency, the toolkit included a complete set of instructional tools to ensure that the workshops were productive, easy to perform, and could be conducted in thirty minutes, with thirty to sixty minutes of preparation time for managers. The managers themselves would need no separate training to conduct the lessons. To support this goal, the team developed five supporting components for each of the ten lessons:

1. *Moderator Audio (for managers).* To kick off each session, managers listen to a short introductory audio that overviews the theme, explains the hows and whys of the topic relative to customer service, and offers some background information and examples. The narrative of the audios is delivered by a character named Mark who introduces himself as a coach for managers.

2. *Facilitator Cards (for managers).* The facilitator cards are the heart of the toolkit. For each session, managers receive a complete set of cards to print out. In creating the cards, getAbstract aimed to make them simple and friendly so managers would have no resistance using them to conduct the meetings. The cards are color-coded according to use. Blue cards prepare the manager for the session, providing checklists and a timeline of each portion of the session. Yellow cards contain the content of the session, using bullet points to remind managers what to say as they go through the topic. Red cards contain a complete script of what to say for each yellow card and are intended for managers who are not confident about their speaking or meeting skills. The design of each session encourages managers to tell personal stories and provides examples how to frame them.

3. *Posters (for managers).* For some topics, the manager receives a poster of a graphic that accompanies one of the points they make while delivering the session.

4. *Team Audio (for employees).* This is a ten-minute MP3 audio file that employees download from the company's intranet and listen to before the team session. Here again, the narrator is also the coach, Mark, who relates to employees that he worked for Deutsche Post and tells stories of his experiences with good and bad customer service. His approach is serious but nonthreatening.

5. *Action Card (for employees).* Each session has an "action card" that employees print out as a takeaway reminder of the session. This card contains the essence of the session's message and is the behavioral guideline they are invited to follow.

Exhibit 10.5 shows an example of an action card.

Exhibit 10.5. Employee Action Card from "Mistakes" Theme

How to deal with mistakes.

1. **Stay calm.** No reason to panic. Recognizing and addressing the mistake is a vital step.

2. **Admit it.** Even though it's uncomfortable, just take a deep breath and do it. Say: "I made a mistake. I'm sorry. I'll work to make sure this doesn't happen again."

3. **Fix it.** Don't wait around. Do your best to solve the issue before it gets bigger.

4. **Don't place blame.** It's a waste of time. Deutsche Post solves problems together. Making mistakes is human.

5. **Learn from what went wrong.** Go back, find the root of the problem and correct it once and for all. Then move on!

Making mistakes is human.

Exhibit 10.6. Manager's Toolkit Poster

The New Pyramid

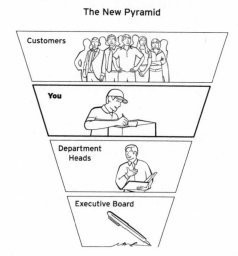

Customers

You

Department Heads

Executive Board

Throughout all of the toolkits, one of the key messages is that, under *First Choice*, management is no longer at the top of the pyramid; customers are, followed directly by the employees who deal with them (see Exhibit 10.6). The sessions reinforce again and again the theme that employees must recognize the crucial role they play in creating customer satisfaction. In the eyes of customers, *they* are DP DHL. *First Choice* empowers them to make customer service decisions on their own, because they are the ones who can best assess the specific context, and they have tools at hand to correct flaws that occur. Employees are told, "We trust you."

Managing the Scale of *First Choice* in DP DHL

To achieve quick leverage across DP DHL, the *First Choice* organization had to develop a sufficient number of internal Senior Advisors (Black Belts in Six Sigma terminology), Process Improvement Advisors, and Initiative Champions (Green Belts in Six Sigma terminology) who were trained in the DMAIC and the Lean methodology. Selected from the divisions and business units, the Senior Advisors would become full-time coordinators and implementor of the *First Choice* initiative in their regions to ensure the application of the DMAIC cycle to specific initiatives. Senior Advisors receive five weeks of training on the theory of Six Sigma, along with facilitation, conflict management, coaching, and training skills. Process Improvement Advisors, who concentrate on preparing, facilitating, and following up on process improvement workshops (comparable to Lean Action Work-Outs in Six Sigma), receive two weeks of training on the theory of Lean in the context of Six Sigma, along with facilitation skills. All Senior Advisors receive an additional five months of hands-on practice working on initiatives.

During the onsite training, the advisors meet cross-regionally and cross-functionally to deepen their learning and achieve formal certification. For each 90-Day Improvement Initiative identified for DMAIC, the Senior Advisors, along with the Initiative Champions and other members of the business unit, perform the DMAIC cycle to evaluate the problem and resolve it. By the end of 2008, DP DHL had selected, trained, and qualified 140 Senior Advisors, 220 Process Improvement Advisors, and more than 7,000 Initiative Champions.

In parallel, managers had to learn about *First Choice* and to support it. In the first year of the launch, more than 8,000 managers were informed about the initiative in executive workshops. To stress that *First Choice* was critical to the company's future, a powerful communications campaign was developed, with voices from the top echelons endorsing the project and emphasizing that *First Choice* was not a flavor of the month but rather a comprehensive transformational project to create a "customer-centric" culture within DP DHL.

A key element in that communications campaign became the *First Choice* booklet mentioned at the beginning of this case. It is directed at the 55,000-plus managers at DP DHL, encouraging them to communicate the philosophy of *First Choice* to every one of their employees and to lead by example, demonstrating a relentless focus on customer needs. The booklet opens with a strong positive message directly from CEO Frank Appel, inviting all managers to give their unconditional support to *First Choice*. It explains the "philosophy" in detail, to make sure that every manager becomes familiar with the five phases and the Six Sigma process. The booklet summarizes several successes that *First Choice* achieved in the pilot tests; its pages seek to inspire readers through a variety of quotes that endorse the mindset of change from contemporary business notables and from famous historical figures:

- "Be the change you want to see in the world."
  —Mahatma Gandhi
- "The journey of a thousand miles begins with one step."
  —Lao Tze
- "We see our customers as invited guests, and we are the hosts. It's our job every day to make every important aspect of the customer experience a little bit better."
  —Jeff Bezos
- "In everything the ends well-defined are the secret of durable success."
  —Victor Cousins
- "Nothing is particularly hard if you divide it into small jobs."
  — Henry Ford

The brochure reinforces time and again the need for every single DP DHL employee to assimilate its message: "*First Choice* is what we want to be. We can only become the best in our industry by keeping our promises and delighting our customers. . . . Everyone's contribution, at every touchpoint, at every interaction, is critical to success."

Measuring Results

First Choice is aimed at creating a deep cultural change through-out the corporation, but its ultimate goal is, of course, to increase business, make it sustainable, and improve the company's stand-ing against its competitors. To evaluate the impact of the process improvement initiatives, *First Choice* looks at all four dimensions of a Balanced Scorecard:

- *Impact on Customers.* Annual customer surveys measure the progress on the touchpoints where *First Choice* Improvement Initiatives have been run.
- *Impact on Processes.* Regular KPI measures are taken, reflecting the progress on the process KPIs that drive customer percep-tion at critical touchpoints.
- *Impact on Employees.* Annual Employee Opinion Surveys are used to find out how well the messages are understood and to what extent *First Choice* directly affects the working environment.
- *Impact on Financials.* A quarterly review of costs and benefits is conducted to measure the financial impact created through *First Choice* Improvement Initiatives.

The Outlook for DP DHL

It took less than eighteen months from the initial idea to the implementation of *First Choice* as a fixture in the manage-ment structure of DP DHL. Today, the initiative has evolved into a smart and comprehensive learning architecture that is designed for simplicity, large-scale utilization, and tangible impact. It brings change systematically and methodically to thousands of its processes in operations that span more than 200 countries.

Over the past three years, nearly 16,000 people became famil-iar with the techniques of Six Sigma and the *First Choice* five-step change process. Nearly 55,000 managers were involved in a campaign of change through communication and learning, and practical toolkits allowed those managers to involve the other 500,000 employees in the philosophy of the project. As this case study is being prepared, *First Choice* goals are familiar to two-thirds of all employees; 50 percent of them state that *First Choice* activities contribute to the success of their immediate working environment. More than 1,000 processes within the corporation have been evaluated and improved. Based on the successes so far, the goal is to manage the transition process from *First Choice* as a project organization to an integral part of DP DHL's business and embedding its various dimensions in the regular performance management instruments.

Conclusion: *First Choice* as a Strategic Learning Intervention

The *First Choice* case is remarkable because of its dimensions and its challenge of changing a global culture in a short period of time. But it is also special because it addresses a number of issues through simple processes that are implemented with a high degree of discipline throughout the entire corporation. The transformational learning architecture designed by Winklbauer and his team is an excellent example how to kill several birds with one stone. The explicit goal is creating customer loyalty, and the sophisticated toolkits and measurement systems support this. This requires employee engagement at the front line, where the customer interaction takes place. The combination of customer focus and employee engagement in a company of this size is already a powerful one. But there is more.

Less explicit, but as powerful, is the impact of the project on the company's leadership culture. By turning the pyramid upside down and enabling the front-line employees to take the lead in dealing with the market, the company becomes flatter. The clearly defined processes relieve the center from the burden of direct operational control, and they empower people, shorten strategic response time, and create countless antennae to sense environmental change.

The case also illustrates the power of processes in changing large-scale systems. While training and communication efforts are important to create engagement, change mindsets, and build skills, they need the enabling architecture of clearly defined and controlled processes to become scalable and effective in such a large organization. The genius of the *First Choice* approach lies in its simplicity and its ability to address several issues at once. While dealing with customer orientation, it also indirectly changes the texture of an organization that carries with it not only the heritage of the bureaucratic culture of a state-owned monopoly, but also the heritage of two challenging mega-mergers—DHL and Exel—that forced the company overnight into global management challenges. By creating common processes across the organization, the front line gets empowered and aligned at the same time.

As such, *First Choice* contributes to cultural post-merger integration and elimination of bureaucracy. DP DHL becomes a faster, more responsive company and increases its ability to adapt to market needs, one customer at a time. As Winklbauer puts it, "We moved from thinking that this would be an add-on program to making it a platform for nothing less than a transformational engine for the strategic change our company needs."

The challenge will be, of course, how quickly *First Choice* can accomplish its goals. After all, the initiative strives to change the hearts and minds of a huge agglomerate that has its roots in a state-owned bureaucracy and that has had to digest a series of major acquisitions in a short period of time that made it a very different corporation. Holger Winklbauer is realistic; in his view, cultural change of this magnitude takes a minimum of five to ten years. And in an environment charged by the short-term pressure to deliver quarterly results, top executives often do not have the patience to allow change to grow roots in the culture and pay off in the long term. On the other hand, the creation of a dedicated *First Choice* organization that reports directly to the CEO is a good sign of commitment and the recognition of the initiative's ultimate strategic importance.

About the Principal in This Case

Holger Winklbauer has been responsible for the successful development and implementation of *First Choice* at Deutsche Post DHL since 2007, directly reporting to CEO Frank Appel. He joined the company's Top Management Consulting group in 2000, became the Head of In-house Consulting in 2002, and a Managing Director of Deutsche Post World Net Business Consulting GmbH in 2003. Prior to DP DHL he worked in procurement at Mannesmann Anlagenbau AG, at the Research Institute for Operations Management (FIR), and at Metro MGL Logistik GmbH. He studied electrical engineering and applied economics in RWTH Aachen University and at the University of Portland, Oregon.

Notes

1. At the time that *First Choice* was started, DP DHL had a third brand, Postbank, one of Germany's leading financial services providers with 14.2 million active domestic customers and approximately 21,000 employees. However, the company agreed in September 2008 to sell a minority holding in Deutsche Postbank to Deutsche Bank AG, and as a result, Postbank is now a discontinued operation within DP DHL and is no longer involved in *First Choice*.

The Author

Roland Deiser is an internationally recognized expert on strategy, innovation, and organizational design, with a focus on building strategic capabilities into large-scale systems.

He was the founding Dean of DaimlerChrysler's Corporate University and is the Founder and Chairman of the European Corporate Learning Forum (ECLF—www.eclf.org), a consortium of more than 60 blue chip corporations from more than 10 countries who have teamed up to share practices and shape the future of Strategic Capability Development.

He is a Senior Fellow with the Center for the Digital Future at the Annenberg School of the University of Southern California in Los Angeles and an Associate Professor of Political Science at Vienna University, Austria. He also serves on the Editorial Board of the *Academy of Management Learning and Education Journal* (AMLE).

Roland is an advisor to Fortune 100 companies and emerging start-ups alike. He is a member of the Advisory Board of Credit Suisse's Business School, and the former Chairman of the Advisory Board of SMAC, Siemens' global early stage investment fund for wireless innovation. He also is, or has been, working in advisory and board positions with several growth companies, primarily in the digital media convergence space.

As an advisor to the music copyright industry, he helped create FastTrack, a global consortium of leading music copyright societies dedicated to building an integrated electronic music copyright management system. He has also served as an expert for the Austrian Government on the development of the country's Film, Television, and Multimedia industry, and for the German Federal and State Commission on the impact of the Internet on the future of universities.

He lives with his wife and two children in Los Angeles, California.

Acknowledgments

As any author will attest, writing a book is a rather large task, and I am grateful to many people for their contributions and assistance. On my list, I want first to acknowledge and thank Rick Benzel, my editor, who worked with me throughout this entire project, from book proposal to final manuscript—and who became a friend in this process. Rick introduced me to Jossey-Bass, helped interview some of the companies in this book, and worked closely with me in writing the business case studies. His professional skills are greatly appreciated.

I particularly thank all the principals of the case studies, who gave generously of their time to provide background and information about their organizations. I list their names here, along with some additional people at a few of the companies who assisted in the process by providing me with extra details, photos, and exhibits: Anna Simioni from UniCredit Group, with help on the photos from Gabriele Tortetta; Marion Horstmann from Siemens, with liaison assistance from Elisabeth Esser; Frank Waltmann and Felix Li from Novartis; Hervé Borensztejn and Alain Hensgen from EADS; Dagmar Woyde-Köhler from EnBW; Michael Roehrig and Ferenc Remenyi from ABB; Andrés Jaffé, Juergen Lahr, and Genevieve Naomi Bon Mendel from BASF; Holger Winklbauer from Deutsche Post DHL, with liaison assistance from Gertrud Zeiss and Verena Amonat; Nate Allen from the U.S. Army; and Ralf Schneider from PricewaterhouseCoopers (now with HSBC).

I further extend my sincere thanks to those people at Wiley and Jossey-Bass who have worked with great professionalism on this book: Matt Davis, who immediately believed in the project and stayed committed throughout the process; Nina Kreiden, who helped me diligently through the book production process; and Brian Grimm, who put much energy into marketing this book and making it successful.

Finally, I would like to thank all the great friends and colleagues from the European Corporate Learning Forum. Their willingness to share the challenging issues of the corporate learning profession and the open and trusting spirit of our discussions are the foundation on which the ideas and lessons of this book rest.

Index

Page references followed by *e* indicate an exhibit; followed by *fig* indicate an illustrated figure.